CAGED

One Woman's Journey from Cult Abuse to Freedom

(An adaptation of a true story)

A NOVEL BY

ROBERT E. HIRSCH

iUniverse, Inc.
New York   Bloomington

CAGED
One Woman's Journey from Cult Abuse to Freedom

iUniverse books may be ordered through booksellers or by contacting:

iUniverse
1663 Liberty Drive
Bloomington, IN 47403
www.iuniverse.com
1-800-Authors (1-800-288-4677)

ISBN: 978-0-595-47350-2 (pbk)
ISBN: 978-0-595-71211-3 (cloth)
ISBN: 978-0-595-91629-0 (ebook)

Printed in the United States of America

iUniverse rev. date:3/19/10

PREFACE

As a clinical psychologist, in practice for two decades, it isn't often that a life story enters my world and has such a powerful impact as Anne's journey has had on me. My decision to write this book involved several important motivations. The first was to share a long-hidden picture of a dark corner of our social fabric. The irony in reporting this kind of story is that it involves competing needs to recount events as accurately as possible, and the commitment to protect the identities of people who have already been victimized and intruded upon by the heinous crimes presented in the book.

The second motivation, to tell this truth, is multifaceted: to tell an important story about a person's life, to educate and increase awareness in the hope of preventing similar harm in the future, and to portray a world of ironies and opposites. Anne's story is about incredible abuse and amazing survival. It is about a seemingly good and trusted community that is at the same time perpetrating evil and harm. It is about the misuse of a religion that could have beautiful and caring value to humankind.

The final motivation was to give a greater understanding of the role and value of the psychotherapy process in providing a safe environment for healing, to further humanize the process, and to help people understand that it is a complex interaction of science and art.

It was a complicated endeavor to tell the truth while simultaneously needing to divert many concrete details. Numerous sources were not available to interview due to the significant legal restrictions incumbent upon legal and social services regarding disclosure of information related to child abuse cases, and the absence of important figures who are no longer alive or would not be appropriate to contact.

When information wasn't available I made a commitment to explore and understand the most likely scenarios and interactions that might have transpired. When identities and locations were changed, I tried to create comparable universes, striving to keep intact the nature of the people and their behaviors, emotions, thoughts and experiences

Conceivably, some of the individuals who were involved in the actual events depicted in this book, whether they be victims, perpetrators, members of the community, law enforcement officials, reporters or treatment providers, will be able to identify some of the real people, places and experiences described in this book, if they choose to read it. This is inevitable. It is hoped they too will strongly consider the impact upon the privacy and emotional and psychological wellbeing of the real people upon whom this book is based, and act respectfully to honor the wishes such persons might have in remaining veiled.

Conversely, any likeness or similarity with other communities, individuals or events is almost inevitably a coincidence, and any such assumptions are highly likely to be inaccurate.

One last area I wish to address is the implications this book has for religion and, more specifically, Christianity. In no way is it my desire or attempt to denigrate or judge religion and its larger role in society. It is my experience and attempt, however, to make a strong statement about the potential for, as well as the danger of individuals to utilize an institution that carries deep trust and great responsibility as a basis for their own evil intent.

The same concerns would apply to other fundamental societal institutions, such as governments, charities, or the press, each of which is granted, de facto, a position of immense trust. This caveat crosses all religions and religious institutions and doesn't discriminate. Western religions, in particular, represent a very complex interaction of restricting freedom and providing tolerance and support for its members to feel loved and supported.

The overall intent of writing this book was not political in nature. However, like many writers of both fiction and non-fiction I know I am making an important statement about an aspect of humankind and how I view it. Anne's journey clearly exposes the great danger and harm that can result from those in power misusing their roles and abusing the very people whose deep trust leaves them vulnerable and comparatively powerless.

With that said, this is also a story of incredible survival, resilience, strength, and ultimately, finding light through the darkness. It is a tribute to the woman upon whose life this book is based, and the attorney who went that extra mile, or 100 miles, to help a very damaged person through a very painful and threatening legal process. It is also a tribute to the art of psychotherapy and its greatest strength, a profound relationship built out of care and trust.

— CHAPTER ONE —

As a clinical psychologist, I am prepared for many forms of behavior and emotion when I meet a new client. One early January morning in 1999, however, as I opened the door from my office to my waiting room, to greet my new client, I noticed that the chairs were empty.

As I began to step back into my office, my eyes fell upon a woman crouched in the corner, her back braced against the wall and her arms wrapped tightly around herself in a protective posture.

There was little doubt that she was either a very disturbed being, someone anticipating imminent threat, or both. As I entered my waiting room, she showed no movement or visible recognition of my presence. So, after observing her for a moment, I quietly asked, "Are you Anne?"

Without shifting or making any sound, the woman almost imperceptibly nodded her head once.

"Hello Anne, I'm Dr. Hirsch," I said.

No response ensued, and I wondered where this might go. At the very least, my work required a basic ability to converse. I had encountered incredible shyness, severe anxiety disorders, profound depression and deep levels of mistrust, but I couldn't recall a client being mute during the initial introduction that occurred in my waiting room.

"Would you like to come into my office, Anne?" I asked.

Her silence continued, but she arose, adjusting her hands further around her head, seemingly to protect her face more, and she began walking toward the door where I was standing.

It was like watching a weak animal having to pass a predator on a narrow mountain path, and I had been cast as the predator. I found myself taking a small step backward. As she slid sideways along the wall toward my office door, she shifted her body toward one side of the doorway, keeping as far away as physically possible from me, avoiding any eye contact. Once she achieved full entry, she stopped in the center of the room, looking lost and appearing to be awaiting directions.

I kept my movements to a minimum, to honor her need for space, while pointing to a chair and inviting her to sit. Very slowly, she placed one hand on its arm while continuing to clutch her body with the other, and slowly lowered herself into the chair, looking like she was in great physical pain. I knew in that moment that a very fragile and damaged woman was sitting eight feet away.

As quietly as I could, fearful of even my voice startling her, I asked, "Anne, have you ever been in therapy before?"

She shook her head slightly from side to side. So far, three to four minutes had elapsed and the only spoken words had all been mine. It was like a reversal of analysis, with the therapist doing all the talking, which was both intriguing and discomforting. But any frustration I felt was diminished by observing Anne facing and leaning into the side of the chair, much like a child might hold a teddy bear. I reminded myself that, also like a child, she was telling me a lot with her body language.

Anne appeared to be in her late twenties, about average height, somewhat overweight, with short, auburn, uncombed hair that lacked any semblance of contemporary fashion. She wore little or no make-up and had a fairly pale complexion. She was dressed in blue jeans, a baggy, cream-colored T-shirt and white tennis shoes. Her look was somewhat androgynous, and she didn't even appear to have house keys or a wallet, unless they were well concealed in a back pocket.

"I'd like to try to learn a little about you, Anne, why you're here today, and how I might be able to help you," I said gently.

Suddenly, words spilled from her, breaking the silence.

"My friend told me you wouldn't beat me if I said the wrong thing, but I don't know that I believe her," she said in a rush.

"What gave you the idea I would ever beat you?" I asked.

"That's what doctors do to people, but my friend said you're different," she answered.

I felt slightly relieved she'd given me a reprieve, but I could almost feel her fear it was so palpable.

"Wow, how brave of you to come here Anne, wondering if you could be physically harmed," I said. "I promise I would never do anything to hurt you physically, and I will do my best to show you I care about helping you to feel better. If I do anything that feels physically threatening though, please let me know. You're always free to stop the session and leave, but I hope we'll get to know each other a little today?" I tried to present my last sentence as a question, so that she, or maybe we, could feel she was making a choice to continue, rather than just relenting.

Anne seemed to hear the words, but I couldn't tell if she'd absorbed their meaning. I continued to feel as if I was talking to a child who needed lots of assurance.

Uncertain if she was clutching her body due to some kind of physical discomfort, I inquired, "May I ask you a question Anne?"

She nodded her head very slightly.

"Are you in any physical pain at the moment?"

She nodded again.

"Are you more physically comfortable curled up and looking down?" I asked.

"You might take it as a sign of disrespect if I look directly at you," she mumbled, her eyes still fixed on the floor.

"Actually, I'll probably take it as a sign that you're more comfortable if you look at me, but I want you to feel safe and at ease, as much as you can right now," I said. To my relief, for the first time, she glanced furtively toward me before looking down again.

"My guess is that you've had a very frightening and maybe traumatic experience," I continued. "Has anyone physically hurt you in the past or in the last couple of days?"

Anne shifted in her chair. "Yes," she whispered, her eyes almost closed.

I paused, waiting for her to steady her nerves.

"Have you been abused previously?"

"All my life," she said without discernable emotion. Her behavior had already indicated a potential history of severe abuse, so I wasn't surprised by her response.

"Do you feel you are in danger now or that someone will try to hurt you again?" I asked.

"Not unless they find me—and they're very far away," she responded, her posture relaxing slightly.

Her responses remained brief and somewhat cryptic, so I chose to continue our interview and return to her physical needs later in the session.

"So, why did you come in today?" I resumed.

Anne sighed. "I was beaten up two days ago, and my friends felt I should get help."

"Have you seen a medical doctor yet?"

"No, I can't go to any doctors."

"Why not?" I asked, trying to conceal my protective concern.

"Because they can hurt you, and they keep body parts in their freezers," she stated matter-of-factly.

This statement sounded pretty crazy, and I wondered if Anne might be experiencing some psychotic thinking. But I was also aware that her friends had encouraged her to come in, yet hadn't accompanied her. I hoped this meant they thought she wasn't so psychologically impaired that she couldn't handle the visit alone.

I resumed my inquiry. "What makes you think doctors keep body parts, Anne?"

"It's what I've known all my life. Everyone in the church believed that," she responded, with a matter-of-fact tone.

"Do you believe it?"

"Yes," she replied, without hesitation. Then, for the first time without having been asked a question, Anne spoke. "But *you* might not have body parts," she said, shifting in her seat before continuing, "because you're not a real doctor."

"I mean," she quickly added, "I don't mean you're not a doctor, but my friends told me you're not a medical doctor, and you don't operate on people or do things to their bodies," she finished in a rush.

I was touched by her concern not to offend me, but at the same time, a part of me also felt sad that she felt so frightened of me.

"I understand what you mean, Anne," I assured her, offering a smile. "Actually, I have a degree called a doctorate in psychology, but it isn't a medical doctor's degree. We don't do anything to our clients' bodies, but we try to help them feel less sad or less afraid and to help them understand their thoughts and feelings." I paused to give her time to hear the honesty in my tone and not just my words. "Actually, I know many medical doctors, and I know they don't ever keep body parts in their freezers," I added.

She remained very still, looking at me intently, which told me she was listening closely.

"And they almost always help people feel less pain," I concluded, trying to help her feel safer. Yet, even though I was trying to soothe her, I realized I had rejected her understanding of the world, and I worried this could affect her comfort with me or her view of my credibility.

Anne gave no visible response, and I surmised that, at best, she viewed my words with skepticism. As often happens in therapy, we had veered from one important path to another, but I felt I needed to further assess the recent assault, so I asked, "Are you injured now, Anne?"

"My chest hurts," she said, placing a hand on her rib cage. "And my right jaw is very sore, she added, lightly touching two fingers along the underside of her chin.

She then held up her other hand and tried to raise her index finger. "This finger feels maybe broken, but it moves a little, so maybe it isn't. And my right leg hurts a lot and has a big bruise on it," she said, reaching a hand down and gently rubbing her thigh.

Her injuries were more pronounced than I had presumed, and indicated a significant tolerance for pain, which I surmised might have crossed over from physical to emotional in nature.

"I know you're afraid, but you really should see a doctor," I reiterated, hoping I might make a dent in the armor.

"No, I don't see doctors. It will get better. It always does in time," she sighed.

So despite my concern both for her physical discomfort and regarding the risk of internal injuries or internal bleeding, I deliberately exuded confidence and a sense of direction. But I felt anxious and off guard because much of her inner being was surfacing so quickly.

"Anne, could you tell me the events that led to your injuries?" I asked, deciding to shift the focus.

She seemed to relax, obviously relieved to talk about something else, something less immediate and less pressuring.

"I went to Oregon last week to testify, and several men from the church broke through the police security set up to protect me." She paused, waiting for my encouragement.

I nodded and smiled slightly. "Go on, Anne," I said.

"They beat me up and broke the leg of one of the policemen assigned to guard me."

She stopped and sat there, unsure of how much detail to go into.

In that moment, I was reminded of how familiar I was with the setting and culture of my work, and how unfamiliar she was with it.

"If you feel comfortable talking about what happened in Oregon last week, I'd like to know about it," I encouraged.

Then, as if a valve had released a floodgate, she began to talk about one of the most incredible histories I had encountered in fifteen years of practice.

— CHAPTER TWO —

"We pulled up to the courthouse in downtown Portland," Anne said, her body relaxing. "The officers stepped out of the car first and opened the door for me." She eased her posture and allowed her body to relax back into the chair.

"I remember stepping out onto the curb and looking up at the large, white, stone building. I kind of always felt afraid, so I didn't feel anything unusual as we began to walk toward the entrance. Suddenly, several men, five or six, maybe more, started running toward us." Anne's breathing quickened, and her eyes darted back and forth. She seemed to be reliving the moment as she shared it with me.

"I recognized Mr. Edwins, one of the men from my church, and knew they were after me. I froze and was too scared to run, and I just knew to cover my head with my hands and arms, allowing my body to take the beating, but trying to protect my head. I had long ago learned to sacrifice my body, but not let them hurt my mind or my soul."

Anne paused, and we looked at each other for a moment, saying nothing. The depth and power of her last sentence hung in the silence. She had dissociated a little as she spoke, but now she seemed to momentarily return from the past, and we both knew she was sharing her will to survive.

"I knew that two policemen couldn't protect me. I knew the power of the people from the church and their devotion. They were willing to do anything and they were doing God's work. Two policemen couldn't stop them. As the two officers turned their backs to me, I felt totally alone inside some inner world, and I sort of passed out or something, because I can't remember …" Anne's voice trailed off and she squinted, revealing her confusion.

"I used to do that a lot. It still happens sometimes. It's like I wasn't even sure if my eyes were open or closed, but I do remember seeing one of the officers fall down on the ground. I suddenly felt a sharp pain in my chest or stomach, and then another one in the back of my leg. And then I fell to the ground and curled into a ball and tried to cover my head and my arms.

"Someone grabbed at my arm and tried to drag me away, and then someone punched my chest and then he hit my jaw. That was the worst pain of all.

"I don't know how long the beating lasted, but I started to hear more people running, and I couldn't tell if they were coming at me or running away. Then, for a moment, I didn't feel anyone grabbing me or hitting me. I just lay there very still, almost like I was dead or something.

"Then someone crouched down beside me, and I grabbed my head tighter to protect against the next blow. But nothing happened, and a hand touched my arm in an oddly soft manner, followed by a voice asking if I was okay. I couldn't move or speak and had no idea what was happening. I remember hearing a man moaning nearby, obviously in pain, and again heard someone ask if I was okay. It was as if the words were in the air, but not able to enter my mind. I wasn't really back yet. My senses could still take in information, but nothing had any real meaning or made any sense yet.

"Then I heard a whistle and several sirens and words that sounded like, 'It's okay. You're safe now.' The next voice was a woman's. She said her name, but I wasn't really there yet. Then, when I felt her hand touch my arm I didn't tense up again and seemed to come back. I didn't feel the need to protect my head and body any longer, and my arms relaxed. I began to try to roll over to sit up and heard the same woman's voice say, 'Please stay still. You might be injured, and I want you to stay still until an ambulance arrives, because you may have internal injuries. My name's Catherine, and I'm a police officer. You're safe now. Can you tell me your name?'

"I had begun to calm down until I heard those words. That's what I'd heard earlier in the morning when I expressed my fear to the policemen protecting me. I began to tense up again and grabbed my head. The policewoman seemed to notice and again gently touched my arm and said, 'Don't worry, there are ten of us here now, and you're safe. The men who attacked you are gone. I need you to open your eyes enough to see all the officers here, so you can trust what I'm telling you.'

"It took a few moments before the officer's words sunk in, and slowly I uncovered my right eye and peeked through my fingers, trying to look around. Things were blurry as my wrists had been pressing on my eyeballs. As my vision cleared, I was able to see several men dressed in blue, and see a woman above me dressed the same. I knew these were police officers and that there were probably enough of them to protect me. I tried to sit up again, but the policewoman again said, 'Please stay down still a little longer. An ambulance crew is here now, and they're heading toward us. I promise I'll stay with you the whole time and all the way to the hospital.'

"Hearing the words 'ambulance' and 'hospital' terrified me and I suddenly tensed up and tried to sit up. There was intense pain in my chest and my jaw hurt terribly, but I was terrified again. As the policewoman tried to gently keep me from moving further, I almost yelled out, 'I won't go to a hospital.'

"The policewoman said, 'But you have injuries and need to be treated.'

"'No, we don't go to hospitals,' I told her. 'I want to go to the airport and go home. Can you just take me to the airport so I can go home?'

"'Let's wait for the ambulance crew to arrive and let them at least check you out,' she said.

"'Okay, but I'm not going to the hospital, and I won't see any doctors. It's not what we believe in.' I said.

"'Who is we?' she asked me.

"'Our church and our community,' I told her. 'I've never seen a doctor, and we heal without them. Doctors are evil and cut humans into pieces and then keep the pieces. This is wrong according to God.'" As Anne said this, I could see the strain and near panic in her face.

"The policewoman responded, 'I see. Can you tell me your name?'

"I said 'Anne,' very quietly, and tried to sit up further. I felt her hands still trying to keep me from moving, but she relaxed some as I continued to sit up further. I think she was doing her best to just keep me from leaving before medical people arrived.

"She then began asking me questions just to distract me, I think.

"'Where will you go when you get to the airport, Anne?' she asked.

"'Boston,' I told her.

"'Is that where you live?'

"'Yes.'

"'Is there someone in your family there we can call for you'

"'No, I don't have any family there. My family lives here in Oregon, but I don't want them to know anything about this right now.'

"'Why wouldn't you want your family to know Anne?' she asked.

"'Because they would think I deserved to be attacked and beaten.'

"Just as the policewoman was about to ask another question, three paramedics arrived with a stretcher and crouched down where I was now sitting, with my knees up to my chest and my arms curled around my knees. The officer moved to the side, allowing the paramedics to face me more directly. I tensed up again and felt myself withdrawing when the medical people crouched next to me. When the female paramedic put her hand on my shoulder, mostly to calm me down, I think, I started to go back inside again and started hugging my body, rather than resist her touch. I had learned to never physically resist others touching me, having never known any real difference between hurting and caring touch."

Anne stopped, still somewhat dazed. It isn't uncommon for trauma victims to have flashbacks so I hadn't been alarmed by her seeming trance as she'd spoken. But it's important to allow clients in that state time to recover their senses, so I didn't say anything.

A few minutes later, Anne looked at me as if remembering where she was, and an expectant look passed across her face for a moment before she habitually cast her eyes down again. I hadn't observed any anger or other emotion during the time she'd been speaking, but I'd found myself very drawn to her reliving of the experience. For a moment I wasn't sure how to respond, having only *my* feelings with which to gauge how to proceed, since I sensed none from her. A part of me knew I was experiencing the feelings Anne was missing, but I needed to stay with her, for now at least.

I felt myself searching for words of support. Finally, I said, "Wow. What a frightening experience. It sounds like there was no one who felt safe or trustworthy."

"I don't think I'd have known what that feels like anyway," Anne, now more fully restored to the present, said. "In a funny way, the men who attacked me felt more a part of me than the police officers."

"Why were they threatened by you?" I asked.

"Because I was there to provide testimony that would hurt them, and they believed I deserved it."

"What were you testifying about?"

"What they did to children."

"And why would you deserve it?"

"Because I was defying God's will, and because women are inferior and deserve it."

"Is that what you believe, Anne?"

"I know my friends think this is wrong, and I'm sure you'll think it's wrong, but it's what I've learned to believe," she said.

"Then it's important that I respect and try to understand your beliefs, Anne," I said, "even if I don't believe you deserve to be harmed."

She just sat there, seeming a little less connected, and I wondered if I had partially shut her down by positing my perspective. For me as a psychotherapist, it was a toss-up between supporting her and helping her to begin to see herself as deserving human kindness. Such complex choices were often unclear, and they were sometimes the most difficult part of my work.

"Maybe it would help if you could tell me about the church, Anne," I said.

Anne again relaxed into the chair, closed her eyes, and began describing the world of her childhood and her community.

— CHAPTER THREE —

Jonas Smith grew up with a preacher father and a mother totally devoted to her husband's calling and position. Young Jonas both greatly feared and idolized his father, seeing the capacity of his role and confidence to influence his flock of parishioners. His father ruled with an iron fist but never laid a hand upon his children. He could instill the fear of God's wrath, and this carried far greater impact. Jonas was the ideal son, a leader in youth projects, who led a mission to Central America after finishing high school at the age of seventeen, and then entered a small, private, Christian-based university, quickly emerging as a strong leader. He studied sociology and psychology, wanting to understand human cultural experience, emotion and behavior in order to enhance his abilities to influence and lead others.

It wasn't long after graduating from college that Jonas felt his calling to lead others in a communal and spiritual life. Jonas had observed the growing disenchantment among the younger adults to whom he had begun to offer support and counseling. Living in Medford, a medium-sized city in southern Oregon, he saw a growing influx of disenchanted, down-and-out, late adolescents and young adults from California and large cities in the East and Midwest, and he saw their coinciding accessibility and vulnerability.

He was running a church-based social service organization, providing a mixture of financial and physical support to homeless people, hoping to bring them into the church to shore up its declining membership and influence. With little external oversight of his financial operations, Jonas was quite free to use church monies at his discretion. From early on, he had been diverting funds to an account unknown to the church elders. He had always known that he would use these funds in some way to increase his influence on the world. In addition, several sizable contributions came from some of the more affluent families of young members Jonas had delivered from drug abuse and street life.

It was with these monies that he initially rented a group of houses in nearby Deerbrook, a community far enough away from Medford to retain its privacy but sufficiently accessible to the larger community to provide access to future members and their commercial needs. The cost of acquiring land in Deerbrook was almost incidental, enabling Jonas to purchase two significant parcels, one being the most central block along Main Street and the other a large parcel of farmland just east of the town. Jonas Smith had very effectively interwoven the tokens of appreciation for his efforts at saving lost souls with the creation of the infrastructure of his evolving social order.

The initial years of the community centered on his adherents' shared alienation and detachment. Over time, however, his sociopolitical focus changed to a religious philosophy. The evolving community easily attracted followers who were disenchanted by the hedonism and perceived breakdown of the social and familial structure in the latter sixties and early seventies. They found Jonas' charisma and fervor attractive, providing him an easily convinced choir.

Early church services had been more like communal gatherings on social issues. They slowly mutated to meetings with more of a philosophical nature, but remained informal and democratic. Jonas eventually began using these meetings to educate and provide greater structure for the community. This evolved into preaching and the gatherings increasingly resembled church services with the introduction of a higher power that slowly mutated into a Godlike figure.

Jonas was brilliant in his gradual approach toward a religious spirituality, building an intensely loyal inner circle of zealots and, effectively, using the power of the inner circle to influence the larger membership. The forum established norms and rules, bringing a sense of government under the same umbrella to the community. It was a brilliant mix of sociology, psychology, spirituality, and corporate strategy. The community grew and developed a stronger role in influencing the daily lives of its inhabitants. There was also a gradual shift in psychological influence, from serving the community to serving the movement's hierarchy. Motivating people to do good deeds gradually gave way to motivating them to obey the evolving inner circle of elders through fear, a fundamental shift that began to give the community a cult-like aura.

In less than a decade, the community grew to approximately six hundred people, mostly families. As they grew in numbers, their economic base expanded greatly. However, the members, in essence, owned nothing. Instead, their food, clothing, shelter, and health care were completely taken care of by the community. Handing over their possessions and incomes to the church was part of living a truly Christian life. This included members who worked outside the farm, most typically in professional capacities, in nearby communities or in the city of Medford. The members' lives were devoted to simplicity and were truly communal in nature. Unless someone ventured off the farm for an outing or to do business, there wasn't even the visibility of money.

Such was the underlying foundation and visible reality of The Christian Movement, a name that Jonas and the movement's elders introduced gradually and intentionally. From the beginning, Jonas had introduced the name "The Movement," and over the first few years had begun employing the name "The Spiritual Movement." As he increasingly, and ever more intentionally, evolved his teaching toward preaching the word of God, he referred to the "Christian principles" of the community. By the time he called for a renaming of the community as The Christian Movement, the change seemed like a natural progression, rather than any sort of leap.

Simultaneously, a physical and financial landscape had also evolved. As integrated as people were with Jonas and his aspirations, virtually no one was privy to how much this community was a well-planned future for his desire for power. It gained greater and greater momentum to become a very successful community, church, and corporate entity, all in one, with Jonas maintaining the leadership of all three.

Men dominated every aspect of the hierarchy, and women were excluded from the ranks of elders and positions of authority. If they had had any real awareness of the burgeoning women's movement across the land, they would have decried it as blasphemous and destructive to the social structure and religious principles that God and Christ had intended for them. It was difficult to ascertain what was more influential in creating their adherence to this way of being. Were they primarily the products of indoctrination and brainwashing or a group of women who had grown up with similar fundamental beliefs and gravitated toward partners and a community that afforded them a familiar environment?

Women were expected to forgo any of the adornments that allowed for attractiveness or femininity. They weren't permitted to wear jewelry other than simple crosses, adorn or embroider their hair, or wear make-up or dresses, except on rare occasions in the outside world. Most of the time they wore uniforms similar to those worn by their male counterparts, with the exception of wearing khaki skirts instead of pants, and neckerchiefs during the colder weather. Overall, their attire diminished any real sense of femininity or individual identity. They made most of their own clothing, with modesty being the criterion.

Outsiders were often disturbed by their military-like attire, perceiving it as encouraging aggression and alienation, but the community leaders felt it dispelled notions of luxury and promoted a sense of equality among all. They believed they had to stand up strongly, with almost a militaristic pride, for their right to believe in true Christianity. They believed they were protecting the teachings of Christ in a world that was losing Christian values.

As time progressed, the central governing body of elders increasingly interpreted and dictated the spiritual, legal, and economic rules that determined life in the community. The intensity and depth of this power and control were typical of most cults. The adherents were entirely devoted to the dictates and values espoused by Father Jonas and his inner circle of elders, who tolerated virtually no dissent.

The movement raised children with a firm hand and a strong belief in physical punishment. The children had few toys, and religious and community participation had priority over familial or peer relationships, engendering authority and loyalty to Jonas Smith and the elders at an early age. The movement emphasized education considerably more for boys, who were inherently more valued than girls, reflecting the adults' social roles and behaviors.

Some members held jobs outside the community, returning each night to the farm and their families or to their communal homes if they weren't married. Their incomes were entirely committed to the movement. There was a position of great trust placed upon those who worked outside to maintain their vows, including a vow of celibacy that was expected of the single members of the church. In addition, like all the members, they vowed to abstain from alcohol, drugs, cigarettes, sugar and caffeine. Others worked in the church's varied business interests in an empire that continued to grow into millions of dollars in net worth.

The movement had been founded around the concepts of communal living and sacrifice for the good of others, popular values and causes in the late sixties and early seventies. Members initially lived in large communal houses committed to rural life and an isolationist philosophy, separating them from the lust, greed, temptation, and socio-political stress that were perceived to be permeating the larger society. The community was composed mostly of families, but there were as many as a hundred single men and women who lived in separate housing.

A prominent role for many community members was to mentor the novitiates who were brought into the community from typically desperate circumstances, such as drug addiction, alcoholism, criminal behavior, prostitution, and running away. For anyone trying to overcome the power of any of these challenges, the farm was as safe and supportive as any inpatient treatment program. The objects that fed their cravings weren't available, and there was constant support for their battles to overcome the "evil within."

However, it didn't take long for these new disciples to feel imprisoned by a new force, that of a devoutly religious community that was as powerful in its control of their lives as their particular vices had been. Only a small minority remained with the community for very long. For most, it was a respite and a place to restore physical strength and nurturance.

The Deerbrook of Anne's childhood was a town identified by its proximity to a larger place, accessible by a road that meandered through verdant forest landscape twenty miles from the city of Medford, Oregon. It was too far away to constitute a suburb, but relied on Medford for its commercial and governmental infrastructure. However, it remained a town dependent upon the social responsibility and volunteerism inherent in its community values and citizenry.

At first glance, a visitor would have been struck by the simplicity of its inhabitants, in many respects unaffected by high technology, international politics, the cultural scenes emanating from the East or West Coast, or many of the problems that plagued urban America. Crime was virtually unknown, a testament to only having to maintain a sheriff, a deputy, and volunteer peace officers. The population was almost entirely white.

Residents dressed in clothes characteristic of rural America, typically in denim jeans, calico, and homemade, knitted sweaters, or the omnipresent uniforms of the members of The Christian Movement.

A visitor would also have noticed that people knew each other in Deerbrook, nodding hello or chatting briefly as they meandered down Main Street. No one seemed in a hurry, and their lives appeared to be free of the pressures of life. There was a distinct sense of having stepped back in time to the fifties, when towns and communities were far more placid, friendly, and safe, and when the culture didn't question inequality of the sexes. Deerbrook was like a seawall holding back the current of the times.

Deerbrook was one of those towns with one main street, aptly named Main Street, with smaller streets feeding off of it and sloping gently uphill on one side and downhill on the other. The town's commercial center spanned three blocks, and most of the buildings that comprised the commercial district were made of brick, reflecting architectural styles from the early part of the century. Almost every structure was either one or two stories high, with twelve- to fourteen-foot ceilings. Many of the windows were arched, with very detailed cornices under the eaves and stonework that showed the skill of masons and craftsmen of a bygone era. On some of the brickwork, advertising that existed prior to billboards and neon signs, although faded, could still be detected.

Distinctly visible in Deerbrook was The Christian Movement church, a large edifice on Main Street in the center of town. The gleaming white structure, with massive columns forming the front porch, extended a full block. It was distinguished from the other buildings in town not only for its immensity, but also for the manicured grounds, which obviously required substantial upkeep. The rest of the town appeared to fan out symmetrically from the church, and an astute observer would easily have intuited that the church, rather than the government, was the dominant and defining force in Deerbrook.

Traveling beyond the few main blocks, the buildings became a mix of wood, brick, and masonry. Many of their names reflected Deerbrook's quaintness and small-town innocence. Some, including the United States Post Office, Deerbrook Hardware, The Deerbrook Hotel, and Mason's Clothing and Fabric Store, still operated under their original names and functions almost a century later. Others, such as the "Food For Thought" grocery store, and the "Cut Above" beauty parlor, made use of witty names akin to those in neighboring Medford— although a cross adorned each side of the establishments' signs, lest anyone forget their religious context.

It was as striking to note what was absent from Deerbrook as much as what was there. There were no hospitals, medical clinics, or physicians. The only commercial establishments were retailers who provided staples and other basic necessities and tradesmen. There were no liquor stores, pharmacies, movie theaters, music or video outlets, or restaurants besides two local cafés. The church housed the only bookstore, and the only banking establishment was the church credit union.

What was visibly present in Deerbrook, however, was an omnipresent fleet of white cargo vans with scriptures adorning the sides, each with one or more men outfitted in various forms of military fatigues, including identical black, lace-up boots and black berets with large white crosses on the front, much like the main church, painted white and adorned with a large black cross. There was little doubt that The Christian Movement was integrated into almost every aspect and nuance of the community.

Deerbrook was one of many towns off the beaten path that found their populations dwindling as the elderly founders died off and the younger generation was pulled toward the stimulation and opportunity of the larger cities. However, the growth and power of The Christian Movement continued to allow it to remain populated and economically viable.

It was a community whose residents were familiar enough with their neighbors that an outsider entering the town, usually someone related to a local inhabitant, or the occasional driver who got lost and meandered into town, would have been easily visible to locals. A visitor interacting with Deerbrook's shopkeepers, or just asking for directions, would have found the locals polite but not overly friendly. People in Deerbrook were generally guarded and suspicious—not enough that an outsider would have suspected something was amiss, but enough to have made anyone passing through feel less than welcome in the town.

Traveling east of town, past its commercial center, one would have seen a few houses, but then only land for the next several miles, before coming to a large, private parcel surrounded by fencing. A sign that said "Welcome to The Farm" was inviting and offered a sense of serenity.

The main road leading in traveled for half a mile through a working farm. There were several large barns, facilities for dairy cow operations, several large chicken coops, orchards, corrals for horses, and storage buildings. The smell of dairy cows, chickens, horses, and hay was pungent, and at various times of the year, was overwhelmed by the noxious odor of fresh manure or sulphur used as fertilizer.

On a typical rainy day, very common to southern Oregon much of the year, a visitor would also have experienced a dampening chill, paralleling a deeper sense that something just wasn't right. Heading along the main road, the first lane veered to the right and headed into a wooded area, where overhanging trees quickly eclipsed most daylight and concealed the road beyond.

Just at the intersection of this road and the main road, there was a sign that read "Camp Deerbrook"—one of the service adjuncts to the main farming business of the community. Several other roads, both to the left and right, led to a sizable group of small residences, spanning four or five blocks off the main road. All the hundred or so houses were uniform in size and style. There were no street signs, and the roads were identical in width and length. None was paved, and all of them sloped to allow for runoff of the area's significant rainfall.

The main road ended in the center of the farm, where several buildings comprised the community's commercial, administrative, and social functions, along with a food cooperative and several large communal dwellings. The most striking edifice was a church similar in appearance to the one in town, painted white with a large black cross on the front. There was also a sprawling brick school. In contrast to all the other wooden structures, the brick construction appeared to reflect the community's devotion to its children. The overall effect, a visitor might have noted, was one of enterprise and devotion to the communal society.

The farm community operated as a true form of socialism, with everyone living and working together for the good of the whole, enjoying economic equality, being responsible for the needs of the community, and being provided for by the community. The houses were nearly identical in size and style, all painted one of three pale colors. Even the gardens lacked individuality and were defined more by the commitment to producing food staples rather than indulging in something as frivolous and hedonistic as flowers.

It wouldn't have taken long for a visitor to notice the complete absence of alcohol, tobacco, televisions, radios, or more than an occasional newspaper.

There were no baseball diamonds, basketball courts, or football fields. The Christian Movement shunned competitive sports, although it encouraged individual recreation and physical activity— as long as it was of the passive variety. Painting, creating "tasteful" and "appropriate" music, embroidery, reading "appropriate" books, walking, cycling, cooking, and swimming, for example, were acceptable, as each served to maintain solemnity.

The devotion to healthy eating and physical exercise contributed to the ability to survive with very limited access to outside medical providers. The prohibition against access to most outside communication prevented people from being influenced against their community's way of being.

In contrast to the consistently visible modesty and simplicity of the community, The Christian Movement was a financial empire with known revenues in the neighborhood of twenty million dollars annually and a net worth that was virtually impossible for an outsider to calculate. Assets were held in the names of numerous corporations that had interwoven relationships. Many of these financial entities enjoyed freedom from taxation, as was typically afforded to religious institutions. A large portion of their business dealings were done with cash, making it extremely difficult to truly assess revenues, income, and the ownership of assets. In spite of taking great advantage of these benefits or loopholes, there was nothing that visibly indicated any improprieties in the movement's business or financial dealings. The group's wealth seemed more due to a very strong work ethic, virtually free labor by the members, and Jonas Smith's very good business acumen.

Venturing down the second road to the right, the second house from the end on the south side, which is how the inhabitants referred to their addresses, one would have come to the Martins, a couple whose most striking feature, to an outsider, would have been their age difference. Mr. Martin appeared to be in his late fifties and Mrs. Martin in her early thirties. The difference in their ages would have been less striking within the community itself, where a number of the elders married much younger women or, in a few cases, teenage girls. As church elders, they were able to attract the movement's neophytes, initially appealing to their vulnerability and wielding considerable power as males and dominant members of the community, a role they justified by interpreting the Bible to reinforce the subordination of women.

The Martins' marriage was typical of those in The Christian Movement. They dressed in plain clothing or in similar khaki camouflage fatigues, with the quintessential black cross adorning their shirts on the upper left side and black, military-style boots. One significant difference was the adornment of ribbons below Mr. Martin's black cross, almost identical to those worn by military officers or combat veterans who have been recognized for their achievements. Women were not allowed to earn or wear any such symbol of

stature or influence. Their outfits were always very clean and pressed, one of
Mrs. Martin's wifely duties.

On this particular day in the summer of 1970, however, Mr. and Mrs.
Martin are dressed differently. Instead of donning their usual khaki, they are
attired in their Sunday best during the middle of the week. Mr. Martin has
donned a black suit and starched white shirt buttoned all the way to the
top, and Mrs. Martin is wearing a very simple black dress, plain black flat
shoes, and a black scarf to cover her head. A simple white cross provides her
only adornment. To the observer, they would appear perfectly attired for a
funeral.

This morning, the Martins are scurrying around the house, obviously
frazzled and in a hurry. They have packed up their young daughter, a
beautiful two-year-old named Shauna, and their five-year-old son, Jacob, who
is considerably more boisterous, a typical reflection of the autonomy instilled
in boys in church families.

Today is very important for the Martins, who are heading out on the
four-hour drive up to Portland to pick up their new daughter at Providence
Community Hospital. While Mr. Martin readies the car, Mrs. Martin takes
the two children to a neighbor's house. This is her one moment to express her
joy to her woman friend, in private, since such natural feminine and maternal
expressions are shunned around males in the community. After a brief directive
to the children to behave, which is virtually unneeded considering their fear
of Mr. Martin's wrath, Mrs. Martin returns to their small house and joins her
husband for the silent journey to Portland.

finger on anything of serious concern. Mr. Martin cut into her thoughts. "Is there anything else you need us to do here?" he asked curtly.

"No, that completes the adoption process, Mr. Martin. I wish you the best with your new daughter."

"Thank you. Let's go, Mother," he said, and the couple turned toward the door. Mrs. Johnson sadly realized that his way of addressing his wife was an accurate reflection of how Mr. Martin valued her, more for her role of motherhood than as the partner and human with whom he shared his life. The Martins walked out the door and into the world with their infant daughter, Anne.

Their trip back to Deerbrook was entirely uneventful, with Mrs. Martin holding the child in her lap and no conversation occurring for the entire four-hour ride. If this was a couple experiencing joy, it was a complete secret. As they drove through the verdant forests, Mrs. Martin periodically looked at the sleeping infant whom she held in her lap, but mostly seemed to stare out the passenger window watching the forests go by. Her reflection on the glass portrayed sadness and apathy rather than the normal joy of a new mother.

Upon their arrival back at their home, Mrs. Martin went next door to retrieve the two other children, while Mr. Martin quickly departed for town, leaving Mrs. Martin to cope with their five-year-old son, two-year-old daughter, and an infant whom she had just met. This was her responsibility, and his was to serve his community as a devotee and messenger of God. Such was the beginning of little Anne's new life. From her very first day, little Anne had come to represent and reflect Mr. Martin's stature in the church. If there was any emotion toward this little girl on his part, it was eclipsed by her role in his goals.

As for Mrs. Martin, she knew to show little affection or emotion toward her daughter in front of Father. Her love and protection of Anne, as constrained as it was, remained a secret at best. We are each dealt a life, and there is little fairness to that process. We are also each dealt abilities to cope with adversity, and there is little fairness to that process. Little Anne was definitely dealt a very poor hand in the nurture department. What nature had dealt her would be revealed during her lifetime.

— CHAPTER FIVE —

I'd been so enthralled by Anne's description of the world she had come from that we'd run out of time for the session and I hadn't yet assessed her general mental state and any immediate risks. "This is such important information," I explained, "and it will obviously take a few sessions to have a good understanding of your life, but I need to ask about some other things. I know you're in physical discomfort from your injuries and that you are very frightened of hospitals and medical doctors, but …"

"I don't want to see any medical doctors or go to any hospitals," Anne interrupted. I found myself both surprised and impressed by her sudden boldness. Her fear of doctors appeared to even outweigh her fear of me.

"All right," I said in what I hoped was a soothing tone, "but if your pain increases, please call me, and I'll put you in touch with someone who would be very caring. Noticing that her eyelids were red and her face looked a bit puffy, I asked, "How often are you crying?"

"I cry all the time—every day," she said.

"How are you sleeping?"

"It's hard to sleep, because I have terrible dreams and I wake up shaking and very frightened. And I'm afraid to fall back asleep. When my jaw and chest stop hurting, I'll sleep better, and the dreams sometimes aren't as bad. I've been taking high doses of herbs from my friend Mickie. My mind doesn't seem to want to stop, and sometimes I have coffee to keep myself awake so I can think things through."

I mulled over this confusing approach to sleep for a moment. It seemed somewhat reflective of her overall disorganization, and I wondered if she was describing obsessing as a means of trying to cope. "It sounds like it can be hard to let things go and just relax," I said.

"My friend Mickie says I'm being really obsessive. She said I'm pretty ODC or something. I'm always making sure everything is clean and in order. Sometimes I start vacuuming at three in the morning when I can't sleep, but I found that wakes everyone up at the house." Anne smiled as she said this, and I was glad to see she had retained her sense of humor. "Mickie laughed when she saw me ironing my underwear, and I think that's when she said I'm ODC."

somewhat animatedly described getting smashed several times with Mickie on a recent trip to Ogonquit, Maine, reminding me of the way my buddies and I would have described getting smashed in our college years. It was one of the indicators of Anne's delayed emotional and psychological development. Most of their drinking occurred in gay and lesbian establishments, and this felt much safer to Anne. Her description of her alcohol intake triggered a couple of potential red flags for me. Her admissions of several recent episodes of intoxication, along with her propensity to treat her emotional symptoms with substances, were concerning.

"Would you be willing to keep a log of your drinking for the next couple of weeks so we actually know how much you're drinking?" I posited.

"Yeah, I guess that would be okay," she replied, almost with enthusiasm for having something concrete to work on.

Not wanting to confront her drinking any further today, I inquired about her health history. Anne indicated a history of allergies, periodic back pain and a history of malaria, acquired during mission work for the church in Kenya. She also indicated a significant history of depression and serious episodes of either anxiety or panic attacks, the last one having occurred that morning in contemplation of coming to our session. Her panic included fears of being beaten or yelled at by me if she said the wrong thing. Her description of her symptoms included her whole body shaking, difficulty breathing followed by hyperventilation, significant sweating, great difficulty concentrating, her mind racing and intense fear that she was being hunted by members of the church. The duration of these events or attacks was usually less than half an hour, further supporting the impression of panic attacks.

Her first such attack had occurred within a week of leaving the church, and she had endured them as frequently as daily in recent weeks. I was struck by the timing of the development of her panic disorder. It had begun after she left a world in which she appeared to have experienced significant distress and trauma. Somewhat ironically, life on the farm had provided a certain consistency. Although she had been abused there, her world—good or bad—was predictable.

Once she had left the church, however, her life had become much less certain. This fit with the terror of uncertainty that forms the essence of panic attacks. In addition, by cooperating with the legal authorities, she had become terrified of retribution from members of the church. She had no means of predicting the nature, severity or timing of such actions.

She shared that the attacks were increasing in intensity more recently, but she couldn't attribute them to any specific event that might have frightened her. They mostly seemed to come "out of the blue." Her most intense panic, she said, occurred in large groups of people, especially if she felt trapped in a crowd. But such attacks were more a result of her fear that the panic would occur in public, rather than being evoked by the crowd itself.

I found myself wanting to share with her how much she was describing classic panic disorder, maybe to help normalize what she was going through, but I feared she might think I was diminishing her experience. I was still quite intimidated by her seeming fragility and hypersensitivity to everything I said or did.

Anne said that Mickie would grow frustrated when she refused to go to a concert or a dance club, but such events were far too threatening for her. She was also fearful of one of the hospice patients where she worked part-time as an aide. She described him as a tall man who reminded her of Jonas Smith. She had asked to stop working with this man because she frequently suffered nosebleeds while caring for him. This struck me as not only unusual, but also as a powerful somatization of her emotional state.

She also described several other men who frightened her easily, each one being depicted as tall. Sometimes she had a sense that a couple of these men might be violent, but she couldn't explain anything behaviorally or verbally that would support her hunches. I couldn't tell if these were paranoid thoughts or a keen sensitivity to danger, either of which could be stemming from a history of abuse and violence.

There was so much more I needed and wanted to know about Anne, but I sensed that she'd had enough for one day. I reached for a document on the table beside my chair as a way of transitioning, and said, "We're going to need to stop for today, Anne."

"Okay," she said, her tone flat.

"Are you comfortable to meet with me again?" I asked.

"Yeah, I guess so," she said, her tone letting us both know how tentative she was.

"Well, how about if we set up a time to meet in a couple of days?"

"We need to meet in a couple of days?" Anne asked, looking surprised. "My friends said we'd probably meet once a week."

"I think it's important that we meet again later this week if we could, so that I can complete my assessment and we can begin to help you feel less afraid," I said, not feeling comfortable waiting a week without having a better handle on her emotional stability or risk.

"When do you want to meet?"

"How about Wednesday morning at ten?" I offered, looking at my appointment book.

"Yeah, that would be okay," she agreed, having no apparent schedule to consider.

"Great. Here's a card with our next appointment time on it," I said, holding it far enough away that it became a cue for Anne to stand up to take it. She stood very slowly, keeping a hand over her head, and very cautiously reached to take the card. I released the card as Anne took it, and I moved a couple of steps sideways to open the door, making sure to give her plenty of physical space to feel safe. "Goodbye, Anne, I'll see you on Wednesday," I said as she passed.

After Anne departed, I sat back down in my chair and stared blankly into space for a few minutes. I felt amazed by the power of this woman's fear, yet somehow sensed an incredible bravery underneath her terror. I was very aware of needing to be extra cautious about everything I said, and I reminded myself of the importance of being sensitive to Anne's fear without infantilizing her. But I felt off my game, not having done my normal intake. And I knew Anne's case would remain a complex task for a long time to come—if she hung in with therapy.

— CHAPTER SIX —

During my years of working with Anne, I had the truly good fortune of living four blocks from my office in Boston's South End, a neighborhood that had transformed tremendously over the past twenty years. Once on the edge of the "safe and desirable" Back Bay neighborhood and the more impoverished neighborhood of Roxbury, west of the city, it was now a gentrified mixture of two-hundred-year-old brick facades that had skyrocketed in value. The neighborhood had become a thriving and chic community, with an increasing yuppie population along with young, childless professionals and an entrenched guppie (gay urban professional) community.

The South End had an array of very trendy shops, purveying a multitude of culinary arts, floral designs, pricy galleries, upscale restaurants featuring international and American cuisine, pet boutiques, and—unlike Deerbrook—many other non-necessities of living.

Walking along the tree-lined streets of the South End provided a valuable transitional phase each day, allowing me to shift from the multi-tasking of home life to the highly focused role of psychotherapy. Having reached my forty-eighth birthday, my hair now had that salt-and-pepper look that distinguished me as an older man, someone shopkeepers now called "Sir." Along with my reading glasses, which despite my initial resistance, I had inevitably succumbed to, my hair certified that I had become a member of an age group I had only imagined my parents belonging to. What most confirmed my aging, however, was my increasing invisibility. Once the object of visual attention, I was now mostly unnoticed. Yet I was very proud of so much of myself and my life, and that is where I usually placed my focus and energy.

On this particular day, when Anne would meet with me for her second session, my walk was especially fruitful, affording me the time to ponder her case. Being both a new client and my first client of the day, she was naturally the focus of my thoughts this morning. As I strolled along on this unusually sunny and mild morning for March in Boston, I considered what Anne had told me in our first session. Anne had presented an incredible story, but I had no idea yet that it was only the tip of an iceberg. As I arrived at my office, a first-floor, private space on Tremont Street, I saw Anne waiting for me. Dressed in a T-shirt with the word "BOSTON" printed on it, she was crouched against a tree and appeared to tense up, lowering her head slightly as I approached her. We exchanged a quiet "hello," and she followed me into my waiting room. She stood there, appearing very uncertain, and I asked her to take a seat and give me a few minutes. My sense was that more than honor the request, she meekly obeyed it.

After reviewing my notes from our first session, I opened the door to the waiting room, only to find Anne again cowering in the corner, almost out of my view. I invited her into my office, and she again slowly walked toward the door with her arms protecting her face and head. I backed far enough into the office to give her ample physical space to enter. She came into the room but just stood in the center, appearing to be waiting for me to give her permission to sit on the sofa. I very calmly gestured with my hand and said, "How about sitting on the sofa again, and I'll take my chair?"

Without saying anything, Anne quietly took her seat. She didn't look at me and, as in our first session, held herself with her hands cupping each of her shoulders.

After a brief pause, I asked, "How are you doing today, Anne?"

"I'm okay," she said softly. "But my chest still hurts a lot, and it's hard to eat, because my jaw is still pretty sore."

"Have you thought any further about whether you might see a doctor?"

"I won't go to a doctor, but my friend Tim is a nurse, and he's given me something for the pain. He says that even if I have fractured ribs, there really isn't anything they're going to do. He thinks I should have my jaw checked out, however, by a dentist, but I'll be okay."

"I understand," I said, my tone resigned. "I'd like to find out more about you today, but I also want to be sure you feel you can talk about anything you'd like to as well."

Pulling a paper from her pocket, Anne said, "I got a letter from my father and brought it with me. Would you like to read it?" she asked, barely offering the paper.

I gently took the page from Anne and saw that it was a copy of an e-mail sent two days earlier. I found myself wondering about the impersonal nature of technology now connecting Anne with her family compared to the world she had always known. I began to read.

Anne,

Your life and your actions of the past three weeks are a sin and an abomination to yourself and God. I am ashamed to call you a child of mine and wish fervently that we had never adopted you. Your natural parents had the right idea. I dislike you. But not only do I dislike you; I wish you were dead. You are a disgusting and vile being. Your life is pointless, just like you. You tell your mother and I that you are working on sorting things out, yet you must realize that the only way to sort out anything is through God and submission to his servants. You must be a slave to God and to God's men. Then you will find fulfillment and happiness, even though you do not deserve them. They should have finished you off when they had the chance. Mercy for the sinner is murder from the saints. Think on these things, and know that the moment you return to the fold, you'll be forgiven and loved. I will pray for you.

    Dad.

I was stunned by the letter's vitriol and cruelty. "I wish you were dead" were words reminiscent of what a child might say. It was hard to imagine that a father could feel, let alone express, such vituperation. But more importantly, the letter gave me additional information about what kind of damage might have been exacted upon Anne growing up.

"How did you feel when you read the letter?" I asked, feigning neutrality.

"I don't know. That's how he writes," Anne replied, her matter-of-fact tone more honest in its neutrality.

"Do you think it's a mean or hurtful letter?" I pressed, thinking that I could have asked a more open-ended question instead of leading the witness, so to speak. I had reacted from my own emotional place to what seemed an obvious truth. Sometimes that's okay, but, for now, I needed to be wherever Anne was.

"I guess it is," she replied quietly.

This was not the spirit I had hoped Anne might feel. She showed no anger or even recognition that such a letter might be unusual. I had to remind myself that her normal and my normal were quite different. It wasn't my role or right to encourage or challenge her emotions or perceptions at this stage of treatment, but I still offered, "Anne, I realize you either aren't experiencing or aren't expressing anger, but are you aware that most people would feel angry receiving such a letter from anyone, let alone their father?"

"I know most people would feel angry, but I don't," Anne said, glancing up quickly to see if I might disapprove of her response.

Recognizing her behavior, I gently asked, "Do you have any thoughts as to why your experience and reaction are so different from most people?"

"I guess I just don't feel anger. If I felt angry and expressed it growing up, I would have been hurt more. I learned not to get angry or even let myself feel angry." This was a fundamental insight into her history. Anne had endured what was beginning to look like a very abusive and dangerous childhood, and she had found ways, such as this, to survive.

"I wonder if you would feel comfortable telling me more about what kinds of hurt you experienced growing up, Anne. I should share with you that I may have to report child abuse. But I know this has been reported, and that's why you're a witness. What's also important here is that there might be other children still being abused."

"I don't want anything about my father reported," she said, raising her voice for the first time.

Wondering where that came from, I needed to respond carefully. "Well, I'm not allowed to make that promise, Anne. I realize that might not be comforting enough for you, but I don't want you to ever feel deceived by me. Too many people have hurt you and damaged your trust and ability to feel. I can at least commit that if there is something I feel I need to report, then you and I together can decide how to approach this."

I looked for some kind of acknowledgment, but Anne just sat there, hopefully hearing my words at least, but too afraid or too shut down to express any discomfort or disagreement. "So, why might anyone think that your father should be reported?"

Anne squirmed in her seat but stayed quiet. "I know this is scary for you to talk about, but in some ways you're choosing whether to prioritize our work together as a way to help you or a way to protect him. You've spent your life doing the latter, and maybe this is finally the time to trust another path," I prodded.

She remained silent, but almost visibly gave this some thought. "Do you have to report things I tell you he did to me as a child?" she asked finally.

"Does your father have access to or spend any time around children now, including grandchildren, neighbors, or maybe volunteer activities?"

"I can't imagine he's around children at all. He's eighty-four, and the only grandchildren are in Europe. He also hasn't been involved in anything with me or any children I know of for more than a decade," Anne said, appearing relieved that she didn't have anything incriminating to divulge.

"If you're talking about things from your childhood and more than a decade ago, then I doubt that's a concern, if no one is at further risk," I said.

For the moment, it was most important that I continue trying to learn about Anne's experience, and I would have to assess any decision regarding mandated reporting afterwards. I also knew that numerous authorities and people in social services had assessed both the legal issues and other potential victims involved. Consequently, I might be the only person who was simply there to help her feel better.

"I can at least commit to having us together make any decisions regarding me talking to anyone else, okay?"

"Okay," she said hesitantly. We paused briefly, both of us seemingly aware that we had reached some kind of agreement together.

"Do the police or social services know anything about your father's involvement in abusing you?" I continued.

"No. When I called the police, it was because a nine-year-old girl I was babysitting was being sexually abused. I did tell the police about my history of being abused, but I didn't tell them my father would be involved sometimes."

"Well, would you still be willing to tell me about your history of being abused?"

"I guess so. Do you mean physical abuse?"

"I'd like to understand all the types of abuse—physical, emotional, and, if there was sexual abuse, that would be very important also," I said softly.

"I was forced to have sex often."

"At what age did this begin, Anne?"

"I can remember back to about ages five or six, and it was happening then."

"How long did it continue?"

"Until a few years ago."

"Meaning into adulthood as well?" I asked, realizing she was talking about almost thirty years.

"Yes."

"How often did it happen?"

"Sometimes daily, but usually only a couple of times a week."

"What's it like to think and talk about it with me now?" I asked, searching for some kind of emotional reaction.

"Okay, I guess," she said, her voice flat.

"Can you tell me about some of the abusive experiences, what happened and who was involved?" I asked, feeling a little more comforted that Anne was feeling safe enough to share more with me.

"I was made to have oral sex and sexual intercourse. Mostly, the church elders were involved."

"Anne, you've told me your father was a church elder. Did his abuse occur as part of being with other elders, or was it occurring at home as well?"

"It was both."

"Where was your mother, and what do you think she knew?"

"She knew about some of it, but not all of it. The women in the church would sometimes hold me down, but my mother never did that. She would see the bleeding and the bruises and treat them, so she knew it was happening. I don't think she knew my father was involved, but I'm not really sure. She believed what my father believed and would never question his beliefs or the teachings of the church. I guess I don't really know what she felt about things."

"Were there other forms of abuse?"

"Well, I don't know if you call it abuse, but I was often kept in a cage, and I had lots of other injuries."

"Without knowing what you mean by 'other injuries' or being 'kept in a cage,' I would think these things are forms of serious abuse actually. How do you feel about your childhood when you think about it now?"

"I get really upset sometimes, because I realize how much I gave up, and now that I learn about other people's childhoods being fun and happy, it's much harder to know," she replied, a hint of sadness in her voice for the first time.

"When you think of what you gave up, what do you focus on?"

"I gave up just being a child, getting to play, go to school with other kids, knowing what it was really like to feel loved or have someone believe in me. I didn't ever think I did anything right, and I learned to believe I was evil. Even my mom saw me as a child of Satan," she said, looking downward and ashamed.

Not sure whether it would add to her sense of loss, I kept to myself my own thoughts of what else she had given up: any sense of safety, unconditional love from a mother and a father, possibly ever having any positive sense of sexuality, and even being part of the twentieth century. I also didn't want our session to end on such a negative note. Therapy was still new for her, and I wanted her to be able to see my office as a healing place as well as a place to reflect upon and share her pain.

So I asked, "Can you think of anything good about your childhood when you look back now?"

"Yeah, we got to feel superior to outsiders, because that's what the church always taught us. And I got to drive a tractor, milk the cows, and babysit other children. I really liked doing all those things."

Her tremendous ability to find something good in the midst of so much pain and adversity struck me. This was such a part of emotional and psychological survival. Seeing we were out of time for the day, I felt good about stopping on this positive note. "I'd like to learn much more about all of this, but we're out of time for today," I said. "So how about if we stop in a few minutes."

"Okay," she said, almost looking a little disappointed.

"I wanted to ask if you were able to keep a log of your drinking this past week."

Anne reached into her pocket and extracted a folded piece of paper. She unfolded it and somewhat cautiously handed it to me. As I reviewed the information in front of me, I was aware that my estimation of her drinking was indeed closer to what she had recorded in her log than to what she had previously told me. The log indicated at least some drinking daily, and that she'd consumed thirty drinks during the past week, including beer, wine, and hard liquor. It also showed two episodes of ingesting enough alcohol to have likely produced considerable intoxication.

"How do you view your drinking at this point?" I asked.

"I was kinda surprised at how many drinks I've had in a week," she admitted. "It was, like, thirty drinks, and that seems like a lot when I really think about it."

"Does the amount of drinking concern you?" I asked.

"I hadn't thought about it, I guess, but compared to Mickie and some of her friends—they really drink—it doesn't seem too bad."

I didn't feel quite as confident using that perspective, but as much as I wanted to address this further, I noticed we were past our allotted time and needed to stop. "Well, I've got to stop for today. How about meeting next Tuesday? Could you come in at 11 a.m.?"

"Okay."

"You've shared a lot today, and I appreciate your willingness to trust me. We'll pick up here next week. I hope you have a good weekend and continue to heal," I said.

"Okay. Is that all for today?" Anne said, as she shifted in her seat. I sensed that my expression of appreciation and the more personal expression were quite foreign to her .

But she stood up slowly and seemed almost disappointed to have to leave, a marked contrast to her intense fear at the beginning of the appointment.

I stood up, walked to the door, and opened it, making sure to provide enough space for her comfort. Anne walked out, with her arms at her sides, swinging slightly, and her head raised enough to almost catch my eye.

— CHAPTER SEVEN —

Anne left my office and headed down Tremont Street to meet her friend Mickie at a nearby coffeehouse. It had taken a lot of determination on Mickie's part to resist Anne's pleas that she sit in my waiting room during her appointment. But, as was often the case, Mickie's tenacity and position of trust had prevailed.

Mickie had become Anne's closest friend since Anne had arrived in Boston six months earlier. They had talked about many things, laughed a lot, and often discussed Mickie's difficult relationship with her girlfriend. Anne had met Mickie after she had begun working as an aide in a hospice a few miles away near The Fenway, a large city park and wooded area that separated the inner city of Boston from Brookline and its less dense suburban communities. Mickie, a nurse there, had taken an instant liking to Anne, drawn by her passivity and naïve understanding of the world, which allowed Mickie's extroversion and outward expressiveness an audience and an acolyte.

In contrast to Anne's shyness and cautious approach to any social interaction, Mickie was boisterous, chaotic, and opinionated. She was also very open about her sexual orientation as a lesbian. Anne had never been around anyone she had known to be a lesbian, but had no particular reaction nor any discomfort with it. She had no real concept of herself as a sexual being, never having participated in any sexual behavior that was chosen or felt caring. Nor did she have any sense of a sexual identity or anything she understood as sexual attraction to either gender. She knew that she enjoyed looking at women and that they would hold her gaze longer than men. She felt safer and more comfortable with gay men than straight men, believing men to be stronger than women, but knowing gay men wouldn't sexually abuse her. She enjoyed several close gay male relationships in her new life and had insisted upon seeing a gay male psychologist. She also felt far more accepted in the gay community, where pain and rejection were part of the lexicon. Mickie had shared that histories of physical and emotional abuse were prevalent among her friends, allowing Anne to feel more normal. So Anne had begun hanging around with Mickie and her partner, along with their group of friends.

Lesbians seemed to give noticeably less focus and power to sexual behavior than men typically do. So the fact that Anne didn't have any real sexual orientation and didn't engage in or ever talk about sexual activity was not of great concern. She came across as quiet, anxious, and sometimes sad, but she had become a good friend of Mickie's. Mickie was sort of a ringleader among her group of women friends, and this provided greater inclusion for Anne.

None of the women, except for Mickie, knew that she was in Boston as part of a witness protection plan. They only knew from Mickie that Anne had relocated to Boston after a very abusive history and that she wasn't ready to talk about it. And, as much as they were inclined to have fun and be themselves, they were also very caring and respectful to allow Anne her process and her pace. Their nature and values were inherently geared to include another woman who was facing demons, either internally or externally, into their little clan. They had paid much too high a price for being excluded in their own lives to perpetuate their experiences onto other women. Still, despite feeling accepted, Anne often found it very difficult to relate to these women.

Anne had grown up in a very sheltered environment, with no formal education, almost no exposure to the outside world, and little humor or frivolity. Her own sense of humor had evolved as a private means of coping with pain and fear. Seeing these women joking together was a strange cultural experience. Similarly, Mickie and her friends would often discuss political or social issues with which Anne had no familiarity. In Anne's world, women didn't discuss political beliefs or values in any public setting. On occasion, she would ask Mickie what something meant or what they were referring to, but for the vast majority of the time, she remained in her own naïve world, not wanting her ignorance to be obvious. They would laugh hysterically at sexual jokes or innuendos that were foreign to Anne, furthering the alienation and confusion she had felt since leaving the familiarity of The Christian Movement. At times, she would attempt to laugh on cue when others did so, always striving to be courteous and avoid upsetting anyone or appearing stupid.

Anne walked the two blocks down Tremont Street with her head tilted slightly downward to avoid any semblance of eye contact, but to still be able to scan the environment for danger. She rarely felt safe walking down the street, especially alone, and was anxious to meet up with Mickie. The potential of threat had become as normal to her as the assumed absence of it was to everyone else. Most particularly, she was very fearful of men. As she approached the coffeehouse, she saw Mickie sitting at a window table talking with two other women seated with her. Anne felt her breathing begin to relax just at the sight of Mickie.

Along with friendship, Mickie had come to represent a sense of safety to Anne, a protector of sorts who possessed the aggression and toughness to follow through if needed. Anne felt what would be considered a crush on Mickie, without any physical or sexual arousal. It was a mixture of childhood feelings toward a mother who could provide protection and an adult feeling of just wanting to be connected and cared about.

Anne entered the coffeehouse and cautiously approached Mickie's table, not having met the two women with whom Mickie was talking. As she drew within a few feet, Mickie looked up at her and smiled, recognizing Anne's typical hesitation with strangers. "Hey, girl," Mickie called out, and the two other women shifted their gaze to watch the approaching Anne, smiling to make her feel more comfortable.

"Have a seat," Mickie said, pushing out the only other chair at the table with her foot. "Meet my friends, June and Aileen." The two women nodded their hellos.

"This is Anne," Mickie continued. "She's just been to see her shrink."

Anne felt embarrassed and uncomfortable with Mickie's announcement. Just having met with a doctor, let alone starting to reveal a lifetime of secrets about herself, her parents, and her community, seemed very disloyal to her family and the church, and she felt incredibly exposed. To have her private life, which felt so shameful, publicly revealed was very difficult. This sort of pronouncement, however, was not unusual for the brash Mickie, who seemed almost to take pleasure in shocking people. Anne was far too shy, introverted, and needing the friendship to challenge Mickie by expressing her discomfort.

The two women almost simultaneously said "hello" again to Anne who, very quietly, said "hello" back, although she had no idea which woman was June or which was Aileen, and her shyness and carefulness would keep it that way. Whenever she encountered them in the coming months, she would simply consider them as a pair named June and Aileen.

"How'd it go?" one of the June/Aileen pair asked.

Although she knew that the question had perhaps been asked for lack of anything else to say, coming from a complete stranger, it seemed very intrusive to Anne. "Okay," she answered, sending a clear message that she wasn't seeking to talk about her therapy session in public.

The women took the hint, but they didn't seem offended. "Well, we gotta run," they said, and turning back to Mickie, they nodded their good-byes to both Mickie and Anne.

Anne's relief was short-lived, as Mickie immediately asked, "So how was shrinkland?" even before June and Aileen had made their way to the door. Anne sank into an empty chair, conscious of feeling slightly miffed that

Mickie seemed oblivious to her discomfort with the topic, but relieved it was just the two of them. So she said, "It was okay; he's nice, kind of like Nathan, my attorney."

"So, what did you talk about today?" Mickie, whose curiosity outweighed any sense of propriety, continued.

"I showed him a letter I got from my father, and he was wondering why I'm not angry."

"You mean the prick?" Mickie cursed. As supportive a friend as Mickie was, she was limited in her ability to hear about the abuse without becoming enraged and vilifying Anne's family, especially her "demented fuck of a father." Anne couldn't see that Mickie was expressing anger that she herself could not express, and so she felt very uncomfortable with Mickie's reaction. It was intolerable for her to view her father as evil or demented, because she needed to honor him. Knowing that revealing her father's abusive behavior led to anger and dislike of him felt disloyal and disrespectful. So the second time she found herself sharing some of her abuse history had been the last. Both women knew they could no longer discuss the elephant in the room.

Anne ignored Mickie's outburst. But, to placate her, she added, "Then we talked about some of the abuse. I think Dr. Hirsch was kind of freaked out hearing about some of it. He seems pretty cool. I told him about some of the things they did to me."

But despite Anne's attempt to pacify her, Mickie grew more tense and responded as she usually did. "Well, let's get out of here," she said. "I've got to show you this really cool jacket I'm thinking of buying Allison for her birthday." Allison, Mickie's partner of the past eighteen months, was a source of both constant stress and endless needs. Anne couldn't understand why Mickie was with her. Anne had no real sense of the power of physical or sexual attraction and, otherwise, couldn't find any attributes that might hold sway over Mickie's affections. She also had never seen anything that resembled a healthy or balanced relationship, so a somewhat dysfunctional one seemed normal.

But she felt relieved to be back on less intimate ground. Mickie, a trust-fund kid, showered Allison with gifts, and one of Anne and Mickie's typical days off together was shopping for Allison and hitting the only real women's bar in Boston. It was the closest thing to intimacy Anne had experienced, drinking with Mickie, shopping and socializing with Mickie's friends. As the two women stood and headed out, each understood that the really deep and painful stuff was still off-limits in what was otherwise a close bond.

However, for Anne, there was a constant underlying sense of being disloyal and undeserving as well as an awareness of how naïve and sheltered her life had always been. She also had a constant awareness that virtually every behavior in which she and Mickie engaged constituted a violation of everything that God, her parents and her community expected of her. She continually feared retribution and eternal damnation, but this was also challenged by her freedom from abuse and her chance to be a part of the real world.

— CHAPTER EIGHT —

I had many things to give me purpose in both my personal and professional lives, and one of them was my incredible dog, Madison, who accompanied me to work most days. I had been taking Madison to my office a couple of times a week for several years and found his presence very well received by almost all of my clients. For me, Madison was like a magical being that brought constant joy and playfulness to my life. When I found a client to be less than comfortable or enthusiastic about a dog's presence in the therapy session, I would leave Madison at home for that part of the day. And, perhaps being overly protective of Anne's fragile state, I intentionally had not brought him in during any of our sessions to date.

But on the morning of my fifth session with Anne, my intuition told me that Madison's presence might be comforting to her now. I was rarely wrong about who might or might not be comfortable, either because they had discussed the importance of their own pets in their lives or because I sensed they might feel safer with animals than with people. So, on this particular morning, I brought Madison along, and, as I reached my office and said hello to Anne, who was fearfully crouched on her usual perch on the stairs, her face immediately brightened when she saw his eager, open face. She stood up and took a couple of steps closer and crouched down to his level to put her hand on Madison's head, petting him very gently. She seemed so naturally safe with him, markedly in contrast to her discomfort with me. I knew I had found a valuable new alliance with Anne, having brought my co-therapist to work.

"What's his name?" Anne asked, her eyes and posture less guarded than she usually was with me.

"Madison," I smiled.

"Does he come to work with you often?"

"Most of the time. How about if we go up to the office and I'll show you his diploma?"

Anne looked at me skeptically, a slight grin tugging at her lips. I jiggled Madison's leash trying to divert him from his intense desire to go toward any other living object, be it a plant, animal, insect or human, so that I could insert my key into the door. As I pushed it open, Madison suddenly bounded into my waiting room, almost pulling me over. A little flustered, I turned to

Anne and said, "Give me a couple of minutes to look over my notes and get settled."

Grinning slightly at my obvious awkwardness, she said, "That's cool. Can Madison stay here with me while you get ready?"

A few minutes later, when I opened the door to my waiting room, they were still playing on the floor. When Anne walked in, I pointed to a diploma on the wall and watched as she read it. It said that Madison had received a "Dogtorate" from "I Lick U" and contained all the usual language, in English and Latin.

For the first time, Anne actually laughed, albeit very slightly, and uttered, "That's so cool." In that moment, our fragile bond deepened a little. I had learned that two things both comforted and connected her to me—Madison and humor. They would become foundations of our relationship over time.

"Can he sit on the sofa with me?" Anne asked once we were settled in my office.

"I'm sure he'd love to do that," I smiled. Almost as if he had taken a cue, Madison immediately turned and leaped onto the sofa, turning around two full times before finding a comfortable position. Anne sat down facing Madison, resting both hands on the sides of his neck, and he laid his big head in her lap. The two had begun a friendship that would endure for years.

Trying to maintain the lightness of the moment, I joked, "He's really good about confidentiality. No one has been able to get any information out of him yet."

Anne laughed slightly again. "That's really cool," she smiled.

"Have you ever had a dog, Anne?" I asked then, attempting to ease our conversation toward her past once again.

"No, we weren't allowed our own pets. I guess my parents didn't really relish the idea. But I was close with some of the cows and sheep. I'd hang out with them and get to know some of them like a pet. You could do all the same things. You walked them and fed them and petted them and helped them if they got sick. I even named each of them, and they sometimes responded to their names. But they were never allowed in the house, although sometimes I was allowed to spend the night with a couple of my favorite ones. I knew they wouldn't hurt me. I still feel much safer with animals." She paused and looked directly at me, adding, "And we shared having to be kept in cages or fenced in and sometimes being hurt and not understanding what we had done to cause it." Anne then shifted her gaze downward again, seeming a little surprised at herself for having said so much.

After a brief, but seemingly long pause, I asked, "How are you today, Anne?"

Looking at a piece of paper in her hand, she said, "My father sent me another letter, and I brought it to see if you might want to read it." She remained still, cautiously awaiting my response.

"I'd be glad to read the letter or have you read it to me if you would like," I said. "But first, I was wondering if you might let me know how you're feeling physically and how your injuries are doing."

Anne seemed to relax a little and responded, perhaps a little too quickly, "My side is still pretty sore, but my head doesn't hurt anymore, and the bruises on my leg are a little better."

I sensed from the rapidity of her answer that she knew her improvement would counter my attempts to get her to seek medical attention, but all I said was, "I'm glad you're feeling a little better. Would it be helpful for me to read this letter now?"

She nodded with a childlike quality and handed me the letter.

I began to read, and soon felt my pulse quicken with anger, an anger that, so far, was completely absent from Anne's discernable emotional expression. This letter began, as had the previous one she'd shown me, without an endearment.

Anne

You mentioned that it was Father's Day on Sunday, so I thought I would write to you with a few "Father's" memories of my own.

I remember your body quivering with fear when you finally realized that you would obey me no matter what.

I remember your screams as the other men had you and how I loved to see your terror.

I remember your fat little ugly face.

I remember you crying when I told you I hated you.

I remember enjoying your shame as your brother watched you stripped and beaten.

I remember your red face and embarrassment when you were publicly admonished.

I remember your attempts to leave.

I remember your readmissions to The Movement.

I remember how you have never succeeded at anything and never will.

I remember your stuttering, pathetic attempts at trying to express yourself.

I remember your loneliness (even though it does not surprise me).

I remember your lack of submission.

In the future, I will remember a daughter who disappoints me constantly, who doesn't have the guts to stand up for the truth, and who whimpers and whines her way through life.

Thank you for such a happy Father's Day and at least for some fond memories.

I put the letter down slowly, unable or unwilling to conceal the sinking feeling it had elicited. I was stunned, a rare reaction after all the stories I had heard. As I looked up, I noticed that Anne was staring at me, obviously waiting for my reaction. Yet, before I could even ask how she felt about the letter, she handed me another one. "This is my letter in response. Do you want to read it too?" she asked.

"Yes I do, especially knowing it's an expression of your feelings," I said, trying to temper my personal reaction, as she handed me the letter.

First I want to say that I love you very much and want our relationship to be a positive thing for both of us. Recently, I've been hurt by some of the e-mails you sent me and need to resolve this with you. I understand how you may not realize that the e-mails I sent you are aimed at helping me grow and mature, but they come from a place of love and concern also.

I realize that I am not the person you want me to be and that it is hard for you to accept my choice to live outside the Church family. I am glad that you see that. "I can think of no good reason as to why you left the Church," you have stated. I know you feel I have made some unwise decisions in my life, and in some instances, you are right. In order for me to learn and grow as a person, you need to respect the decisions I do make, whether you think they are right or wrong. This does not mean that I do not value your input and advice, but it is no longer acceptable for you to continue to write these destructive letters. I know you see me as too delicate to deal with criticism, and at risk of living an unshepherded life, but your letters are not helpful to us now or for the future. I will not read nor reply to them from now on.

I very much want us to have a relationship built both on love and a mutual respect for each other and our different beliefs. I believe that you want that too, and hope we can start to build on and improve the relationship we have."

Anne

I finished reading, took off my glasses, and rubbed my eyes. What I had sitting across from me, I realized in amazement, was a woman who had clearly accepted significant responsibility for the physical, sexual, spiritual, and verbal abuse perpetrated upon her, yet was trying to express a need for mutual admiration and respect for a father who was one of her abusers.

What was encouraging, at least, was her endeavor to set some limits. She had put several thousand miles between herself and her family, and she had protected herself by creating a new identity and hiding her whereabouts from her father. Discouraging, however, was her lack of anger toward him, which I again confirmed by asking, "Anne, did you feel angry reading your father's letter?"

"No, he is hurt by my having left him and the church," she said calmly.

"But the meanness and attempt to damage or hurt you go way beyond any kind of appropriate expression from a father to a daughter, not to mention his denial as to why you left—for your physical and psychological survival," I quickly responded, my voice carrying the only detectable emotion in the room.

"You sound like my friend Mickie. I don't talk to her about much of this, because she becomes outraged and angry or frustrated at me for not being angry. Are you upset with me for not being angry?"

"You know, that's a fair question. I hope you'll continue to check out concerns like this. I'm not angry with you. Your father, in my view of the world, has caused you great hurt, but your view and perspective is quite different. Does it bother you that I see him as wrong and might feel anger toward him?" I asked, intentionally softening my tone.

"I don't know that it bothers me, and I can understand that everyone else feels that way. But it isn't what I feel, and I don't want you to get mad at me and kick me out for not seeing things the way you do," Anne said, looking downward.

"That's not something I could really imagine. It's okay for us to feel differently about things. Often, however, in time, my clients and I come to see things more similarly. I guess we learn from each other. I just want to say that I think it's great and really important that you're at least trying to set some boundaries to protect yourself from his destructive words, as you put it. Do you have to read his letters?"

"How would I know if there isn't something important in them—like if my mother is ill?"

"Well, one option might be to have someone in your life read the letters and let you know if the letters are either more hospitable or contain information you would need to know."

"Would you be willing to read them and tell me if there are things I need to know?" she asked quickly.

I pondered this a minute, feeling the need to try to keep some healthy boundaries around Anne's dependence upon me. I responded, "I would maybe serve as a backup if you couldn't find anyone else. What about your friend Mickie or your friend Tim, who referred you to me?"

"Mickie gets too angry and wants to go and hurt my father. She's pretty volatile, but a really good friend. I can ask Tim. He would probably be cool with it."

"That's great. It's a small step on a path to becoming stronger and protecting yourself," I said, but was taken aback when she replied with what seemed a complete non sequitur.

"I found this really cool sunglass shop yesterday," she said, her tone animated.

Not only was I struck by the change of subject to something fairly innocuous, I was also intrigued by its potential symbolism. I wondered if there was meaning in it. After all, her abusers had observed only their own needs, while hers remained hidden, even from herself—just as sunglasses would hide her from others. But this was therapist conjecture, so I attempted to investigate further, asking, in a deliberately relaxed tone, "I wonder what made you change the subject."

With her uncanny survival instinct for sensing any form of negative emotion or reaction in others, she responded, "Oh, I'm sorry if that wasn't okay. I just thought I'd tell you about this shop. It was really cool."

"It isn't at all wrong for you to talk about whatever you'd like," I assured her. "But sometimes it's important for us to understand why you might change the subject. I was wondering if you had become uncomfortable."

"I guess I felt uncomfortable and thought maybe you were mad at me for asking if you would read my father's letters for me," Anne said, again diverting her glance toward the floor.

"I'm not mad at all, Anne, but I am aware you worry about this fairly often. I think you'll learn to know I'm not like the men who have hurt you and feel safer and more at ease with me over time. Actually, I was just suggesting you might have a friend you could count on as well, since you need that kind of support in your life beyond our weekly meetings, but I'm fine to be a backup as part of our work together." It seemed imperative to tread very softly and to help us find healthy boundaries that weren't defined by her need to actually, physically hide from me or completely depend upon me for her sense of survival.

"So, did you buy some sunglasses?" I asked, sensing that she needed a break from all the heavy stuff.

"Yeah, they're really cool. I'll bring them in next time I come. They are like mirrors when you look at me, but I can see out of them."

It struck me that mirrored sunglasses were a novelty for Anne. The degree to which she had been sheltered was reminiscent of having been in a coma or asleep for the past thirty years.

"Okay," she said, and then sat silently, looking uncertain. "I remembered something my father did one time," she continued after a moment, then paused, waiting for encouragement or direction.

"Yeah, so how about sharing it with me?" I said, using a more playful tone in my voice to offer encouragement. I wanted us to start to feel a little more comfortable together, and she smiled a little in acknowledgment. But I wouldn't have been so casual if I'd had any notion of what was to follow.

"I remember him dragging me naked through the church by my hair after I had been caged for a long time. My legs wouldn't work, since I'd been squashed in the cage for so long. He kept on shrieking that I was deliberately sinning and would pay for it and took me to a room full of the elders. And they all started praying really loudly in tongues, and I understood something about casting the demons out of me. They laid me on the floor, and each in turn got on top of me and prayed intensely. They acted like they couldn't get the demons out, and some of them hit me in the stomach, and one of them kept sticking his finger down my throat to make me vomit out the demons. They got a black marker and wrote the word sinner all over my body and face, so that others in the church would know I was a sinner and stay away from me. Then my father took me home and made me stand in the kitchen naked while my family ate supper. My legs hurt so bad I fell over and just wanted to die right then."

I found myself just sitting there, feeling sort of lifeless, as if the air had escaped my body. I looked at Anne, and I am sure I communicated my despondency. She very slightly relaxed her lips, seeming to sense my empathy, and I mustered the energy to ask, "Would it be helpful to talk more about this now?"

"Not really," she said, "I just thought you'd want to know that I remembered that."

What was a memory and, therefore, familiar to Anne was really upsetting for me, and it took me a moment to shift from my emotional space back to her. "I very much want to know and am glad you trust me enough to share this with me," I managed to respond. We sat there silently, sort of looking at each other, yet trying not to stare at each other, and I decided to give her, or us, a break.

Remembering a notation I had made at the end of our previous session, I said, "You know, I realized at the end of our last session that I don't really know anything about you actually leaving the church. How were you able to leave?"

"I didn't really leave. The police took me away after I called 911 and reported that one of the children I sat for was being molested by her father when I walked in on them. They took me away for my protection since Jonas and my father and the other elders would be very angry and probably try to hurt me. I was then put in a safe house and didn't have any contact with my family or anyone connected to the church for quite a while." Anne shared this very powerful event without any discernable emotion.

"So, that explains why you're in witness protection," I commented, nodding my head.

"Yeah," Anne responded unenthusiastically.

"I was wondering if you'd be okay to talk a little more about some of your own childhood memories."

"I guess so," she said, the quietness in her answer revealing her reluctance.

"All right, but let me know if you feel uncomfortable again, and we can decide whether to talk about something else. It's important for us to balance the need to know more about your life with your need for comfort, but I won't always know when we're crossing that line. I was wondering what you might recall or have learned about your childhood that wasn't painful or abusive, like playing or having friends or pets that were important to you?'

Relaxing back into the chair, Anne said, "I would help out with some of the farm animals, looking after them and helping with feeding, getting the cows in, and collecting eggs. We used to bake cow poop in the sun, shaping it into small balls and throwing them at each other." She grinned. "Gross, I know. That was really fun."

This was the first I had heard of anything fun or playmates in her life. "Who was 'we,' Anne?" I asked. "Did you have friends that you played with regularly?"

"There were a few other girls I would play with. Since we didn't go to school, we were able to play in the afternoons after our chores were done. We ran around and played on the farm. The boys had balls and sometimes we could play with them, but mostly we found things to make our toys out of. When I was old enough, like eleven or twelve, I was allowed to milk the cows and let them in and out of the barn by myself. It was the nicest part of my childhood, being with the animals, and no one ever bothered me or tried to hurt me there. Another thing I remember having fun with was going outside when it was dark and throwing dishrags into the air and watching the bats swoop down for them," she finished, with a slight smile of reminiscence.

"I'm really glad to hear there were times and places that you were able to feel safe and happy," I shared, wanting to encourage her moments of good memories.

"I was mostly happy at home with my mom. She was mostly nice to me, and my father was almost never around during the days, and my brother was in school or doing other things."

I recalled that Anne also had a sister and made a note to ask about her later.

Then I continued. "You told me when we first met that the church ran a summer camp. Was that for the kids in the church, and did you go to it?"

"It was for the church kids and kids from orphanages and things like that. I was able to go there for two weeks each summer. The camps were really religious, but you got to row on the little lake, and they mostly left me alone and would abuse the other kids."

"And none of these kids ever reported this when they returned back to where they were living?"

"These were like the worst kids, the ones that couldn't be placed or no one wanted to adopt. And they were often abused in their homes, and no one would have believed them probably anyways. They really liked coming to the camp and being outdoors and stuff, so they wouldn't maybe want to ruin that."

"So, what looked like a humanitarian deed was also very much the opposite?" I commented.

Anne didn't say anything, but simply gave me a slight smile, acknowledging our mutual awareness.

"So, what other kinds of chores did you do?"

"Well, there was the socks and underwear box that was communal for the whole house, and I'd take out socks and darn them. And I'd help my mom with the laundry. We did the laundry for five houses, about forty people, as part of our community work. So there was a lot of wash daily. We had an old machine that had a hand-turned mangle. I'd take the laundry out of the soapy water and hand it to my mom to put it through the mangle. I remember when I first got to leave Deerbrook and went to Portland for the first time, I passed by a store that had new washing machines and saw that you didn't have to help work the machine like ours. They were really cool. I also saw a dryer and didn't even know there was such a thing. We had to hang the laundry outside when it wasn't raining (which wasn't too often). Usually we did it the covered way, which was indoors. You see, there was this hallway that led to the prayer room, and we would hang the laundry on hooks on the wall."

My curiosity and intuition were triggered with her serendipitous mention of a prayer room. "Could you tell me about the prayer room?" I asked.

"We had prayers each morning and each evening and had to sit very quietly and absolutely still while my father said prayers. He often spoke in tongues, and we didn't know what he was saying in the prayers. We knew when to say 'amen,' but didn't speak otherwise. If we made any other sounds or giggled, we would be beaten for not respecting God."

"I know you lived in a pretty small house, so having a prayer room in that space must have meant it was a pretty important thing?"

"Most of the houses had prayer rooms, and this was sort of a requirement in the church since you had to pray several times a day. It was also my father's place to have his privacy."

"Obviously, prayer and devotion were extremely important to your father," I said, although admittedly with an underlying feeling of sarcasm that, in retrospect, felt more like an inappropriate expression of my anger.

But Anne responded with a slight grin, "Yeah, I guess so," she said, seeming to appreciate my sarcasm and maybe even the complexity of my effort to navigate my beliefs and hers.

"Would you do things with your sister and brother, Anne?" I asked, wanting to continue learning about her daily life.

"Sometimes my brother would come outside with me, but my sister wasn't there anymore," she replied, her tone almost dismissive and seeming to reflect discomfort regarding her sister.

"Where was your sister?" I probed a little further.

"She was dead." Anne said calmly, but looking very sad.

"This is your sister Shauna?" I asked, quite surprised since this hadn't surfaced when she described her childhood history in our first session.

"Yes," Anne answered , shifting in the chair, her eyes moving from me back toward the floor.

"Can you tell me how she died, Anne?" I pressed gently.

Anne remained quiet and continued looking down, wrapping her arms around her chest.

"Does this make you uncomfortable, Anne?" I asked, although her discomfort was obvious.

"Yes," she said, almost imperceptibly.

"I understand. We can talk more about it another time and go at whatever pace you're okay with. Would that be all right?"

"I guess so," she whispered, giving me a furtive glance.

"So, your dad wasn't around most of the time?"

"No, he would come home for supper. But even when he was around, I kept out of his way, because he was angry a lot of the time."

"Did you think he was angry with you?"

"Yeah, he was often angry with me, even if I wasn't doing anything. So I just tried to be invisible."

"What would he do when he was angry with you?"

"He'd yell or tell me I was a sinner or the devil was in me, and I knew what that meant."

"What did it mean?"

"It meant they needed to cleanse me and get the evil out of me."

Knowing what that implied, I didn't need to push Anne to travel back to that place. "Would he ever hit you or physically abuse you when he was angry?" I asked instead.

"Not in front of my mother. Somehow she let him know that wasn't okay—kind of what she could see wasn't okay. But if she wasn't around, then it was different."

"Did your dad ever do anything with you, like play or read to you?"

"Not really. He mostly did things with my brother, or he wasn't around. He did teach me to read, though."

"So, that's why you're able to read some now?"

"Yeah, but I'm not very good, and it takes a long time."

"How would he teach you to read?"

"He taught me to read the Bible, and he would give me lists of words to underline. That's how I learned each of the words. It was really kind of a slow way of learning."

"Did you ever get to leave the farm for any length of time without your family, like when you had reached adulthood?"

"I went to Africa for three years as part of our missionary program."

"Did you do mission work?"

"I mostly did janitorial stuff. It was really great there. We lived in huts by the hospital, but I had so much freedom, and the people were really nice to me and no one hurt me."

"Did anyone know about your history and what went on in the church while you were growing up?"

"No, I knew not to talk about it, and I kind of thought everyone's life was probably like that."

"Why did you go home, since you liked it in Africa?"

"The program ended, at least for us. They kicked The Christian Movement out of the larger church that ran the missionary program, because they thought our beliefs and rituals were wrong. So we ended up going home."

"I gather this was one of the better times of your life?"

"Yeah, I was really afraid at first, because I didn't really know what to expect. But, after a while, I realized they treated me nicely, and no one tried to hurt me or have sex with me. It helped me learn to be mostly on my own and not afraid of change."

"So, the question that begs to be asked is that since you had learned to have this confidence and felt safer away from the church, why didn't you leave after your mission?"

"Oh, I would think about leaving, even dream about it. But I didn't really have any skills or any money. And I knew I'd end up homeless like the people we rescued. And I feared God would punish me, or the elders might come after me and punish me."

Looking at the clock, I realized we only had a few minutes remaining, and I very much wanted to follow up on the log of her alcohol intake that she had provided at the end of our last session. "Well, if we might shift gears for a few minutes, you shared with me about drinking last week and indicated that you drank as much as thirty drinks the previous week. I wanted to ask how you view your drinking. Does it feel okay and in control for you?"

Anne thought for a moment and then said, "I guess it's okay. We just have lots of fun drinking together."

"I understand that and certainly know it can be a big part of social life. But, in all honesty, thirty drinks in a week is a very significant amount of alcohol and could be contributing to some of the anxiety and depression that you're experiencing."

"Are you upset with me?" she asked.

"What makes you ask that?"

"You sort of look disappointed and maybe think I'm wrong to drink that much."

"Well, I don't know what makes me look disappointed. On the contrary, I think it's very important that you're being honest with me and are willing to talk about it. I don't really look at things as right or wrong, though. That's a kind of moral judgment. I look at whether things are helping or hurting your life. Since we're almost out of time, I'd like to make a suggestion and ask you to try something. How about reducing your alcohol intake to no more than ten drinks this coming week? That means you can have a drink or two every night or just go out and drink a lot a couple of nights. What's most important is whether you or the alcohol is in control. If you can reduce and manage your drinking, then you may be in control. If not, then the alcohol or the emotions that lead you to drink are in control. How does that sound to you?"

"I guess that's cool," she agreed. "Do you still want me to write down how much I'm drinking?"

"Yes, I'd like you to keep track of that for a while." I paused and then added something that I often say to clients when we set goals. "I very much hope and want you to be able to do this, but I want you to make a promise—that if you end up drinking more, you will still come in next week and be honest about it. If you don't do as well as your goal, then we'll talk about it. But I don't want you to be worried about me being disappointed. Can you commit to that?"

"Yeah, that's cool," she replied, although her tone was more ambivalent.

"Then, on that note, let's stop for today. Thank you for sharing things with me and for letting me know when something is too uncomfortable. So, how about if we continue to meet this same time each week?"

"Okay."

Even though she still worried too much about my approval and was struggling with what to share, I realized that Anne appeared more engaged and more comfortable talking with me overall. Committing to a consistent weekly time was a further step toward solidifying our relationship and a commitment to treatment for her.

"Then I'll say good-bye and see you next week, Anne. Please call me if you feel the need before we get to meet again," I added, reflecting my continuing concern and uncertainty about her fragility.

"I'll be okay," she said. And, as she stood up and headed toward the door, she seemed just a little taller than she had previously.

After Anne departed, I found myself thinking about her drinking for a few minutes. My intuition told me this wasn't about alcoholism. Other than the quantity she was consuming, she seemed to be more caught up in the social drinking excesses of her friends and the bar scene, but she didn't present any of the other hallmarks that defined alcoholism so far. The test of her ability to manage her drinking and reduce it by two-thirds would help define whether she or the alcohol was in control.

Sitting at my desk, lost in thought, I wondered about the last hour and the kind of tragedy and pain my client was presenting. I had a foreboding sense of doom regarding Anne's sister, that she in some way had suffered greatly, as had Anne. I also found myself wondering about this "Christian" community, committed to providing care for young people on the one hand and somewhat ritualistically abusing children on the other hand. I hoped that there might be information on the Internet regarding the town, its inhabitants, or The Christian Movement and its leaders.

— CHAPTER NINE —

That evening I decided to do some research and was surprised to find a plethora of articles concerning such a small and obscure community. As I scanned the list of articles on the Web, I was struck by several mentions of the word "cult" in place of the terms "church" or "community" that Anne had been using. One article was titled "A true vision inside the Christian Cult" and had been published in both the town's local newspaper and in several more prominent newspapers.

Last week *The Oregon Journal* exposed the "reality behind the myth" regarding The Christian Movement, a religious community in the town of Deerbrook, about twenty miles east of Medford. It reported that as many as five young people between the ages of eighteen and twenty-five had died in circumstances that were deemed mysterious and investigable.

Until recently, authorities had not connected the deaths. However, detectives with the Medford Police Department noted the unusual proliferation of deaths among people under thirty, occurring within months of each other and within the same vicinity.

The leader of the community, Jonas Smith, is a preacher who has been investigated for what the Medford Police Department said was, "very questionable and seemingly bizarre religious and teaching practices." Several authorities on cult phenomena and brainwashing have deemed him to be a powerful figure, and one has gone as far as calling him a "sociopath with maniacal aspirations." Smith, the article reported, has been known to "redirect the minds of his followers to make them his flock of slaves."

It has been virtually impossible to find any substantial evidence or witnesses to any prosecutable criminal activity on Smith's part or on the part of his community elders, but "there is little doubt that people have suffered under his control," according to Professor David Williams, an authority on cult behavior who has studied Smith and The Christian Community.

A second article had been published in *The Ashland Journal.* The research for this expose involved sending a young undercover reporter, Janice Woods, to pose as a distraught and destitute young woman. Her very youthful appearance allowed her to present herself as a seventeen-year-old who had run away and was desperate for safe shelter. Ms. Woods, using a fictitious name,

Jeanette Dodd, appeared at the central church building for The Christian Community in Deerbrook and was referred to a Christian worker, ostensibly a woman who served as a social worker for the church and community.

In order to further create a more accurate portrayal of an angry and rebellious runaway, Ms. Dodd smelled of tobacco and alcohol, knowing this would reinforce her appearance of desperation and present her as someone in need of spiritual guidance.

Ms. Woods wrote the following in her exposé:

> The very tall man with frighteningly dark eyes moved toward me with a scowl on his face. He pushed his finger into my shoulder as I was standing in line outside the community eating hall. Even though I'd had an eerie feeling in the community during my first 24 hours, for the first time I became truly frightened, as he went into a rage yelling, "Why weren't you at this morning's prayer meeting? Here we are, offering you a home, food, clothing and the love of our community, only asking that you participate in our teachings and community services, and you don't even show enough respect to do that."
>
> I was absolutely frozen, aware of the absurdity of his rage, but feeling far too threatened to not take it seriously. This man was huge, and no one reacted except to lower their heads and look away from us. It was as if we were being left all alone in a crowd and no one dared incur his attention, let alone the wrath of Father Jonas Smith.
>
> Time stood still. I hadn't known what to expect from my experience in the community, but real danger wasn't something I had anticipated in this assignment. But then, as if this rage had never transpired, he calmly put his two huge hands on my shoulders and said, "However, it is our calling not only to teach, but to be forgiving. Have some food, Jeanette, and afterwards one of our esteemed church elders, Mr. Carson, is going to help you better understand the few things we ask of outsiders we adopt into our community, so that you may become a part of us."
>
> As calm and ostensibly inviting as this might have sounded, it was an eerie portent of things to come. As I took my food tray up after what was a very good and healthy meal, a kind, fatherly man put his arm gently on my shoulder and said, "Hello Jeanette, I'm Mr. Carson, and Father Jonas has asked me to spend some time with you to help you feel more acquainted with our community."
>
> I had traveled, within a 15-minute period, from calm to intense fear to calm, from being suddenly yelled at by a stranger to being nurtured with good food by a seemingly kind, older man, who

appeared to genuinely desire to help me feel more comfortable with the community ways.

Mr. Carson gently escorted me outside and told me we should go to one of the prayer rooms in the main church, so we could have quiet. My instincts said to be at least wary, if not frightened, but the reporter in me prevailed over my intuition, and I went with him.

The moment we reached the room, he began, "We know where you went, Jeanette. You were seen walking into town and were watched. We know you went to find cigarettes and alcohol, for these are tools of the devil, and he is still within you." His voice raised in anger as he made this statement.

I had actually headed into town to have a chance to use a pay phone to call my editor and let him know I was okay, an agreement I had made to be able to participate in this assignment. If he didn't hear from me on any given day, he was going to contact the local police or, if need be, come look for me himself. He had been opposed to this undertaking out of concern for my safety over journalistic success, but I am a strong-willed young woman and was able to prevail. I knew that no one could have actually been watching me, as Mr. Carson had stated, because it would have been reported that I had made a phone call, and nothing like that was stated.

After Mr. Carson's angry tirade, he suddenly calmed and said, "If you wish to live within our community and have safety, shelter, food and our love, then you must attend all the prayer services. Don't you want the Lord to come into your life and help you be saved?" He stared at me with piercing eyes that unnerved me and left me frightened to say anything other than "yes." My guard was now up, and I sensed that these emotional u-turns were a concerted effort to confuse me and create an increased need for the more supportive moments, a tactic known as "good cop, bad cop." Yet, even though I assumed his approach was intentional, I was very uncertain as to my physical safety and ability to leave if and when I chose. After all, I was here to investigate alleged and suspected abuses.

When I had initially met with the social worker the day before, I had asked about the rules, as a rebellious teenager might. I was told, "We don't have rules, but live in a community and respect the community elders and others, and honor the teachings of the Bible and God." I had just learned that there were not just rules, but demands you had to obey lest you incur the wrath of the elders, who weren't nearly as kind as they could look when needed. These people were good actors, and I began to understand how they could fool the authorities.

"Two of our community sisters are going to help you become adjusted to our ways of life, Jeanette," Mr. Carson said. "You will stay with them in one of the guest houses, and they will help you attend church and understand our customs better." At this point, he walked over and opened the door, and two very plain-looking, middle-aged women came in and said hello, both smiling and seemingly kind.

I spent the next 24 hours with these women watching my every move and directing me to prayer services three times the following day, most of them led by Father Smith, with the elders always in attendance. Father Smith came up to me all three times to inquire as to my comfort and to ask me if I felt grateful to God and the community. I falsely said "yes" each time, trying to stay in his graces and be able to continue to experience this strange community.

But I realized that I had missed my opportunity to contact my editor and had to make a decision to either risk going into town to somehow call him or face having the police show up, a move that would blow my cover and terminate the investigation. Ultimately, I concluded I had no way to further protect gathering a story, since my editor would act to protect me without the prearranged contact. So, I opted to sneak out during the night, at least not alerting the community to the upcoming exposé.

I had already seen enough to understand that any lost, disenchanted or disconnected adolescent was at great risk to be taken in and psychologically overwhelmed by these people. My emotions were kept in a constant state of confusion, and within only a couple of days I had felt threatened enough, especially if I were truly in a survival mode requiring food and safe shelter, to at least try to conform to the expectations of the leaders. I also had little question that much more lay beneath the surface of this supposedly quaint, well-intentioned, and family-oriented community.

On a personal note, this was ultimately the most terrifying two days of my life. It is one thing to be cut off from the outside world, but quite another to feel threatened inside the boundaries of one's community, in which women are, in essence, controlled to live for work and prayer, to be subservient, cook, clean, sew, farm and raise the children. These are certainly historic roles for women, but their lack of freedom to express themselves in any other way is eerie.

As I talked with women there, I learned they see themselves as equal to men in God's eyes, but as having distinct roles in support of men, especially the elders, who hold positions akin to royalty. They shared with me that the authority designated to men emanates from the biblical teachings of St. Paul, who espoused the belief that "I suffer not a woman to teach, nor to usurp authority over the man, but to be in silence."

Their prayer services were reminiscent of those common to evangelical sects, but did not include the freedom to choose whether or not to participate. There was little talk or even knowledge of the outside world among these women, and their conversation was never really political or challenging of their circumstances.

I realize that my two days "in residence" only provides a glimpse of The Christian Movement, and I didn't observe any evidence of foul play. But my experience there left me concerned for truly vulnerable persons who turn to the community for physical and emotional support. I was very limited in my access to most of the community and feel that my personal experience and interactions warrant further investigation.

After reading this initial article, I was a bit shaken, realizing that Anne was a victim of this powerful force and her whole world had been subsumed within it. As upsetting as this felt for me, the article provided a better understanding and a validation of Anne's life history. Feeling inspired, I moved on to a second article. It had been written fifteen years earlier and was titled "The fortune behind the misfortune."

Behind the Christian Community and its founder, Jonas Smith, is a business and property empire worth millions, if not tens of millions, with holdings that include farming, health food stores, leisure clothing, hardware stores, a nursing care home, several markets, publishing and recording entities that develop and purvey religiously oriented publications as well as music and transportation and hauling companies. In essence, it has most of the resources that provide for a self-contained residential and business community. The actual net worth of this community of 600 has been estimated at $40 to 50 million, with an annual income exceeding $5 million, but it is enshrouded in secrecy. It appears to be a well-run corporate empire that enjoys significant tax breaks as a religious institution. One explanation for the significant accumulation of wealth is that the "free" labor provided by members of the community enables a phenomenal net profit from its various enterprises. The return on their efforts is, in essence, comparable to slave labor and sweatshop wages, which would be illegal in any businesses operating outside the umbrella of a religious institution. The members of the community sacrifice all luxuries and make significant sacrifices to adhere to the teachings and principles of their leader, thus mitigating the funds needed to provide for their lives. They possess no net worth, as far as can be discerned in any legal sense, accepting on faith that their needs will be provided for. However, in any legal sense their labor and dedication builds the net worth of this little economic empire, but not their individual assets or security. This very system perpetuates itself through devout loyalty and their inability to choose independence from the system. There are certainly parallels that could be drawn with the system of Southern slavery.

A third article was written by a reporter who had contacted the heretofore clandestine community to openly request the opportunity to visit and assess for himself the controversy regarding alleged cult-like practices and their military-like appearance.

He arrived at one of the community houses, expecting Norman Bates, from 'Psycho' to answer the door. Instead, a plump woman in her mid-sixties, with a sweet, welcoming manner opened the door. The house was cozy and warm with comfortable furniture and happy residents dressed normally. There were no signs of military-style clothing, nor any indications of coercion or restricted freedom. They served lunch while he was there, and the food was good and healthy. They were emphatic in their denial of any pressure to remain in the community and denied or significantly downplayed almost all of the rumors he brought up. Several of them attested that their literal survival was attributable to their involvement in The Christian Movement. The men and women seemed of equal status in the house, although they acknowledged that men and women held their "rightful" places in the eyes of God and their community. Each of them shared a unique story, typically involving a struggle with addiction, homelessness, being destitute, or spiritually void, only to find safety and recovery within "the Movement," as they often referred to it. None of them could have imagined leaving to face a world they perceived as being fraught with greed, violence, and isolation.

I was struck by the enormous difference in the experiences of these two reporters, differences that reflected the swirling controversy in the press. I made a note to ask Anne about her perceptions of this latter exposé, since it clearly contradicted her description of her community.

After finishing this third article, I looked at the time on my computer and was disappointed that I needed to turn in for the night, having been mesmerized by these journalistic revelations and the foreboding nature of their content. In one respect, my own life had intersected with this new world about which I was slowly becoming familiar, and my intuition told me that much more sinister truths would be revealed in the coming months. Even though I had no reason to challenge Anne's credibility, these published accounts created an even stronger foundation of truth for her reality. Only once before in my practice had publicity regarding a client coincided with treatment.

— CHAPTER TEN —

One day, when Anne and I had been meeting for a little more than two months, I found her sitting in my waiting room, shaking and visibly much more upset than she had been the previous week. She waited for me to invite her in, instead of rising when I opened the door as had become her custom, and walked slowly into my office and sat down cautiously.

With her arms crossed over her body, she kept her eyes down and said, with awkwardness, "I'm having one of my attacks, I think. I took an Ativan in the waiting room, but it hasn't helped yet. I know I said I don't use medications, but on bad days I need it."

I remained quiet in response and simply nodded my understanding.

"It makes me relax," Anne said, glancing downward.

As much as I had some concern regarding her medical choices, I was impressed that she had lobbied her point. "So, what have you been experiencing physically and emotionally that defines an attack?" I asked.

"Sometimes they just seem to come on all of a sudden, but I've been a lot more stressed and scared, and I've been picking at my fingers," she answered, holding them out so that I could see where the skin had been rubbed raw. "You see where I even make them bleed?" she asked, sounding defeated.

"Are you aware when you're doing this?" I asked, knowing this was a sign of pretty severe anxiety.

"Not most of the time. I do it mostly at night when I'm asleep and will wake up and they're bleeding," she said, with a look of dejection that seemed to imply she felt little control.

"I guess I've never noticed your fingers," I said. "Is this something new?"

"I used to bite my nails as a child, but my dad would hit me, and he sometimes would rip off parts of my nails. So I stopped biting them. I don't even know why he cared, or if he just didn't want other people to see me doing it. Anyways, I guess that's when I started picking at my fingers in my sleep, but I didn't do it when people were around—I don't think."

Just the image of her father ripping off parts of her fingernails gave me a queasy feeling. Listening to the actual abuse and imaging the pain and blood were really difficult for me. And then I looked at Anne and saw how calmly she was describing this part of her childhood. "I understand. It sounds like what you did was to avoid further pain. Have you ever tried to stop doing it?"

"How would I stop something that's happening while I'm sleeping?" she asked, looking a little annoyed.

Her skeptical look made sense, and I felt like I had lost her rather fragile faith in me for a moment. Trying to recover, I responded, "Well, the first answer might be to reduce some of the stress you're experiencing. There are other options as well, like wearing some kind of light gloves for a while."

"Would that work?" she asked with a puzzled look.

"It might. It's something we sometimes do with babies—and I'm not calling you a baby—when they scratch themselves at night. It doesn't really change behavior, but it protects them from hurting themselves. Behavioral change often means prioritizing the prevention of harm or injury and figuring out later why it occurs."

Anne's face relaxed a little, as she seemed to accept this explanation. "Maybe I'll get some gloves and see what that's like," she said.

"And along with that, maybe you and I can work on some other techniques to cope with all you're feeling," I offered. Seeing her face brighten, I continued. "I could begin to teach you some relaxation exercises, and we could begin to look at some of the thoughts that underlie some of your painful emotions. How about if we take the last fifteen minutes today and begin working on some of these strategies?"

"Yeah, that would be cool," she agreed, with an eagerness in her voice.

Getting back to her current emotional state, I inquired, "Did anything happen this morning that might have frightened you more than usual, Anne?"

"No, I was fine at home, but I began to feel really scared as I walked out of my apartment to come here."

"Do you think being out among people felt scary, or could coming here to talk about things be frightening?"

"I'm not sure, maybe both. I'm scared of so many things," Anne responded, with a look of sadness.

"You told me last time we met that the attacks began again about six weeks ago, and I was wondering if we might talk about that time a little more."

It took her a few seconds to answer, but then she said, "I guess so." Her reticence, I knew, reflected her uncertainty and discomfort with most topics that could connect to real feelings. I softened my voice a little, trying to help her feel a little more at ease.

"One of the things that's struck me as important in your story was that you came to Boston six months ago, and that much change might have produced a lot of anxiety for anyone, but you describe the attacks as having begun several months later. Can you tell me a little about coming here and why you ended up coming to Boston?"

Looking relieved by the chance to reflect back, rather than dealing with her current emotions, Anne seemed to perk up a little and began to recount the history of her new life in Boston. She explained that when the authorities and her attorney strongly encouraged her to relocate away from Oregon, the initial hope was that she would go to California, in part to make it easier to return to Portland to provide testimony. However, Anne insisted on being as far away as possible and was determined to go to Boston, both because of its geographical distance from Oregon and because she had seen pictures of it on television for the first time while in the safe house.

There had been little else to do during her year there, and television had become an important companion. Having hardly ever seen television growing up, she was both mesmerized and educated by this new medium, and, along with the Internet, television had become her window to the world. Huge and confusing as she found it, she had, nevertheless, become particularly enthralled with several shows, the most notable being *Cheers*, and she watched reruns daily. The fact that the show was set in Boston increased the city's appeal as a destination. The people seemed cool and fun, and they got to sit around and hang out at a bar most of the time, playing jokes on each other. This seemed, as Anne put it, "really cool," since they weren't mean spirited and didn't hurt each other. Even though she was chronologically an adult, her very limited exposure to the outside world left Anne with childlike beliefs—including that people on television were just like real people. Despite all of her fear and history of passivity, she had remained resolute about going to Boston as part of her agreement to remain an important witness.

Another point of disagreement between the FBI, Anne's attorney, Nathan Cohen, and Anne herself was her insistence upon retaining her name.

But Anne's reason for not wanting to change her name was much more emotional and psychological than rational. She had given up so much of herself and her identity in the process of becoming a protected and relocated witness that she needed something that remained of herself. When told that retaining her name posed a danger, she responded that her whole life had posed a danger and she had managed to survive. She knew that some powerful internal sense of self had been one of her ways of surviving. Consequently, her tenacity and the emotional appeal of needing to hold onto some part of *herself* had prevailed, and the authorities accepted that she would begin her new life as Anne Martin, although she did agree to change her date of birth and social security number.

The FBI and Nathan Cohen worked out several other terms of the relocation, including Anne's expenses for one year, which covered housing, food, and an allowance for clothing, health insurance, and health-related expenses. Hearing this, I now understood why Anne wouldn't accept any medical treatment, but would have health insurance. The authorities also agreed to pay for counseling for Anne, should she seek it. In addition, they provided her with $30,000, to enable her to buy a car and to enter an educational or technical school to develop skills toward a career. They agreed to cover any expenses related to providing testimony and/or any civil litigation that might eventually ensue. Nathan Cohen was adept at representing his clients' needs, and Anne felt he was committed to her protection and welfare.

After affirming Anne's decision to relocate to Boston, the FBI took six weeks to make the necessary arrangements, working closely with their colleagues in Boston. Her relocation was unceremonious, only allowing for her to say good-bye to Nathan, who visited her at the safe house the day before her departure. The authorities did not record her destination, and neither Adele nor Nathan initially knew the exact location where she was heading.

The FBI provided Anne with the numbers of two agents, one in Portland and one in Boston, who would serve as contacts for questions, needs, or emergencies. Since Nathan would continue to represent Anne, the agents gave him the number for a cell phone that they had provided to her, and they told Anne he was the only person from her past with whom she was to have contact unless the FBI served as an intermediary. This included contact with her family, who remained intricately connected with members of The Christian Movement, even after having left the community and Deerbrook following Anne's decision to testify against several of the elders and Jonas Smith.

The authorities strongly cautioned Anne to avoid any contact with her past, emphasizing potential jeopardy to her relocation and safety. The entire agreement felt somewhat akin to a restraining order, Anne told me, and she confided that she'd known from the outset that she intended to have contact with her family, especially her mother, whom she missed a great deal. She would cross that bridge, either openly or surreptitiously, after getting settled in her new life, having learned long ago when to simply be quiet instead of protesting.

On a rainy Monday morning in December, federal agents escorted Anne to the Portland airport and put her on an indirect flight to Boston, first landing in Phoenix and requiring her to change airlines. This was an added precaution, just in case someone from The Christian Movement happened to be at the Portland airport to observe the destination of the flight she was boarding.

Anne was incredibly excited about flying to her new life, attesting to how little fear she had for things that might typically arouse anxiety in others. She arrived in her new city nine hours later, with only an address for her new home and not knowing anyone. Although keeping it secret from the FBI and even from Nathan Cohen, she had made a few contacts over the Internet, hoping to have a couple of friends in her new home. The FBI agents had given Anne detailed instructions as to how to proceed once she arrived in Boston, and she followed them to the letter. Upon arriving at the terminal at Logan Airport, she went to baggage claim and retrieved her luggage, consisting of two large suitcases and two boxes of knickknacks she had acquired during her year after leaving the church. Most of these had come from outings she had taken with the various police personnel assigned to her over the year. Also in the boxes were materials for making quilts, a pastime she had enjoyed since her early adolescence.

She loaded all of her worldly possessions on a cart and slowly managed to push it outside to a taxi line. It was shockingly cold, and there were snow flurries coming down. It was just turning from dusk to dark, and she felt somewhat surreal, having virtually no idea where she was and not knowing a soul within three thousand miles.

The ride from the airport to her new residence in the town of Arlington, a suburb about fifteen minutes outside of Boston, took about thirty minutes and ended on a quiet, nondescript, tree-lined street. After the driver took her luggage from the trunk and set it on the curb, she paid him the exact amount he had indicated. As he took the money, she noticed he seemed quite annoyed and somewhat rudely turned and got into his taxi without saying a word. It would be several weeks and several similar reactions later before Anne understood the custom of tipping. This was one of many cultural practices that she had never been exposed to, having never having had the freedom to venture beyond her limited environment.

Anne found herself standing on the sidewalk as the snow flurries came down around her, looking up at a two-story, white, wood-framed house with a large front porch flanked by two doors. She had been told her front door would be the one on the left, so she hauled her worldly belongings, the two suitcases and the two boxes, up onto the porch and dug inside her backpack to find her key. She opened the door and walked inside. Although Anne felt, at this moment, very much alone, her isolation was nothing compared with the sense of loneliness that would set in more deeply over the coming weeks.

"It's almost as if you arrived from a remote island somewhere, or another planet, and are seeing earth for the first time," I commented, as I imagined the depth of aloneness she was describing.

"I didn't understand the world at all and don't really know that much now either, and I actually used to feel like I'd dropped in from another planet," she agreed. "When I was in the safe house, I got to sometimes watch the reruns of a show called *My Favorite Martian*, and I kind of related to the Martian guy."

I laughed. "I loved that show growing up. It's strange because when I was a little kid, it seemed so cool and magical, and now I'm seeing how difficult it really can be. He also had a really good friend to live with, but I imagine you have been much lonelier most of the time."

"I was completely alone for at least the first three months, and I cried a lot. I missed the church and the structure my life had there. I wanted to go home. I still feel that sometimes. I was terrified I wouldn't be able to make it on my own. I missed my family," she said, looking up at me for a reaction.

"It makes sense you missed the world you knew," I assured her. "Apart from the loneliness, what frightened you the most about having to make it on your own?"

"I don't know, mostly that I didn't understand a lot about how people lived or many of the things they'd talk about, and I was afraid I'd look really foolish and say or do the wrong things. I was terrified of men and being hurt again. I had never had to really shop for food or buy clothes or find my way on buses. And I feared I was betraying God and the church and would be punished for being a sinner." The look of fear on Anne's face portrayed how powerfully she feared retribution.

"In some ways, you had spent most of your life living in fear, but I gather this was a different kind of fear."

"Yeah. In the church and Deerbrook, I actually learned to know what could or would happen and had learned to shut out the physical pain and the emotions when someone was hurting me or punishing me. But when I got into the world on my own, I didn't have any idea what I might be facing, and instead of people being there, even the ones who would often hurt me, there was no one."

"I understand. So, what happened after those first months, Anne? You have some friends now, so, where did you begin to meet people?"

"Well, none of those people I'd contacted through the Internet before arriving ever wrote again, so, after I'd been in Boston a few months, I took some of the money they'd given me and enrolled in a school in Cambridge that provided training for home health care, and that's when I first met Mickie.

She was teaching a course on hospice care. We became instant friends and started doing everything together."

"That had to feel very good to have a friend and some social support," I prompted her.

"Actually, the panic began then. I was having to face people and try to figure out so much, and I felt so stupid and so weird about my past. Mickie and I would go places, like a club or a bar or a restaurant, and I would start to freak out and we'd have to leave," she admitted.

"So, the isolation was very lonely and depressing, but beginning to develop a social life brought on a whole new emotional experience—anxiety," I reflected.

"Yeah, I guess it was anxiety. Some days I didn't want to leave the house all day, and I would just sit there."

"When we face a choice of something that causes strong depression versus something that causes strong anxiety," I explained, "the anxiety will usually trump the depression, because it's a more powerful feeling. I believe that intense fear is the strongest feeling we probably can have, at least in terms of a negative feeling. Some people say grief is as strong or stronger, but anxiety is powerful."

"What do you mean by 'trump'?" she asked with a puzzled look.

I should have realized she wouldn't know this word. "I'm sorry. That's a term from a card game. Have you ever heard of a game called Bridge?"

"I don't think so."

"Well, knowing the game isn't important. 'Trump' means conquering or being stronger. When something trumps something else, it's stronger and takes over. So, in my thinking, your anxiety was a stronger feeling than even the loneliness for a while, and you stayed home. But I have a feeling that after several months, the loneliness and sadness became stronger, and it sort of became worth facing some of the fear of being in the world at that point."

"Yeah, that's kinda what happened," she agreed. "I was crying all the time and felt lonelier as the weeks went by. And I would call Nathan every couple of days, since he said I could. He kept encouraging me to just try to go to a few places, like a coffeehouse, and to check out nursing schools, since I had said that was something I thought I'd like to do. I guess all of that led me to start getting out of the house a little, but starting school changed everything." Anne rubbed her hands together, as she relived the anxiety of pushing herself into the world.

"So, why did you choose hospice care?" I asked.

"Because I knew it would be flexible and allow me to go to school, and I got to help people."

"Did you consider trying to find a counselor or therapist to talk to?"

"Not really, though Nathan suggested it. But I was afraid it would be like the prayer services," she said after a moment, looking down and revealing her discomfort.

"What do you mean?" I asked, sensing she was about to reveal another horrible experience from her childhood.

"Well, the elders of the church performed prayer services to try to help me."

"Can you help me understand what kind of service you are referring to, Anne?" I prompted gently.

"They would try to deliver me from the evil that had taken over my soul and my body."

"When did this take place?" I asked, sensing this was another difficult topic for her.

Moving around somewhat anxiously in her chair, she replied, "The last time was when I was seventeen."

Deciding to push her a little, I asked, "What would happen in these services?"

Staying silent, Anne looked down toward the floor, communicating to me that she may have reached a limit for today. Trying to take the pressure off of her, I offered, "I understand you may not want to talk about this now, and that's fine. When you're ready to, we can talk more about the prayer services." Then, after hesitating a few moments, I added, "I have a thought, but I want you to feel free to decide what you want to do, so this is just a suggestion for you to consider. I wonder if you might be more comfortable writing about the prayer services. Sometimes that can be easier than talking and may even be a way to let out some of the feelings."

Anne remained very quiet for a few moments and then said, "I don't write very well. We were only taught to write a little. But Tim might help me."

Her simple statement opened up a whole new direction in the session. "So, did you attend some school?" I asked.

"No, only the boys could go to school," Anne responded, looking surprised that I didn't recall that.

Acknowledging her reaction, I asked, "So, tell me again, why were the boys allowed to go to school, but not the girls?"

"Mostly because the girls were supposed to serve the community doing things that didn't require real education. Women mostly raised the children, took care of the homes and the animals, and worked in the shops in town. We were sometimes taught things to help us be better at our jobs."

"To be honest, you have a good command of the language and a strong vocabulary for not having attended school. Maybe that is something you'll do now."

"I'm not intelligent enough to go to school," Anne quickly clarified.

"Why do you think you're not intelligent?" I asked, feeling her sadness.

"Because I can't read or write well, and have always been told that I'm too dumb to learn anything," Anne said, looking right at me as if she had offered proof for her belief.

"Who told you that, Anne?" I asked, very much wanting to challenge a belief that didn't actually question her religious faith.

Anne hesitated for a moment and then said, "My father has always told me that."

Masking my intense dislike of him, I responded, "Well, I have a very different perception of your intelligence. I'm not saying you have the knowledge and information of someone who has been in school, but I'm quite certain you have the ability to learn and acquire a lot of knowledge." I paused and watched her for a reaction, but found no change in her expression. I glanced at the clock and said, "Well, before we shift to a relaxation exercise, I wanted to ask your thoughts about something I read regarding the church."

"Okay," Anne agreed, sounding a little reluctant.

So I shared a synopsis of the reporter's visit to the communal home I'd read about, wanting to get her take on it.

Anne smiled slightly. "When a reporter expressed an interest in visiting the farm or the community," she explained, "Father Jonas was usually very inviting, because he was adept at staging such visits. Particular members of the community would pose, almost like actors, in a house, and they would present a very positive view of the community."

I wasn't really surprised, considering the cunning that had effectively allowed the community to elude the authorities for two decades.

"So, what do you think made people stay when they wanted out?" I asked, my curiosity prevailing over the pragmatics of needing to stop for today.

"Well, there weren't really any physical restraints. I mean, we had fences, but they couldn't really keep anyone from leaving. The chains and locks were really our fears and being so dependent. We would go to hell and be ostracized forever from the community and lose contact with everyone, friends and sometimes even family, and be left alone with a God who now saw us as evil," Anne said. "And you really didn't own anything or have any money or even your own bank account, so it meant living on the streets. I had heard rumors that there was some kind of system that could help you, like the underground that helped slaves escape." She paused and looked more directly at me, wondering if I had known this. She then continued, "Did you know that quilts were used to help the slaves escape the South?"

"No," I responded.

"Yeah, the women who were in the underground would embed maps on their quilts, and they could be used to help someone move north or to other havens that were part of the escape route."

Not having known this, I was struck by the powerful and important use of artistry to save people. The transition felt a little awkward, but I took the next fifteen minutes to teach her some basic muscle relaxation combined with breathing. I asked her to try this twice a day, "like a medication, but instead of a medication," before going to sleep and before beginning her day each morning. I also gave her a list of the ten most common thinking distortions that often underlie depression and anxiety, and asked her to identify the two or three that most fit her thinking. After briefly reviewing the list together, I said, "So, how about if we stop for today and meet the same time next week?"

"Okay," she agreed, standing up slowly and heading to the door.

As she opened the door, I said, "I'll see you next Tuesday." I was comforted to see that she stood more upright and didn't back away from me as she headed for the door. I wasn't sure if she was feeling better or mostly just safer with me. After Anne departed, I found myself reflecting that I just wanted to be someone who didn't hurt her and who helped her to feel safe and trusting. The ability to trust again was something Anne would or wouldn't find, in time. It would be an important challenge for her, and my role was to not betray her sense of safety and trust.

— CHAPTER ELEVEN —

Anne and I had continued to meet weekly as we headed into our fifth month together, and, lately, I had been seeing a different Anne. She possessed considerably greater energy and occasionally smiled.

As she entered my office this morning, she handed me a piece of folded paper and then quietly sat down. Before unfolding the paper, I looked toward her and asked, "So, what's this?"

"It's what I wrote about the prayer service," she said, with the pride of a child who's come home with a good report card.

I certainly remembered having made such a request a while back, but was surprised that Anne had taken this step, considering her reticence and discomfort regarding talking about it and the length of time since the subject had arisen.

"Would you like me to read it now?" I asked, smiling to show my appreciation.

"You can if you want," she replied, a little surprised being offered a choice.

So I unfolded the paper and began to read.

The prayer services were done to deliver me from sin, a sort of exorcism although it wasn't called that. It was called a delivery, and they spoke in tongues. While they were praying and speaking in tongues, they would have me undress and touch me. Then they would penetrate me from behind, in my anus. It was always terribly painful, and I would be beaten if I cried or screamed, so I screamed inside, and a couple of times I actually passed out from the pain. I would think of being somewhere else. They believed that "buttfucking" purged the evil from inside. Sometimes this was done as a punishment, and at other times for no particular reason. There were always at least three or more elders present, and Jonas was always there leading the service. This happened many times, starting when I was about fifteen, and the last time was about two years ago.

I finished reading her words and was shaken by the power of her simple description of this horrible ritual to which she had been repeatedly subjected. I was also struck by her use of the word "buttfucking," certainly not expecting it to be part of the vocabulary of a Christian community. I decided that she had probably learned the term at the safe house or among her friends in

Boston, and that asking her about it would create more discomfort for her. I looked up at Anne, her face showing no emotion, and found myself holding back a tear from forming in my right eye. "Wow, I'm so sorry you had to endure this," I said. "Now I understand why it must be hard to think or talk about." But, as I said this, I thought how hollow my words sounded, sort of my way of just finding something to say. I felt like I wanted to apologize for men and everyone she should have been able to trust.

Anne lowered her eyes, but I saw a glimmer of appreciation mixed with her sadness. It was a cross between a smile and a slight frown, expressions that often coincided when she glanced toward me and saw the emotions I often felt in my work with her. Anne was clearly both interested in and comforted by my reactions to her traumatic history.

"How did it feel writing this, Anne?" I asked, wanting to regain my role and my composure.

But her response, "Okay, I guess," provided little to help me comprehend how she perceived such cruelty and wrongdoing. She had blocked any emotional attachment to the physical and psychological pain she endured, and it now almost seemed as if she relied upon others' reactions to understand which feelings she would otherwise experience.

Anne looked up toward me. "I brought in something to show you," she said. "It isn't very good, but I thought you might want to see it."

Guessing that I was about to accompany her down another powerfully emotional path, I very much wanted to see whatever she had brought, but I wanted to brace myself for another upsetting part of her history. So, while I merely responded, "I'd like to see anything you'd be up for sharing with me," covertly I wondered where my edges of comfort were.

Anne picked up her backpack from the floor, triggering Madison to sit up at the mere possibility that she would extract some kind of treat. She unzipped the main compartment and pulled out a cloth-like object, arousing my curiosity but thoroughly disappointing Madison, who couldn't smell anything edible. Then Anne unfolded the cloth, revealing a quilt she had made. Its left side consisted of black and white vertical stripes, reminiscent of prison bars, inside which crouched the silhouette of a person sitting motionless on the floor. On the right side, she had created a rainbow, within which another silhouette appeared to be flying upward, a marked contrast from the defeated looking figure on the left. Although I suspected that the rainbow represented the gay community's chosen symbol and a symbol of freedom from oppression in other groups, such as Jesse Jackson's Rainbow Coalition, I wanted to hear Anne's interpretation of the quilt.

"So, can you tell me about it?" I asked, my words sounding rather cliché.

With surprising enthusiasm, given her characteristic reserve, Anne explained that this was actually the first of several quilts she had made. It had become an important pastime since taking a quilting class when she first arrived in Boston. She described the earlier quilts she'd made as being "fun ones," but now they had begun to reflect her memories and her feelings. She had kept the first one and given away the others, usually to homeless people, because it was impractical to keep them all in her small apartment, and because doing so had become a way of getting rid of an issue and its accompanying painful emotions. She had made the quilt she showed me the previous evening, finding herself unable to sleep, and described it as being about her two lives—one when she would be kept in a cage, the life at times almost drained from her, and the other as her new life in which she was free and felt like she could fly. She explained that the stitching had a big, jagged zigzag between the two sides and was red, because it represented going through fire to get to the other side and freedom.

For a moment I sat there stunned, realizing I was seeing a new world, a very different way to express inner feelings and one's journey. I had seen people do this with writing, painting, and music. Now I had seen the therapeutic value of quilting. I loved the opportunity to be exposed to other forms of healing, a gift that often occurred in my work.

"So, do the rainbow colors represent the rainbow in the gay community?" I asked, my curiosity overcoming my supposed commitment to wait for Anne's interpretation.

"I don't know. I guess so," she said, her raised brows reflecting her own uncertainty.

"You really did all this in one night?" I asked incredulously.

"Yeah, but I use a sewing machine to do all the stitching," she responded, in a matter-of-fact tone that obviously, and typically, denied the truly impressive person I saw in front of me.

Knowing a little less about a sewing machine than the workings of a nuclear power plant, I was still amazed.

"Why don't you think it's very good? I really like it!" I exclaimed.

For the first time I could remember, Anne's face momentarily lit up, but just as quickly, she reverted to a look of skepticism.

"You really think it's good?" she asked with a questioning look.

"Yeah, I think it's great, both the artistry and the creativity and meaning," I assured her.

Again, her face lit up, and I could feel the power a parent has to instill pride and self-respect in a child.

Since we were already talking about the quilts as a means of helping her cope with the stress she was experiencing, I decided to ask about the relaxation techniques we had talked about a few weeks earlier.

"I like the muscle relaxation breathing thing, but sometimes I'm too upset to do it," Anne acknowledged.

"I absolutely understand what you're saying," I told her. "When your mind is overwhelmed, one's thoughts overpower the body's ability to calm itself. But once you've really learned these techniques well, you could take back that control. I know the learning process is the challenge though. Are you finding it easier at any particular time?"

"Yeah, it's easier before I go to sleep. In the morning, I sometimes wake up so upset from things I've dreamed that it doesn't work as well."

"Then continue to do it each night," I replied, "and maybe only try it on the mornings it might be a little easier. I'd rather you really get good at the technique and then apply it to more challenging conditions."

"Okay, I can do that. I looked at that list you gave me, and I kind of do most of those things," she said, referring to a list of cognitive distortions I had given her.

"I'm really glad you're taking the homework stuff seriously, because that's where any real change will happen in your life. As for doing all those things, welcome to the club. When I had to initially learn all the mental health disorders in graduate school, I thought, 'Shit, I have all of them,' and like you, we all do all of those distortions to some degree. So, what would be the two strongest ones for you?"

"Well, if I have to pick two, then I'd say mindreading and catastrophizing," she answered.

"I couldn't agree more," I smiled. "So, give me an example of mindreading."

This time she gave me a somewhat sarcastic grin, the kind that said you know what I should answer. "When I think you're mad at me," she said.

"Bingo. Great minds think alike," I responded, mirroring her grin. "What about another example?"

This time Anne pondered for a minute and then said tentatively, in a questioning tone, "I don't know, maybe when I think everyone thinks I'm really weird or stupid or something like that."

"I couldn't have thought of two better examples," I nodded, to offer encouragement. "So, what about catastrophizing?"

"When I think everything is going wrong and won't ever get better."

"That's almost the definition of catastrophizing. Can you also think of something specific you've thought that with, that could affect your emotions and cause anxiety and depression?"

"When I get into one of those panic places, I feel like I'm going to die or have a heart attack."

"That's actually a great example, because you truly aren't going to die or have a heart attack, but your thoughts make the panic worse. So, I want you to continue to be aware of whenever you do either of these things, and the next step will be to begin to challenge the thoughts as you recognize them. I want you to challenge them by asking one simple question, no matter what the situation: Do I actually have evidence, other than my thoughts, to support or prove my worst fears right now? Does that make sense?"

"I think so," Anne said tentatively.

Using our relationship to bring something to life whenever I got the chance, I continued, "So, an example is that when you think I'm mad at you, you would ask, 'Do I have evidence right now, —and I mean real evidence— something I can see, hear, taste, smell, or touch, that says he's mad right now? And, do I have evidence that even if he is, that he's mad at me?' So, keep working on the relaxation exercises and identifying and challenging the thought distortions, and you will definitely see them becoming helpful, and, most importantly, it will become within your power to change your thoughts."

Anne looked a little tired, and I sensed she had absorbed as much teaching as she could for today. It seemed like an apt time to switch gears, so I said, "I wanted to find out more about the legal services you've been provided and what's happening on that front, especially since our work together may end up connected to it."

"I have a lawyer. His name's Nathan Cohen," she said, her posture relaxing with the shift to a less emotionally laden topic.

"I remember you referring to him before. How did you find Mr. Cohen?"

"I guess he was assigned to me by my social worker or the district attorney's department."

"Is this related to you being a witness and part of the witness protection program?"

"Yes, but he's also representing me as a victim of abuse and violence," she said.

"So, do you like working with Mr. Cohen?" I asked.

"I was very frightened when I first met him. It was only a few days after I had called the police and been taken away from the church. I had never known any kind of lawyer and wasn't really sure what they even did. He was very kind, and one of the other residents said she was sure he was gay. I didn't really know what that meant, but when she explained that meant he had sex with men, and not women, that helped me to feel safer."

This had inadvertently helped to pave the way for Anne to feel more comfortable with me. "I'm glad you're able to feel safe with Mr. Cohen," I said. "Would you be comfortable for me to talk with him?"

"Yeah, that would be okay," she readily agreed.

Since Anne seemed to like the idea, I then asked, "I wanted to ask you some questions related to your identity. I guess there's some uncertainty on my part regarding your sense of your sexual identity. Is that okay with you?"

Anne responded quietly, "I guess it's okay, but I'm not sure what you mean by my sexual identity."

I didn't find this a surprising question for a woman whose only sexual experiences had been forced upon her and who had been sheltered from so many aspects of human behavior by a church that had inhibited sexual awareness in children, while simultaneously forcing some of them into sexual activity. I also found myself concerned that this might be too heavy and too confusing an issue for Anne at this stage of therapy and her emotional development.

"I'm aware that your closest friends seem to be lesbians, and that you feel more comfortable with me and with your attorney because we're gay men. And I know that you were severely sexually abused by men, and that the idea of sexual involvement feels very far away from something you might imagine for yourself. But I still don't know if you're more attracted to men or women, neither, or both. In some ways, it may not matter, but in other respects I want us both to know who you are and what things feel like for you. I know this may not be something you're ready to talk about ..." I trailed off, a little uncertain as to how she would respond.

"I'm not sure what you want to know," Anne said cautiously.

I smiled slightly, realizing how convoluted my inquiry had become. "I understand, and maybe it would help if I ask some questions to guide us in this exploration. I guess my first question is whether you find yourself physically or sexually attracted to men or women more," I asked.

"I like looking at everyone, and you can learn a lot just looking at people. But I guess I find myself more attracted to women, but I don't ever want to have sex with any of them," she said, her tone sounding firm.

"Do you ever imagine being in a relationship with a woman?" I continued.

"Not really. I look at Mickie's relationship, and it doesn't look very good to me. I also can't ever imagine having to touch someone a lot."

"When you were younger, do you also remember being attracted to women?"

"I wasn't at all aware of it until I was about fourteen, but by the time I was fifteen, it went away."

This was one of those unusual responses from Anne that often led to powerful places and the darker corners of her past. "Do you know why it went away when you were fifteen?" I asked, trying not to sound surprised by her unusual response.

"Yeah, because I was stoned."

Somewhat perplexed by this unexpected response, considering her sheltered environment and having heard no other indications of drug use as a minor, I asked, "Can you tell me more about being stoned and how often that occurred?"

"That was the only time."

"You haven't said anything before about drug use, Anne. Is this something you did with other friends within the church?" I asked, a look of confusion on my face.

Anne squinted, and she looked at me quizzically. Now we both appeared to be perplexed. "Why do you ask if I did drugs?" she asked with a defensive tone.

"Because you said you got stoned."

"I'm not sure what that has to do with drugs," she replied.

I had an odd feeling. Obviously we were missing each other's point, but I still couldn't understand the confusion. I was surprised she had used the term. After all, Anne's very sheltered history had inhibited her knowledge of cultural idioms. Now I was even more surprised she'd used it without knowing it pertained to drug use. "When you said you got stoned, were you referring to smoking marijuana or pot?" I asked.

Anne raised her eyebrows again, skeptically this time, and said with conviction, "I've never taken any drugs, not even any medications until recently."

Totally confused now, I asked plainly, "Then what were you meaning when you said you were stoned?"

"When I was fifteen, several of the elders accused me of flirting with boys and harboring thoughts of promiscuity toward some of the older ones. They referred to it as a 'spirit of lust.' It wasn't true at all, and I tried to tell them that I didn't even like boys, that I kind of liked girls. They began screaming at me and yelling things like 'sin of homosexuality' and 'sinner.' I was frightened, because their anger usually led to hurting me in some way. I wasn't sure what I'd done or said that was wrong, but that usually didn't seem related to them hurting me. It was more about telling me I was a sinner or harbored the devil inside me. I knew I was in trouble though. They put me in a cage, like they often did prior to penetrating me or hurting me, and kept me there overnight. The next morning was Sunday, and people were gathering early for church. They took me out to the central courtyard behind the main church.

It was a large cement courtyard where they held big events. There were maybe a hundred members there, and they formed a massive circle. They took me to the center of the circle, and I was very confused. My eyes were still adjusting to the light, and my legs were too stiff to walk on my own after spending the night curled up in the cage. It was the same cage I had always been kept in, but as I got older and grew, it became impossible to even move inside. They forced me to kneel and made me sit up and put my hands on my head and left me there, and then people began to throw stones as hard as they could. Some of them really hurt, especially a couple that hit me in the face. I tried to protect my head, and then I passed out. I think that maybe one of the stones may have knocked me out, and there were several really large bumps on my head when I woke up. I remember going into a trance like I often did, so I can't remember how long this went on before I passed out, maybe a few minutes. Maybe the trance was how I passed out. I don't really know."

When Anne finished sharing this recollection, I found myself more upset than at any time before in listening to her history. Although she had calmly recounted these atrocities, I was deeply, and somewhat visibly, stunned, my hushed tone reflecting my sadness. "Wow, I really missed the boat on that one. I guess I couldn't even imagine in modern times in the Western world that this could still happen. It's something I think of maybe in a Moslem land or from five hundred years ago. I'm sorry. I understood 'stoned' to be only about drugs, and I'm so amazed and sorry this was done to you." I felt bad for accusing her of using drugs, knowing how difficult it must have felt for her. Later, upon further reflection, I was able to forgive myself a little for what had been, after all, a reasonable assumption, and to credit myself for being human and not omniscient, something I had to allow myself to realize more often.

I noticed that Anne just smiled very slightly, ironically a smile of sympathy for my pain. She had learned that when people heard of such events, it was difficult for them, and wanted to soothe their sadness far more than cause them any pain. The smile was her way of nurturing. "Oh, that's cool. Thanks. I didn't mean to upset you. It was a long time ago," she said.

"I'm not upset, more surprised, and, well, I guess angry, so that probably qualifies as upset," I said, not feeling comfortable with the focus on my feelings. But, if I wanted her to be open and honest, I couldn't try to hide my more obvious feelings, I decided. "I don't want you to feel you need to protect me," I continued. "I'm fine to hear about whatever happened in your life and even to feel bad for a little while. Like you, it becomes less uncomfortable with time, because time helps us to adjust to almost everything we face in life, both good and bad. I have a deal for you. I won't push you to feel things I think you should feel, if you can allow me to feel whatever pain or sadness

I might feel for you. Let's just let each other experience things however we need to for now."

Anne seemed to like this concept and replied, "That's cool. I kind of like that idea."

"So, besides your friends Mickie and Tim, do you feel you want to be connected to the lesbian community?"

"I don't know. I know this will seem bizarre to you, but I really miss the church and my family. I don't feel anyone really knows me here, except you, but you're not really like a friend or my family."

"I find nothing bizarre about that, and I imagine that any community where you spend your life, no matter how painful, is still home—until you find or create a new home and a new family. When you say you miss the church, are you talking about the community or also about missing the spiritual part of your life—at least the good parts?"

"Kinda both, I guess," She said wistfully.

Pondering whether to present an idea that might feel intimidating, I decided to at least mention it. "Well," I said, "I have an idea for you to at least think about. Do you know what MCC is?"

"A couple of Mickie's friends were talking about it. It's some kind of a church that lets you be gay. I don't know what the letters stand for."

"MCC stands for Metropolitan Community Church, and there are MCCs in numerous big cities in the country." Then, thinking about the implications of her image of the church as being a place that allowed people to be gay, rather than as being a place of worship, I continued, "I guess I view MCC as a place for worship and social opportunity in our community, and these have always been intertwined in your past. It might allow you to reconnect to what's valuable to you and offer you a very different experience and sense of God. But I guess I'm assuming that belief in God is still part of how you're spiritual. Do you still believe in God after all you've faced in God's name?"

"I don't really know how to answer that. I'd be frightened to say I didn't believe in God, and I'm pretty sure I do, but it's really confusing. Does this church require you to believe in God?"

"Well, I'm probably not the person to answer that, since I don't attend it, but it's a church for the gay community and a lot of people whose lives have been seriously hurt in the name of religion and God, so they are probably very open to their congregants finding their own ways to answer what they believe in. Maybe you could even ask these friends who were talking about it if you could go with them one Sunday."

Anne didn't say anything, and I knew to leave this as a seed that I had planted, although I was pleased that she expressed more curiosity than fear about the concept. In any case, it seemed like a good note on which to end the session, so I said, "How about if we stop here for today and meet the same time next week?"

"Okay," she said, standing when I did and heading toward the door.

After Anne departed, I put in a call to Nathan Cohen, while things were fresh in my mind.

— CHAPTER TWELVE —

It was 9:30 on a Thursday morning in early December of 1997 in Portland, Oregon, and Nathan Cohen had just entered his office in the Government Plaza Building. At age sixty, Nathan had been a civil servant, so to speak, for thirty years, having entered into the role right out of law school.

He had devoted his entire career to the service of protecting children, a calling that made great natural sense, since he had grown up in an intensely loving and devoted Jewish family in Chicago. Nathan had been taught early in life that one of adults' primary roles was to love and protect children, and as the recipient of such devotion, he knew its intrinsic value.

Nathan had grown up with both financial security and self-esteem and knew he wanted to do something valuable with his life. His family's affluence enabled him to pursue a vocation that fulfilled his values rather than merely his financial needs, and when it came time to attend college, Nathan had little doubt as to where he wanted to go and what he wanted to do. He had wanted to travel "out West" as long as he could remember, so, at age eighteen, he headed to Palo Alto, California, where he had set his sights on Stanford University. Nathan wasn't an ordinary freshman. Compared with most of his classmates, he chose to devote far less free time to parties, attending football games, and social events. Instead, he was deeply engaged in social work projects, helping homeless people and runaway youth and contributing his energy to the developing political causes of the latter half of the sixties. His strongest social connections were with his "brothers and sisters" on the front lines of the war on oppression. Like most of his "compatriots," Nathan's view of the world was also indelibly shaped by bongs and psychedelics. He truly felt his mind was expanded by such enhancements, widening his peripheral view of the world, deepening his attachments to his "comrades," and allowing him to see beyond his narrow experience in ways he believed he would not have otherwise.

He had known since childhood that he wanted to practice law, as a means of helping people far less fortunate than himself, and Nathan's path never seemed to veer toward any other direction. In the beginning of his senior year at Stanford, he applied to the Boalt Hall School of Law at Berkeley. He didn't apply to any other law schools. Berkeley was the place he wanted to be, both for its eminence in the legal world and for its sociopolitical positioning in the growing antiwar and antiestablishment movements, which were inextricably linked and appealed to his very essence and tenets. By early spring, Nathan was offered a place in the first-year class of 1969.

Yet, even though he was at the center of the sixties era and surrounded by people who considered being "hippies" to be part of their calling, Nathan didn't think of himself that way. He kept his hair short, and, unlike many of his peers who scorned cleanliness as being conventional and who favored loose clothing, he adored having showers and wearing tight-fitting attire. So he stuck out as an oddity in the burgeoning social movement centered at Haight and Ashbury, being far too neat and polished in comparison with his peers. Indeed, Nathan himself wondered why he was different. In particular, he wondered about his sexual attractions.

Since high school, Nathan had been aware that he found other guys attractive and that he didn't think about girls with the same aggressiveness or sexualized focus as did his straight male friends. He had remained celibate through his college years, devoting his emotions and love to his passions and his friends, even though by the time he entered law school, he had been enveloped in a social and cultural milieu that accepted every form of physical love—men with women, men with men, and women with women. Nathan gradually grew to accept in himself what he'd long suspected: he was gay. His maturity and the acceptance he felt from his peers and family, ultimately, provided peace with his identity, allowing him to have stronger and more intimate relationships. It was late into this decade of his acceptance of himself as a gay man that he met Cliff. They shared many values and became instantaneous best friends in a relationship that would last a lifetime.

Following Nathan's four years in law school, a path that was prolonged an additional year by his commitment to the antiwar movement, he and Cliff decided to move up to the serenity and beauty of the Pacific Northwest. They contemplated several smaller communities, including Ashland, Oregon, and the large metropolis of Seattle, Washington, but found themselves most attracted to Portland, Oregon, which appealed to their need for a city that felt manageable enough in size to not feel crowded, but large enough and liberal enough that they could feel comfortable as a gay couple.

Once in Portland, Nathan took his first job with the American Civil Liberties Union and spent five years dedicated to protecting the freedoms and equality of people from every walk of life. From the start, his colleagues viewed him as a devoted attorney who was able to balance professional efficacy with passion for his clients.

His time with the ACLU confirmed that his calling was in public service, and when he felt ready to move on to a different type of challenge, he took a position in another public service sector, the Victims Rights Program, where he became an advocate both for the rights of children who were abused, neglected, or caught up in legal or custodial conflicts and for adult victims of violent crime. Nathan had been privy to what he thought were the most heinous atrocities toward children and adults, injustices that resulted in tremendous physical and/or emotional damage to his clients. However, after more than a decade working for victims' rights, he received a new case with which none of his previous work could compare. It was a case that would become very important and personal for him.

It was a Monday morning when Adele Cantor, a social worker in Child and Adult Protective Services, came into his office and asked if he had the time and interest to represent a woman named Anne, whom Portland police had brought to her over the weekend. Adele indicated that Anne appeared to have been the victim of some kind of cult-like religious community as well as a witness to the abuse of at least one minor. Adele told Nathan that Anne's community was located in a small town outside of Medford, Oregon, several hours away from Portland, and that the authorities had decided to relocate her to a safe house in Portland for greater protection. Adele also said that the district attorney had advised her a change of venue would likely be granted for an upcoming trial in which Anne would need to testify.

Ironically, both the defendant's legal team and the local prosecutor agreed upon the relocation, for very different reasons. The amount of publicity in the Medford area was of concern to the defense since there was a strong presumption of guilt in the public arena long before a trial was to begin. On the other side, the local district attorney had concerns about members of the jury being connected to The Christian Movement, even peripherally, and being highly pressured to support the church and its members.

Nathan took a moment to review his calendar to be certain he could take on another case. "Okay," he concluded after a moment. "I can take it. It actually sounds very interesting."

"Great," Adele said. "Here's her address at the safe house. Just so you know, the D.A. was unusually adamant that her location be kept very secure, even from anyone else in my office. I guess they're concerned that members of her community might come after her." She handed him a scrap of paper with the address written on it, which she had kept separate from Anne's file, knowing that other employees in her agency had access to client files and not wanting to take any risks.

"I'll review the file," Nathan said, "and try to meet with Anne tomorrow."

After Adele departed, he sat down at his desk, opened the file, and began to read Adele's intake notes, from within which a rough sketch of his new client, whose full name he learned was Anne Martin, began to appear. Initially, Nathan read, Anne had refused to respond to questions regarding the community in which she had been living. She remained mute with regard to any question that might reveal any wrongdoing or implicate anyone with any crime other than the physical abuse of a child she had been babysitting. It was the abuse of this child that had propelled Anne to call 911, but once the police arrived, Anne was silent and only pointed upstairs. According to what the police had told Adele, as they had entered the residence, the child's father had been standing a couple of feet away screaming at Anne. The police report further stated that, "she appeared terrified but remained frozen, standing by a phone that had obviously been shattered by the child's father in an attempt to stop her phone call to authorities."

Once they had arrived at the Medford Police Headquarters, however, Anne had begun to answer some of their questions, providing vague information to the detectives regarding a history of physical, verbal, and sexual abuse of others in the community. She wouldn't identify anyone in particular, however, and it wasn't clear to police whether or not she herself had been abused, because she wouldn't cooperate by responding to questions regarding her own history. But she expressed that witnessing the abuse of the child had motivated her to call for help. Adele's notes clearly indicated a woman who appeared terrified and extremely shut down. It was her intuition and her hunch regarding Anne's reaction in reporting the abuse that led Adele to strongly suspect that Anne had been partially inspired to act based on her own history of abuse as a child. And, from what Adele knew of religious cults, it also seemed that Anne might have felt undeserving of help herself, but would have seen the value of rescuing another, as this might have felt more in keeping with the cult's stated philosophy.

It was on this assumption that Adele asked Nathan to review the case and take on representing Anne as both a witness and a potential victim. Otherwise, Anne would have been referred to the district attorney's office for legal representation as a witness to a serious criminal matter.

The department had consistently used female police officers and social workers to interview Anne, but could not provide her with female legal representation, since there was only one attorney in the office to serve the mostly female clientele. Consequently, Adele had approached Nathan Cohen because, without anyone ever having explicitly said so, she and her colleagues believed that, as a gay man, Nathan might provide a sense of safety to Anne. He had consistently demonstrated remarkable rapport with traumatized victims and terrified witnesses during his tenure with Child and Adult Protective Services.

As Nathan continued to read, he noticed an additional document in the file that potentially confirmed Adele's suspicion. Adele had retrieved a report regarding Anne that Social Services had filed thirteen years previously, having suspected her of being a victim of abuse. That report, too, had noted Anne's "mute and completely uncooperative behavior." Anne initially had resisted any physical examination, refused to provide any details regarding her family or her community, and was eventually released back to the custody of her parents, the report concluded. "This girl is clearly refusing to provide information. It appears highly likely she has not only been abused, but also highly controlled, both physically and psychologically, creating an intense loyalty and/or fear regarding her perpetrators," the interviewing social worker had written.

In spite of having been forced to undergo a physical examination, Nathan knew that without Anne's cooperation, as the only available witness to the alleged abuse, they would eventually have been obligated to send her back to her parents. He finished reading the report and sat back in his chair. He could see that his new client would require both his legal protection as a witness and his psychological support as an abuse victim. This dual role was exactly what most inspired Nathan about the case. It was the type of assignment that gave him a true sense of purpose, and there was something about this young woman that struck a chord of great interest, enormous compassion, and a powerful desire to protect her. He wasn't sure why he felt so connected to Anne, but he sensed something very impressive and strong in her. "Anne," he mused, "is not a 'victim' or just a survivor, but someone who was determined to live."

— CHAPTER THIRTEEN —

Nathan's clients typically had experienced recent significant physical and/or emotional trauma and were highly sensitive to any type of threat, whether it be an elevated sound, a rapid movement by another person, or even a furtive glance. Rarely had any of them had time to receive counseling that might have alleviated some of these intense fears. In fact, most of Nathan's clients had come his way due to an intervention on the part of Child and Adult Protective Services, and, in essence, Nathan was part of that department's early response team that treated these walking wounded.

Even though the agency used the word "victim" in its title, none of the staff did so with clients, unless they referred to themselves that way. Nathan and his colleagues considered the term "victim" to be highly sensitive, often denoting how a client viewed her own ability to overcome or to have prevented trauma and/or feel safe in the future. In its most negative sense, the word could imply a mental disorder, and so a truly good attorney working in the victims' program had to be a caring therapist as much as a legal advocate. Nathan Cohen was the essence of these dualities.

The morning after reviewing Anne's case report, Nathan awoke enthusiastic to undertake what he sensed would be an important and rewarding endeavor. He navigated through side streets just outside downtown Portland, arriving at the front door of a small, nondescript, brick house. It was an ugly combination of brick and wood, needing paint, considerable repairs to the porch railings, and a very green thumb. Obviously, the exterior décor of a building funded by social services for victims of crime had little budgetary priority. Usually when Nathan met with victims of violence, they had been either women housed in a shelter or children who were in foster care settings. Meetings with protected witnesses, such as Anne, however, were often in more clandestine settings.

Yet, although the house was inconspicuous in appearance, Nathan felt concerned, wondering whether it was obscure enough to protect her. Still fresh in his mind were the case file addendum notes from the police investigation, which indicated a significant possibility that members of Anne's community would attempt to prevent her from testifying. Hiding a witness from a divinely inspired, self-righteous community with ample resources was a considerably greater challenge than hiding a witness from an abusive spouse. It was more akin to protecting someone from a gang or from organized crime, whose reach and capability would far exceed that of an individual, often extending into other organizations and into the street community.

Further, although Anne's location was only known to a very few people besides himself, people who were sworn to confidentiality and committed to her protection, Nathan worried about other residents at the safe house to whom Anne might divulge her story and identity. She would certainly have been strongly cautioned regarding talking with anyone, but her fear and emotional state could affect rational behavior.

It was with these thoughts in mind that Nathan climbed the stairs to the porch and rang the doorbell. He could hear sounds inside, but no one answered the door. He looked at his watch. After a minute passed, he knocked, twice. Silence. Then he heard footsteps. Whoever it was approached the other side of the door and slid back a small vent that allowed a view of anyone standing on the porch.

"Who is it?" came a question from a brusque female voice.

Nathan cleared his throat a little, his normal composure being affected when he met a new client, and especially their guardians, as they were as fiercely protective of their charges as he was.

"My name is Nathan Cohen. I'm an attorney with Adult Protective Services," he said, his voice louder than normal, to provide certainty. "I'm here to see Anne." Nathan knew to never use her last name in any potentially compromising setting.

There was a brief, hushed conversation, and after about thirty seconds, the front door opened and a middle-aged woman in a police uniform opened the door. The buckle securing her weapon in its holster was undone, he noticed, indicating she didn't want to frighten him but wasn't taking anyone for granted. "May I see your identification?" she asked with an authoritative tone.

Nathan put down his briefcase, slowly took out his wallet from his back left pocket, being careful not to give her cause for concern, and handed her both his license and a business card, which she studied with a practiced eye, noting facial features that would be hard to alter, including the shape of Nathan's ears and his jaw line. Nathan stood respectfully while she did so, recognizing that, unlike bouncers, bank tellers, and store clerks, her focus and accuracy in comparing the person with the photo were considerably more detailed and vastly more effective.

Finally convinced that Nathan was indeed the attorney whom Adult Protective Services had indicated would be coming to meet with Anne, she handed back the license. "Thank you for your cooperation," she said with a smile.

"I appreciate that you take our mission seriously," Nathan said sincerely. And, on that note, she invited him into the safe house for what would be the first of numerous visits.

Nathan's first glimpse of the interior of the safe house was less than inspiring. The front door opened onto a small hallway with a narrow stairway to the second floor. An archway, the one decent architectural detail in the house, led into the living room, a long narrow room with a large bay window that would have looked onto the front garden had it not been shielded by a dark green drape that was frayed at the bottom and left the room continuously darkened. The carpet had once been beige, but had been stained so many times over the years that it now resembled a shade of gray. Only two of the four walls matched in color, the furniture was well beyond lived-in, and the sofa's springs had yielded to history. At the near end of the living room was a cheap pine wooden table with four matching chairs, and directly opposite the bay window was a door that led to the kitchen. The kitchen was a hodgepodge of old appliances and chipped Formica surfaces that had accumulated years of grease and stains that were a permanent part of the décor.

Overall, Nathan thought, the room didn't reflect living as much as existing, a sentiment he surmised was not lost on its residents, who, had they been emotionally stronger and not as frightened, might have registered complaints. Yet, in spite of the room's impoverished, dilapidated appearance, there wasn't a lot of clutter, and the place was relatively clean, at least, as much as possible given the age of the furnishings, Nathan allowed.

The officer gestured for Nathan to sit down on the sofa, with a slight shrug of her shoulders by way of apology for the worn sofa. "Not exactly a budget priority," she smiled. Her softer voice and kinder expression encouraged Nathan to feel she now saw them on the same team. "I'm Myrna," she said, snapping the buckle closed on her holster, looking from her gun to Nathan. "I hope you can understand we're not taking any chances."

Feeling relieved by the gesture and her relaxed posture, Nathan crossed the room to the sofa and carefully sat down, lest he collapse into an abyss of musty fabric. He briefly found humor in the contrast of his Brooks Brothers blazer with the dilapidated sofa, a natural concern, he mused, for a posh gay man.

Attired in his usual outfit—casual slacks, a lightweight pullover sweater, and a blue blazer— he hoped he reflected professionalism, but not a stuffiness that would intimidate Anne. He set his briefcase down on the floor, wanting to appear less formal and official than he would if he kept it in his lap or on the sofa.

"Make yourself comfortable, Mr. Cohen, and I'll go upstairs and bring Anne down," Myrna said after Nathan took a seat. "She's quite anxious about this meeting and has a lot of fear of most people, so you'll want to give her lots of space, so to speak."

"I understand," Nathan assured her.

A minute later, Nathan heard a door open at the top of the stairs. But it was several minutes before he heard footsteps slowly descend. Nathan felt his own nervousness increase, realizing from the slowness of Anne's descent how frightened and fragile she must be. As she reached the bottom step, he saw a visibly frightened woman, in an oversized T-shirt, her auburn hair cropped shapelessly, pause and continue to hold onto the flimsy railing. Rather than look at him, Anne focused downward and remained silent. She slowly released her grip and walked cautiously toward a chair across the room and sat down, never looking up at Nathan.

Remembering Adele Cantor's description in her report of how frightened Anne was, Nathan quickly took the initiative, hoping to take off any pressure Anne might feel to do so. "Hello, Anne," he said as softly as he could. "I'm Nathan Cohen, and I'm an attorney. Adele Cantor asked me to meet with you to provide legal support." Rather than get up, as would have been his customary manner, he remained seated so as to not intimidate her. At six feet two inches, he could be quite imposing, and he was aware that, to a frightened woman who had likely been abused by men, standing up would almost certainly alarm her. Then, since Anne did not respond, Nathan inquired, "Did Adele tell you that I would be coming here to meet with you?"

Anne very slightly nodded her head.

Slightly encouraged, Nathan asked, "Would it be okay if we talked for a little while, Anne?"

Without looking directly at Nathan, but raising her head slightly, Anne responded, "Yeah, it's okay." Just hearing her voice, which sounded soft and timid, like a child's, drew him toward her emotionally.

Noticing another resident enter the room on her way to the kitchen, Nathan asked, "Would you be okay if we talked somewhere that offered more privacy?" And then he immediately wondered if this suggestion would frighten her more or offer comfort.

Looking toward Myrna, Anne said, "I guess we might be able to talk in one of the upstairs rooms?" Her answer sounded more like a question.

Myrna asked, "Do you feel comfortable talking upstairs with Mr. Cohen, Anne? I can go upstairs with you if you'd like."

But Anne very quietly said, "No, it's cool. I'll be okay," and for the first time, Nathan observed an underlying bravery and confidence in her, despite her obviously fragile state. Anne turned toward the stairway, and Nathan rose and followed her up the stairs to a bedroom, which he assumed was probably hers. There were two twin beds, each made neatly, and two small, nondescript, old pine dressers, upon one of which sat an older model television, with a greenish, convex screen, and dials, the likes of which Nathan hadn't seen in thirty years. In contrast to the drab interior downstairs, this room was adorned with almost offensively flowery wallpaper. It looked like a tasteless attempt to bring artificial cheer into the world of a dying child.

Anne sat at the foot of one of the beds, and Nathan sat down across from her on the other bed, again deliberately placing his briefcase on the floor. He looked toward her and asked, "So, is this your room, Anne?" trying to engage her with small talk.

She had to turn her head slightly to look in his direction before answering. "Yeah, me and another girl's. She isn't here right now. She went with the other officer to the store for cigarettes, I think."

Trying to keep the conversation light to break the tension, Nathan asked, "So, how are you two working out as roommates?"

"It's cool. She's really quiet, so we don't talk much. She seems nice, though. I only got here four days ago, so I don't know her much. But I know she likes to cook, 'cause she made dinner the other night, and it was pretty good."

"Do you have any hobbies like that?" Nathan asked, trying to ease her into talking about herself.

But all Anne offered was, "Nah. I mostly just watch TV."

"So, how are you feeling today?" Nathan asked, when Anne offered no further comment.

"Okay, I guess," she mumbled.

"And, how do you feel about this place?" he asked, thinking that no one could really like it.

"It's kinda cool. Everyone's really nice. When I first arrived, there was a policewoman with me almost all the time, but after the first couple of days, they would let me hang out by myself more. We all get to help cook, and we can tell jokes, so it's kinda fun."

"I know it must feel confining," Nathan commented, enthusiastic to keep the conversation going.

"Yeah, it's hard having to stay inside so much. We can go out into the backyard, since it's really private, but they don't let us go out front, and we can't go anywhere by ourselves. When I got here, I just wanted to go home, and I cried the first couple of days."

"I'm sure this isn't easy," Nathan said, his voice soft and caring.

"But a couple of the officers are really cool, and they taught me some card games. They're kind of more like friends than police," Anne volunteered.

"How are the other residents treating you?" Nathan asked, with a somewhat hidden agenda—to see if Anne was revealing too much.

"The other people staying here have been kind, but they've asked me lots of questions and I was told not to talk about anything except to you or my social worker or the police. I think they think I'm here because I was beaten or something, but I haven't talked about anything," Anne responded, looking at Nathan for approval.

"That's important, Anne," Nathan said, nodding his head slightly.

"For the most part, they're cool with that, but then they ask questions again later. It's kind of hard to not answer their questions, but I'm being careful," Anne offered, her confidence growing with Nathan's nod of acknowledgement.

"I know it must be hard to not talk or express any of your feelings, Anne," Nathan said, "but it's crucial that you not discuss your situation or the case at any time, except with me or Adele Cantor, at this point. You just don't know who might share something important somewhere, even accidentally. People will respect your right to privacy if you remain firm and consistent."

Observing no response from her, Nathan continued, "I'd like to ask some questions about what you witnessed that led to your being here. Is that Okay with you?"

"Yeah, I guess so," Anne mumbled, looking downward.

"I know some of this may be hard to talk about, but it's very important that I understand everything accurately, and I know you've already talked about this with the police, the district attorney, and Adele Cantor. One good thing is that once I get to know you better and learn about what you've been through and witnessed, I can also speak for you. So, maybe you won't have to go through everything again, at least for now. I'm also asking that you trust me and be really up-front and honest with me, and I realize I'm a stranger right now and that isn't easy to do."

Anne shifted her glance downward, almost as if she had been scolded, and said, "I never lie. It's a sin against God. But there are some things that I don't want to talk about, and that's not the same as lying."

"No, it isn't," Nathan responded, wondering what nerve he'd struck. "And if I ask about something you don't want to talk about, how about telling me that and we can decide where to go from there?"

"Okay, but I'm not talking about my father. The police and the social worker tried to get me to talk about him, but I wouldn't."

Not having read anything in Adele's notes regarding her father, Nathan wasn't sure what Anne was talking about. Obviously, however, she had things she wanted to hide regarding her father, and he could only guess that this was the nerve he had hit and that maybe her father had abused her in some way.

Having taken the time after reading Adele Cantor's notes and the police report, Nathan had done some research on The Christian Movement. The various allegations, to date, and considerable speculation regarding psychological control and abuse led him to believe there were other perpetrators within The Christian Movement and that their prosecution would allow both for justice to prevail and for the protection of other victims. So far, however, Anne remained the only known source to provide this information. He also knew he had to earn her trust and not be overly zealous and overshadow his other mission, providing her legal counsel as a witness and support as a victim. As complex as all this might seem, he found himself very motivated by the challenge and dual roles.

"Well, I wasn't necessarily going to ask anything about your father, but maybe later we could talk about why talking about him is so off-limits. Remember, you can say you'd rather not talk about something; that's your way of having some control over what we talk about."

"Okay," Anne agreed, reluctantly.

"Okay. So why don't you tell me what you observed at the Jenkinses' home that led you to call the police?" asked Nathan, taking a pad from his briefcase. He wanted to preserve Anne's words as accurately as possible for future testimony.

After a moment, Anne looked up a little and told Nathan what happened. Anne used to babysit Amanda, who is now ten, and her brother Eric, who is twelve, for two hours in the afternoons when their parents' work shifts overlapped. One day last week she had come to the house, as always, and walked inside. She called out for Amanda and Eric, but there was no answer. So she looked in the backyard, saw their bicycles, and figured they were upstairs playing in their rooms. She went upstairs and entered Amanda's room, only to find her father on top of her, certain he was penetrating the young girl. When she looked down, she saw Eric under the bed, hiding and very frightened. Anne was afraid if she tried to stop Mr. Jenkins that Amanda might get injured, so she ran downstairs, where there was a phone in the entryway, and dialed 911. By the time an operator answered, and Anne yelled, "You have to come now," Mr. Jenkins was there. He grabbed the phone and slammed it down, then hit Anne in the face with his fist, screaming and shouting. She was terrified and froze. Mr. Jenkins then picked up the phone and tried to call someone. But then he slammed down the phone and broke it, as he continued to scream right in Anne's face and slap her again as she stood there motionless, having withdrawn somewhere deep inside of herself.

Two police cars arrived quickly, and the occupants raced from their cars into the house. As two officers entered through the front door, their weapons drawn, the first thing they observed was Mr. Jenkins slapping Anne. They lunged forward, grabbed Mr. Jenkins, threw him to the ground, and placed handcuffs on him, as Anne stood motionless, pointing toward the stairs and staring at the floor. They pulled Mr. Jenkins to his feet and escorted him to the living room, as he continued to scream, "You little whore, you're going to pay for this."

Two more officers entered the house, and one of them gently took Anne's arm and escorted her out to the front porch, away from the screaming Mr. Jenkins, while the other officer, a policewoman, observing a young girl at the top of the stairs, bleeding, called for an ambulance as she ran up the stairs. Even with all the chaos surrounding her, Anne remained in an almost catatonic state, simply responding to the officer's physical cues to follow him outside.

Despite being completely enthralled with Anne's recounting of the events, Nathan interrupted her to ask a question that could have important legal ramifications. "Anne, since you appeared to be in some kind of trancelike state, by your own description, were you still able to know what was going on around you?"

"Yeah, I sort of withdraw inside, but still know things are happening around me, and I seem to know to protect my head and my body, and later on I can remember things that were happening. I just don't seem to feel things any longer. That was a place I often went to when I was really frightened."

Nathan knew that Anne was describing dissociation, but didn't feel comfortable delving further into this with Anne. He needed to stay in his role as her attorney and allow this to be addressed in some future therapy.

"What happened after that, Anne?" Nathan encouraged her.

She again seemed to withdraw inside herself and continue. A second policeman joined them on the front porch, while the first officer, who had identified himself as Dan, helped Anne sit down on the porch swing. He then kneeled down and asked Anne about any injuries, while the other officer took out a pad and wrote things down. Dan asked about how to reach the children's mother, but Anne didn't respond and just stared down at the porch, feeling confused and afraid to say almost anything at that moment. In part, she was frightened for Mrs. Jenkins, who not only had to learn that Mr. Jenkins was hurting Amanda, but would also have to face his fury and threats.

Right about then, an ambulance arrived, and Anne was startled by the siren. She was terrified of the medical personnel who came rushing up to the house, and she curled into a ball in response to her fear, wrapping her arms around her body to protect herself. One of the paramedics entered the house while the other turned toward where Anne was sitting, slowing down his gait in response to her obvious withdrawal. Having treated numerous victims of violence and abuse, the paramedic was familiar with Anne's fear of being touched by anyone, even someone trying to help. When he knelt down to talk with Anne, both he and Dan were surprised to hear a muffled voice say, "I don't want to see any doctors." The two men looked at each other, their eyebrows raised.

As the paramedic gently reached toward Anne to push her hair back and look at a gash on her forehead that was bleeding, Anne twisted to the side but didn't offer further resistance. He pulled his hand back a little, knowing she probably had the legal right to refuse treatment. Dan then became a little more firm, telling Anne that since she was a witness to a crime, he needed to ask some questions and he needed her to cooperate with the paramedic and, at least, allow him to evaluate her injuries. Anne paused, looking directly at Nathan for some kind of prompt, not sure if she was going on too long or talking about what he wanted to know.

"So, what happened then?" asked Nathan, recognizing the uncertainty and wanting her to continue with her account of her experience, in part to assess her ability to recall and describe the events of that day. He knew this went to the heart of her ability to testify, and he would ask more about what she had witnessed regarding Amanda later.

"Dan said I needed to go with them to the emergency room, and I kind of shut down and wouldn't talk to anyone. I thought they maybe also wanted to get me away from there and maybe thought I was in danger if the church elders found out what I'd done." Anne then stopped talking, again waiting for Nathan to direct her further.

"Did you leave with them at that point?" asked Nathan.

"Yeah, we went to the hospital," Anne said, with a defeated look.

"Have you seen Amanda or her mother or father since that?" Nathan asked, wanting to cover any angle a defense attorney might use to prejudice Anne as a witness.

"I didn't get to see Amanda again, or any of them," Anne said, with a sadness in her voice.

"So, what happened at the hospital?" Nathan asked.

"A woman doctor, a nurse, and a policewoman came, and the doctor looked at my face and put some ice on it where I'd been hit. They were really nice and gentle, and I thought that would be okay, since that was something my mom did if I got hurt."

In that moment Nathan observed a childlike quality in the softness of her voice and her calm smile. He softly asked, "What happened after that?"

"The policewoman told me we needed to go to the police station. I became very frightened and asked if I was in trouble or was being arrested. She assured me I had done nothing wrong and had done the most right thing in the world, and she said they wanted to ask some questions and find a place for me to stay." No longer focusing on the physically threatening moment of that day, Anne looked more directly at Nathan as she recounted this part of her experience.

"So, what did that feel like for you, knowing you had to stay somewhere for your safety?"

"Actually, I wasn't sure if they were going to put me in jail still, and I just wanted to go home. But I knew it wasn't safe to go home, and I knew they somehow knew this," Anne said, a resignation in her voice.

"What would have been dangerous about going home?" Nathan asked, knowing he was pushing her a little. Anne stiffened, uncomfortable with Nathan's suspicions about her home environment. "I gather you don't feel like talking about something here?" he asked cautiously, knowing he was treading on thin ice.

"I don't want to talk about my family," Anne replied, with a firm tone.

"Well, can you at least tell me if you think that's why they felt you were in danger?"

"I don't really know, maybe a little," Anne responded, her voice more acquiescent.

Not wanting to further intimidate Anne, Nathan asked, "Would it be okay to talk about the church elders at least?" His voice softened.

Looking relieved, Anne said, "Yeah, they probably knew the elders would be furious with me for calling the police, especially Father Jonas. They have their own system for dealing with people in the community, and never involve the police or anyone from outside."

"Okay, so let's talk a little more about the actual events that led you to call the police. The details and your experience are very important, since you're a witness and may need to testify."

It was the first time Anne had heard this. She grew very still, and her face drained of color. Nathan saw the intense fear and immediately realized he had errantly presumed someone might have informed Anne of this. "I'm sorry, Anne," he said, trying to calm her. "Hasn't anyone told you before now that you might be required to testify as a witness?"

Anne replied in her quiet, meek voice, "No. Do I have to? Can't you just tell them what I've told you?"

"That isn't how the legal system works, I'm afraid," Nathan responded, his growing empathy for the terrified young woman strengthening his resolve to help her and protect her as best he could. "But we can cross that bridge when we come to it, and it will be a while, probably several months, before a trial would occur—that's if there is a trial." This did little to assuage Anne's fear.

"So, would you be okay to tell me what led you to call the police?" Nathan asked cautiously, treading the difficult line between protecting Anne emotionally and supporting this very important legal case.

"I just knew that what he was doing was wrong. He was hurting Amanda, and I was frightened for her. I knew I had to stop this," she blurted, somewhat defensively, as if she thought she had to justify her action.

"You did the right thing, Anne," Nathan interjected quickly, wanting to be certain she felt he was in her corner. "When you said, 'I had to stop this,' did you just mean stop Mr. Jenkins, or did you mean something larger?"

"I think I felt both at the time—that I had to stop Mr. Jenkins, and I had to try to stop …," Anne's voice trailed off, "everything." Anne grew silent again and glanced down, seeming to realize she had said more than she had wanted to.

"What do you mean by 'everything'?" Nathan asked. Again, encountering silence, Nathan prompted, "Anne, there were more incidents of abuse, weren't there?"

She continued to look toward the ground and slightly nodded her head.

Nathan simply said, "Okay. It's okay you've let me know that, Anne, and maybe we can talk more about it later. Would that be okay?"

Looking up toward Nathan with obvious relief for a reprieve for the time being, Anne said, "I guess so."

Nathan knew she was very conflicted about revealing other incidences of abuse, but he was fairly certain this "slip" wasn't an accident and was her way of cuing him to go there. He also knew that his priority today was to clarify what she had witnessed regarding Amanda's sexual abuse, and he didn't want her to become too upset or too afraid to answer his questions regarding that particular history.

"Were you frightened when you made the call and Mr. Jenkins began screaming at you?" he asked.

"I don't really remember being scared. I just knew what I had to do. When Mr. Jenkins was hitting me and shouting at me, I just went into one of those places where I don't feel anything."

"You told the police that when you went upstairs and entered Amanda's room, you saw Mr. Jenkins lying on top of her and penetrating her. How do you know the word 'penetrating'?"

"It's a word the police and social workers kept using when they asked me questions."

"I thought so," said Nathan, knowing it was more of a legal or clinical description. "Can you remember exactly what words you used when you first told this to the police?"

"Yeah, I said he had his thing in Amanda."

"How could you tell this from where you were standing?"

"Because his pants were down, and he was on top of her," Anne said defensively. And I could see the pain on her face from where I was standing."

"How could you tell this wasn't just pain from having him on top of her, crushing her with his weight?"

"I could tell," answered Anne, a certainty in her tone.

Nathan believed that Anne understood Amanda's pain and abuse were wrong, wrong in a way that, possibly, she couldn't view her own history as being. This continued to confirm Adele's suspicions and the need for him to approach interviewing Anne as both a witness and a victim. Nathan, the lawyer, decided to take his shot.

"You know, this is the third time you've said something that pretty clearly leads me to believe that you've been abused, and I'm fairly sure that you're holding this inside and have very mixed feelings about telling me about it. But it's very important for me to know to be able to represent and protect you."

Anne's silence, combined with her slumping shoulders and looking back toward the floor, was the best confirmation she could provide at the time. Nathan had stated his belief, and she had done nothing to refute it.

Nathan paused a minute before continuing, to give Anne, who seemed on the verge of shutting down, time to compose herself. He was conflicted, but needed to obtain whatever information she could provide. He also knew she'd be facing far tougher circumstances in a courtroom. So he decided to push a little further. "I'm going to assume that your silence means I'm not wrong, Anne, but I'll ask this question another way. I know you won't lie, so I'm asking you to tell me if I'm wrong in my belief by nodding your head yes. If you don't, you're telling me I'm right."

Anne didn't appear to hear him. Her head hung down, and her arms were wrapped tightly around her chest.

He knew he was forcing the point and putting pressure on her, but the attorney in him also had a crucial role in advocating for both his client and for justice, at times having to prevail over protecting Anne from her fears and pain. This was one of those moments, one that required great instincts, timing, and sometimes just luck. "Anne, I know I'm pushing my point," he said, trying to conceal the trepidation in his voice. "But I see us as a team, and sometimes I'm going to ask for your help as my teammate."

The idea of being part of a team was a concept that had worked for Nathan before with victims of abuse who couldn't trust anyone to really be on their side. This approach had the potential to backfire, however, because most of the time the people who had violated his clients were those in whom they placed absolute trust—husbands, partners, fathers, or their mothers, who, often in their eyes, had failed to observe the obvious and/or to protect them.

Slowing down his words, he said, "I need you to tell me, with words, just one word even, if you have been physically or sexually abused by people in The Christian Movement. I need you to answer yes or no. Have you been abused?"

Without changing her posture or downcast expression, Anne very quietly said, "Yes."

"Did this happen when you were a child, an adult, or both?" Nathan asked quickly, not wanting to lose the possible momentum.

"Both," Anne responded almost robotically.

"To your knowledge, were other children also abused?"

"Yes," she whispered, looking more upset.

"Anne, thank you," Nathan said, her monosyllabic responses not lost on him. "I know this was difficult for you. I don't need to ask more about it today. Just know that you're no longer all alone. As a team, it's something we share." He started to reach a hand across the distance between them in an attempt to solidify the image of working together, to shake hands. But from the way she held back, he knew any touch remained unwelcome, if not intolerable. Nathan just hoped he hadn't threatened her further with the gesture. He was trying very hard to do this well.

Shifting gears, Nathan continued, "So, let's talk about what happened at the police station."

Anne perked up, sitting straighter and looking toward Nathan. They had entered less threatening territory. "They took me to a room, where they asked me all the same questions again, and afterwards, they asked me to read what I had said and to sign it," she said with a questioning look.

"Did you understand why you were signing it?" Nathan asked, picking up on her look and wanting to head off any possible problem with the police procedures a defense attorney would exploit.

"Not really," replied Anne, shaking her head.

"It's really just about having you confirm that the statements are true, to the best of your knowledge, and are yours, sort of like signing a check to confirm it is you agreeing to make the payment."

"I've never written a check," Anne said with a childlike innocence.

"Of course, I should have thought of that," Nathan said, nodding softly.

"That's cool," Anne responded, with a slight smile. "Should I continue?" she asked, her initiative surprising Nathan.

"Please," he said, offering an appreciative smile.

"After I signed the thing, the policewoman told me they had decided it would be good to have me around in case they had more questions. I knew they were avoiding telling me I was in danger, but I knew I was. They asked more questions about other things that had happened on the farm and at the church, but I wouldn't answer. I was afraid I'd be in trouble if I didn't answer their questions, but I was more afraid to tell them anything other than what had happened at the Jenkins' house. I was so angry with Mr. Jenkins for what he had done to Amanda, that I almost told them about other things," Anne said, a slight scowl on her face.

"I think the policewoman saw I was getting overwhelmed and starting to cry. So she kind of stopped them and asked me if I'd like to lie down and rest, and when I said yes, she took me to one of the cells. She was really nice and explained that it was the only place I might be able to lie down and sleep, and that the door would be open, but I couldn't leave the area or go outside without being with one of them. I asked her if I was in jail, and she gave me a little hug," Anne said with a smile. "She said I definitely wasn't in jail like someone who had committed a crime, but was there for my protection until they could find a safe place for me to stay for a while." Anne paused, looking somewhat forlorn, and glanced at Nathan.

"So, what was that like—to sleep in a jail cell?" Nathan asked.

"It was kinda strange at first, but I stayed there for two nights. It was actually pretty cool. I got to see lots of things going on and even play cards with a couple of the policemen, and they brought in pizza and ice cream and were really nice to me."

"It sounds like you made some friends there," Nathan said, allowing them both to smile. "So, did anyone meet with you the next day or two to ask any more questions?" he continued, feeling good that they seemed to have developed some rapport and were making progress.

"Yeah, the next day a woman who said she was a police psychologist came, and we took a walk. I didn't really know what a psychologist was, but she was really nice, and she even gave me a donut, which I thought was really cool. She asked me to talk about what had happened at the Jenkins' house, so I told her everything again. She tried to ask about other things in the church, and I could tell she was getting frustrated when I wouldn't answer. Eventually, she suggested I take a vacation and have a break from the church and the farm. I was pretty upset, but I kind of think it also felt good. I knew I was in deep shit."

"What does that mean?" Nathan asked, a little surprised by the phrase "deep shit" coming from Anne. Like the word "penetrating," it didn't feel like hers.

"I kinda felt like I was blowing the lid off of everything, and everyone in the church would be furious with me," Anne said, looking more serious.

"Did you think they would be furious with you for calling the police on Mr. Jenkins or because you might tell the police about other things that had been kept a secret?"

"Both, I guess."

Anne had begun to look tired, but Nathan had one more thing that he wanted to inquire about before they finished, knowing it could be a sticking point with the defense. "I'd like to go back to when you found Mr. Jenkins on top of Amanda. Why do you think Amanda's father wasn't concerned you might catch him abusing her, since you arrived there at the same time daily?"

"I don't know. Maybe he thought I wouldn't check upstairs, or he didn't realize what time it was, or maybe because these things are kept within the church and no one calls the police."

"It took a lot of courage then for you to make that call," he said, his gaze more intent. He had little doubt that it was more about her latter theory.

"I don't think of it as courage. I just wanted to protect Amanda from getting hurt anymore."

"That was still very brave of you," he said with even more conviction.

Anne didn't respond and appeared uncomfortable. She moved in her seat and looked downward, needing to deflect the praise.

"I can understand that much of this is very painful and difficult for you to talk about, Anne, and I realize it's very uncomfortable to tell me about the abuse. So if you'd feel safer, I could try to find a woman lawyer in another department, and she could consult with me. That might feel safer and a little easier for you," Nathan offered.

Again she surprised him, this time with the rapidity of her response. "I don't want to talk with any women," she almost pleaded. "They're worse, and I'd feel less safe."

Perplexed, Nathan asked, "Why are women worse and less safe?"

"Because sometimes they would hold me down," she replied, just as quickly as before.

Stunned by this response, Nathan needed a minute to absorb this information. "I'm sorry, Anne. I assumed only men were hurting you," he said, his voice deflated and somewhat at a loss for words.

Anne grew quiet and looked down toward the floor, her brief burst of candor apparently over.

Nathan was actually surprised that Anne had said so much already, but her sporadic disclosures, followed by withdrawals, told him his hunch had been on track, and that Anne was both very fearful and in great need of talking about what had happened to her. In an attempt to direct them to talk about the proverbial elephant in the room, he pushed a little further, asking, "What were the women holding you down for?"

Anne remained silent. She placed her hands together on the upper part of her chest and curled her body into a circle. She almost seemed to be shrinking, Nathan thought, wondering if her position was simply more physically comfortable or whether it was a protective stance she had developed in response to abuse. It was behavior he had seen before in people who were either very afraid of physical violence or were psychologically regressing. Either way, it indicated great distress. Yet, even while Anne sat curled into herself on the bed, there was a part of her seeking to let out some of what she had held inside for so long. This was one of those situations in which Nathan drew the line. Knowing that he wasn't a trained psychologist, he didn't want to trigger a dangerous regression. So, he chose to stop further questions and simply state the assumption.

"Anne," he said, "I'm going to make a couple of guesses. I'm fairly certain you've been abused physically, sexually, and emotionally as a child, by men in the church. I now realize women not only didn't stop them, but participated sometimes by holding you down. So, I'm sure you have little or no trust in men or women to not hurt you further. I'm pretty certain that if I were way off base in my guess that you would in some way tell me I'm wrong. So, I'll just assume my guess is pretty accurate for now. I know Adele is planning to meet with you in the next day or two, and since she's a therapist, as well as your social worker, maybe it would be better for the two of you to try to talk more about all of this. Would you rather talk with Adele, and she could share things with me?"

Anne seemed to relax her grip on herself a little and shook her head slightly. It was barely perceptible, but was discernable enough to indicate she was able to hear him and was still cognizant and not dissociating, as he had started to fear. Wanting to be sure they understood each other, Nathan asked, "Are you saying you'd rather talk more with me?"

"Yes," she said softly.

"Thank you for being open with me about that, Anne. I won't ask you further about it today, but I'd like to talk more about it when you're ready."

Knowing she had reached her emotional limit and wanting to preserve her comfort with him as much as he could, Nathan said, "Well, let's stop for today. I know this hasn't been easy for you, and I want to thank you for trusting me today, Anne. I hope you'll feel more comfortable and realize that we're a team and need to rely upon each other to travel forward. I'd like to come back tomorrow if that would be okay. I think that would allow me to finish gathering the initial information I need. Would that be okay with you?"

"Yeah, I guess so. But only if I can still say I don't want to talk about something," she replied, with a conviction that matched his earlier tone regarding her bravery.

"I'm fine with that, as long as you're okay that I may keep asking. It's sort of like I have ongoing voting power, and you have ongoing veto power," he smiled, really impressed by her chutzpah, the image that most struck him then.

But a perplexed look crossed Anne's face, and Nathan realized "veto power" was an unfamiliar concept to her. In all likelihood, he surmised, she had never voted or been able to learn about politics in her world. "Do you know what I mean by that?" he asked, wanting to preempt Anne having to inquire.

"Kind of," she replied, somewhat timidly.

"It means I may ask, and you may say you can't talk about something for now. But I still might ask again. I guess I want you to know you have power and rights, including with me."

"And I can still say not now again!" Anne said with a real grin.

As Nathan began to pick up his briefcase, Anne asked, "Do you have an office?"

Her question about his world took him by surprise. Not really trying to hide his puzzled look, he answered, "Yes, I have an office downtown. Why do you ask?"

"Could we meet at your office tomorrow?" she asked carefully.

"Would you rather meet there?"

"I don't know. Maybe it would feel separate from here and be easier to talk about things, and I … Well, it would be neat to just go somewhere other than the yard here."

Nathan thought for a moment. Meeting with people in protective custody at his office was complicated, since it was public knowledge that his department represented such people as part of the judicial system. So, whenever there was any potential risk, he would meet with clients elsewhere, as he was doing with Anne. Also, he didn't yet know how sophisticated the members of The Christian Movement were. But, he realized that Anne was looking at him and had been brave enough to make a request for something. Nathan responded, with a caring tone, "Well, my only concern is that since you're providing us with information regarding a member of The Christian Movement, they might try to stop you. That's obviously why you're living here right now and why you're under police protection. And since my office handles such cases, they might think to see if you showed up there."

"Well, couldn't one of the policemen go with me?" Anne asked.

"Oh, that goes without saying. You're to have police protection with you wherever you go. The truth is, the building has good security, and there are security guards who check anyone entering the building. Without an appointment no one can get in, and you can enter into the garage and be safe. But the paranoid part of me," he smiled briefly, "is wondering if these people are sophisticated or motivated enough to do something really clever, like make an appointment somewhere else in the building to gain access. It's actually sort of a loophole in the security system," Nathan said, pausing a moment before asking, "So, what are your thoughts about them being that clever and motivated?"

"Oh, I'm sure they're very motivated, and they're pretty good at making things happen and doing whatever it takes to protect their privacy and secrecy. I doubt I'd be the first person to seem to disappear," she said. "There were rumors every so often about someone disappearing who tried to leave or made some kind of threat to go to the police. I never knew if they were true, but I did see people suddenly gone who were arguing with Jonas or the elders, and I never saw them again."

Nathan made a mental note of this, but he didn't want to travel this direction yet. "Well, maybe we should just continue to meet here," he said. He hated to disappoint her, but he had to put her best interests first.

But Anne persisted. "I'm cool to still come there if I have a policeman with me, and probably only one or two people could sneak in the way you said. I can't hide from everything all the time. I feel like I'm the one in prison."

It was a powerful appeal that carried the truth, Nathan felt with a sadness, and it tipped a scale. He knew he could arrange for security to be more conscientious if he alerted them to the circumstances, so he offered, "Okay, I'm cool with it—as long as you understand that we're making this decision together. I want to honor your needs wherever I can in this journey. However, I need to check to see if they have someone available to bring you tomorrow. So, as soon as I know that, we can either meet at my office or here, if that isn't possible. Is that cool?"

"Yeah, that would be cool," she smiled, for the first time sharing the feeling of being a team.

"So, let's tentatively plan for around 11 o'clock tomorrow," Nathan said. "I'm going to give you a number to reach me in case of any kind of emergency in which you'd need to reach me quickly, Anne. It's a cell phone, and I'm asking that you use it for an urgent situation that can't wait until I'm in the office."

"What kind of emergency?" Anne asked.

"I don't know exactly, but if something happened where you felt you needed my advice, or if you became frightened of something, you could call. We can talk more about this, but I need us to stop for today."

— CHAPTER FOURTEEN —

It was a chilly Sunday morning in early January, a portent of the snow and freezing temperatures that would soon leave a sparkling whiteness over the brick and stone of Boston's South End area. I felt the coziness of a cup of cappuccino and the warm glow of my fireplace. The intensity of interpersonal contact during my work week magnified the importance of personal downtime at least some part of each weekend, and I usually reserved Sunday mornings as my own. On Sundays I typically devoted two hours to *The New York Times*, a portion of which I spent on the crossword puzzle, followed by brunch with friends. But on this particular weekend, my usual brunch group of three close friends had journeyed to the island of Manhattan for a weekend of Broadway theater, part of the continuing education requirements to remain a fully certified, erudite, and professional gay man. So I had chosen to relax and stay put for the weekend.

In part, this was to catch up on billing and paperwork related to my practice, but I was also interested in doing further Internet research on The Christian Movement, as Anne's cult-like background, the seemingly sanctioned child abuse in her community, and the public and legal ramifications of her experience were both challenging and very interesting to me.

This was an ideal morning to be cozily in front of the fireplace, and I opened my Apple laptop, momentarily reflecting on the incredible convenience of Internet technology. I settled into the couch and began searching. Soon, various resources appeared on my screen that promised to provide further insight into The Christian Movement, its history, and the controversy surrounding it.

The first article to catch my attention was an expose on The Christian Movement, written during its earlier years. It highlighted the community's commitment to less fortunate members of society, particularly younger people and those whose lives had been imperiled by poverty, drugs, rejection, emotional instability, and legal problems. Such people had often reached a bottom or crisis point and were very vulnerable and just trying to survive. Their circumstances not only made them perfect candidates for the security and "salvation" the movement offered, but served them well when they eventually helped to recruit new acolytes, because they intimately knew the experience and the language of the down-and-out.

Much of the movement's recruiting success, I gleaned from the articles, lay in its ability to create revival gatherings that brought together old-time religion with more contemporary stimuli, such as music that had a rock sound, disco lights, and powerful emotional overtones. Their revivals at times resembled Pentecostal gatherings, where people were touched by the Holy Spirit and divine powers to heal their damaged lives.

An outside observer, however, would be hard pressed to distinguish whether the community was more motivated to save people or to prey upon them, wrote one reporter. Describing a typical Friday-night recruitment event as being more like a contemporary rock concert than a religious affair, he wrote, "The crowd resembled those at big concert events or raves, and it was certain a considerable number of those present were under the influence of some kind of illicit substance."

The reporter described the movement's rock band, which had two lead guitarists, a drummer, a base guitarist, a highly sophisticated keyboard with synthesizing capabilities, and an impressive sound system on a portable stage. The two lead singers were very talented, and their words carried the intensity and lyrical sophistication of top twenty renditions. But instead of singing about romantic love, existential angst, or any of the other common themes in popular music, the songs were about salvation, the beauty of heaven, sacrifice, and eternal bliss.

Many of the listeners, most of whom were in their teens to early twenties, were caught up in the rock-and-roll rhythm and energy, and it would have been slowly, if ever, that the meaning of the lyrics would seep into their awareness. "It was a very effective means of drawing people in and conveying a comforting message, energetically and enthusiastically," wrote the reporter.

"If the participants had looked carefully, they would have seen identical black crosses around the necks of each performer and the nearby white vans with 'The Christian Movement' emblazoned on the sides, and perhaps they would have realized there was more going on than music," he added.

Between songs and after sets, the article continued, a team of young men and women would pass through the crowd, handing out leaflets about an upcoming revival at which there would be similar musical energy. They had been trained, in part, by their personal journeys that drew them to the movement, to understand who seemed most susceptible to the recruitment message, and they approached each potential recruit as if he or she was a friend. The leaflets also contained information about the possibility of finding a warm meal, shelter, and work within the community. For many of the down-and-out in the crowd, this was very enticing, and those who chose to take the movement up on the offer were easily influenced.

Another article contained strong criticism from a deacon of the mother church to which The Christian Movement belonged. He referred to these organized rescuers as being a "snatch squad" that grabbed people from rallies using every means at their disposal. They lured them to the community, using enticements such as portable bathrooms and buses to transport them to the farm, where they promised they could get a decent meal and sleep in a real bed. The reporter referenced another deacon, from outside The Christian Movement, who viewed the proselytizers as "trolling for squatters," often contacting their "prey" at times when they were obviously vulnerable and desperate, such as when they stood in lines at social service agencies seeking food or work.

As I read the deacons' criticisms, I was suddenly struck by one of those bizarre brain connections, the homonym for prey being "pray." A single letter in a word provided one of the fundamental paradoxes that defined The Christian Movement, I mused.

The article also referred to a state legislator and several respected journals calling for a wide-scale investigation into the church and its practices. They cited a decade-long swirl of rumors about persons disappearing, abuse, holding people against their will, and ex-members having been demonized for repudiating any of the church teachings or for attempting to leave.

Those who had been able to "escape," as some former members referred to their departure, claimed that one needed not only an "escape plan" but also to be very clever and able to tolerate the loss of all of one's friends, supports, and financial resources.

Another reporter discussed the ironic rapidity with which the new recruits "embraced" the community's spiritual beliefs. Many of these recruits had barely given God a thought during the course of their lives, often having eschewed beliefs the movement espoused as the teachings of God, whether by committing crimes, abusing themselves, or living lives defined by lust, addiction, and escape. Yet, suddenly, during their absorption into the community, they found God to have a major role in their shelter, in the food hall where they received physical sustenance, and in the people providing them with care and support. In this way, the article explained, the movement inextricably wove a sense of a higher power into the recruits' very survival. This had a powerful conditioning effect, as community members, either subtly or blatantly, referred to God when distributing food and leading recruits to sleep in real beds, which some had not enjoyed in months.

Recruits also witnessed a community of people strongly supporting each other and working for the good of the larger society. At the very least, the downtrodden newcomers saw people who possessed comforts they had lost. And further reinforcing these influences, a couple of evenings a week, the movement showed films depicting ordinary people who had resisted religion and gone through very painful, life-altering, and life-threatening circumstances but eventually found peace and redemption through a higher power.

The article portrayed how the movement offered communal, emotional, and physical support to recruits, yet quickly dumped newcomers who refused to espouse the church's teachings or to adopt its language, attend services and classes, and change their behavior, abandoning them to the harsh realities from which they had come.

One article detailed an interview with a spokesperson for the church, an elder I assumed, who responded to some of the harsh criticisms of his community. Addressing the military-style clothing members of The Christian Movement wore, he compared them to the Salvation Army, who also wear uniforms, have ranks, ban alcohol, and are heavily involved in social action and rescuing marginalized members of society. He described one of the missions of his community as serving God by serving the needs of the poor, addicts, and youth rejected by their families because they were "broken" members of society. He strongly endorsed the fact that the movement espoused a "holistic" approach, involving far more than just spiritual needs and including food, shelter, employment, physical safety, education, and connectedness to people. He felt other churches ostracized the movement because it chose to take on more responsibility in guiding its acolytes.

Probably the most disturbing article involved the deaths of five young men over a two-to three-year period, all ruled likely either accidents or suicides. Police found one young man hypothermic in a field on the church's property. They found another in an underground water tank, a third lying on a train track, and a fourth decapitated. The movement claimed the fifth young man died of an overdose and was a probable suicide, but his family vehemently denied he had ever been depressed or suicidal and alleged a cover-up. However, during the police investigations, not only members of the church itself, but others in the local community were reticent to say anything negative about the church, apparently fearing libel suits or other forms of retribution. The article alluded the church was managing to stay "just above the law."

After reviewing six or seven articles, I was struck by the extent and endurance of the controversy surrounding the church. There seemed to be little doubt that The Christian Movement had saved numerous lives but destroyed as many souls and vulnerable human beings via its teachings. The myriad of articles I read expressed so many different viewpoints. Some former disciples and parents clearly deemed The Christian Movement to be a highly controlling and damaging cult; other people attributed their survival and discovery of their life's purpose to the movement. The controversy was both damning and compelling, helping me to understand the power Anne's experiences had upon her, and to explain her intense beliefs and devotion to a community that had severely abused her.

Yet, although I read numerous articles citing physical and psychological abuse within the movement, I was struck by the absence of any speculation regarding systematic brainwashing and potentially large-scale abuse of very vulnerable people. The community seemed shielded by a wall of secrecy and seemed to have been able to avoid interference from medical, governmental, and legal systems. In fact, the plethora of information I found confirmed that the movement had attained considerable stature and respect well outside its geographic area, including among social workers and other care providers. They often referred runaways, drug and alcohol abusers, criminals, and others with emotional or behavioral problems, who either resisted, weren't eligible for, or couldn't afford treatment programs, to The Christian Movement.

They also referred unwanted newborns and pregnant teenagers to the movement's adoption program. Organizations housing the elderly welcomed the movement's efforts to provide volunteer services to their facilities. And programs serving and sheltering children who were abandoned or removed from at-risk homes were thrilled to have their kids attend the movement's summer camp. The confidence of these groups enhanced community respect for the movement and detracted from suspicions and concerns.

Anne had never used the word "cult" in our sessions to date, and only a few of the articles I had read embraced the term, but The Christian Movement clearly had the necessary and defining characteristics of one. I further expanded my search that Sunday morning to learn more about cult behavior and abuse condoned and perpetrated in the name of religious extremism. I found myself strongly connected through my previous work, helping gay and lesbian clients to overcome tremendously destructive abuse and horrible self-images perpetrated by extremist religious beliefs and teachings.

My work with Anne had reignited in me that spark of learning and being fascinated by the breadth of human behavior and psychology that I had enjoyed in my early years of practice. I was emotionally very moved by Anne's experience, and the thought that another human being had been subjected to such destruction touched me deeply. I also realized that Anne had known no other way of living, so my perspective and consequent periodic anger on her behalf didn't necessarily reflect how life appeared and felt for her. As much as our work together and my growing care for Anne occasionally impacted my objectivity, they also connected me more deeply to my work and to helping her.

Deciding to engage in one last piece of research, I began a review of the literature on cults and cult phenomena. I realized that if I was to accurately understand my client's background and be able to help free her from some of the painful experiences she had endured, I would have to learn more about cult thinking and behavior.

So, settling back in my chair with another cappuccino, I learned that the term "cult" is generally pejorative and is used to describe certain religious sects or communities that are apart from mainstream religious institutions and the overall societal structure within which they reside.

Cults, I read, are different from churches and sects. While a church is defined as a religious system and usually fits within the mainstream of the culture, and a sect blends spirituality and culture with strict doctrine and behavioral demands, cults follow patterns of behavior and thinking that are unfamiliar to more mainstream religious communities or societies, emphasizing separation and difference from the larger culture. They often close themselves off from the influences of the larger culture, while simultaneously distorting or perverting the beliefs held by mainstream religious institutions and biblical Christianity.

"In the latter part of the twentieth century there has been much greater awareness of and attention to the more destructive nature of cult behavior," one article began. "Cults are seen as detrimental to many, if not most, of their adherents, because they brainwash recruits and members, overwhelming their ability to make rational judgments and decisions. Their primary methods typically include fear, punishment, ex-communication, public scorn, etc. The members typically become devout and unquestioning slaves of the group leader. Isolation from the larger culture is a vital component of the preservation of the irrational, controlling and destructive nature of these systems."

Yet, after all my reading, one question remained in my mind: How could Christianity be used as a justification for abusing children? As disturbing as it was, I found two primary theological sources of justification in the literature. The first involved the belief held by some conservative Christians that children are evil by nature due to the concept of "original sin," thus allowing beatings and physical abuse to bring the child to righteousness. The second involved the notion of "spare the rod and spoil the child," a concept employed in the belief it would make children into persons of value and responsibility to others rather than allow them to become self-indulgent. Further, I read, cults use the patriarchal structure universal to western religions to justify the submission of women and children to the authority of the father in the family and the male elders in the religious community. There being virtually no depiction of what form such discipline should take allowed for individual interpretation that in some cases involved far-reaching levels of physical and psychological cruelty and sexual abuse. This was certainly inherent in the teaching and practices of The Christian Movement.

Nothing in my own religious background or in any of my reading in theological, anthropological, sociological, or psychological literature had provided any full viable explanation for ritualized abuse. I certainly understood the potential for severe psychopathology and mental illness or a history of severe abuse to lead to such behaviors. However, such histories or illnesses affected individual behavior. Anne had experienced systematic, communal abuse, not unlike the atrocities perpetrated during the Holocaust or against blacks in the South or against gay and lesbian people who are attacked and murdered every year. Each such violent phenomenon had been motivated by a fervent belief on the part of the perpetrator that the victim(s) threatened a particular way of life— much as Anne being a sinner, or a force of Satan, was experienced.

Coming to understand why this had occurred to Anne would be part of our ongoing work together. She had accepted "God's will" as the answer to any question she might have had throughout her life about her circumstances, but I had no comparable answer. In fact, perhaps of greater significance, I found myself wanting to help her move away from her explanation, and I wasn't sure if this was right or wrong, helpful or harmful, or in any way within my rights. At least God's will was an answer she could understand and one that didn't unravel her sense of humankind.

The afternoon had stretched well into the evening, and the fire had long since died down, forgotten, while I sat lost in thought. In some ways, I had as many questions as I'd started with. This wasn't the first time, and it wouldn't be the last, that I would need to strive to understand my role while performing it.

— CHAPTER FIFTEEN —

It had been eight months since our first meeting, and both Anne and I had settled into a comfortable routine, each gaining a sense of the other's style, behaviors, and expressions. My clients are obviously aware that I am getting to know them, but are often less conscious of their growing sense of me. There are many revealing clues—the types of questions I ask, the décor of my office, the titles of the books on my shelves, my style of dress, the ring on my finger, or just Madison's presence.

Anne's growing familiarity with me appeared to be increasing her sense of comfort and contributing to her ability to reveal more of what she had kept inside all of her life. Our sessions were evolving into a mixture of dealing with her current physical and emotional experience and relating it to her past.

Anne seemed ready, on this particular afternoon, to focus more deeply, and, since she was my last client for the day, I had the time and energy to devote to what I foresaw would be a particularly demanding session—that is, if Anne was willing to discuss what I had in mind.

We sat in silence for a few moments, about twenty seconds that felt like twenty minutes, and then Anne looked toward me, hoping I would ask a question and define our direction. When I didn't say anything and just lightly smiled, she became a little anxious.

"What are we going to talk about today?" she asked.

"What would you like to talk about today, Anne?" I asked.

Uncomfortable taking the lead, she reverted to how she often coped with anxiety in the office, by looking down at the floor and mumbling, "I don't know."

"Well, actually, I was wondering how it would be to talk about the cages today," I finally suggested, not wanting to increase the growing tension any further.

She continued to stare at the floor, but I noticed that she had started to pick at her fingernails. "I guess so," she said after a minute, with noticeable ambivalence.

Then, since she didn't seem to know where to start, I encouraged, "What can you tell me about your first memory of being put in a cage?"

I had spoken as sensitively as I could, but Anne looked really sullen and didn't respond. Then, seeming to sense her discomfort, Madison groaned in his sleep from beneath my feet, as if having had a bad dream. Having woken himself with his own grumbling, he looked momentarily surprised, stumbled groggily to his feet, lumbered over to the couch, heaved his bulk up, and plopped back down again, putting his big black and white head in Anne's lap.

The whole performance was so loveably cartoonish that Anne stopped picking at her fingernails and smiled faintly. She laid her hand on Madison's head, stroking his ears gently, and when he gave a contented sigh, she seemed to relax too. Only then, with the warmth of my co-therapist close beside her, did Anne finally tell me this part of her story.

"It was when I was around seven," she began, haltingly. "Father Jonas and my father were bringing me down to the cellar beneath the main church. I'd never been down there before, but I knew it was bad ... I could just feel it. Some of the church elders were there, too, and that was always bad. Whenever I got hurt, they were the only ones around.

"When we got to the cellar door—it was this little wooden door behind a bush—Father Jonas pushed aside the bush and shoved the door open with his shoulder. He had to stoop to go inside, and it was dark, so he had to turn on a flashlight.

"Then someone—I didn't know if it was my father or one of the elders— pushed me from behind into the opening. It was cold, and the walls were kind of gray and damp. And there were spider webs between the stones in the walls."

Anne sat stock still, as if she herself had become the wall. Only her mouth moved, and her words had become toneless. She seemed to, once again, be starting to dissociate. I felt increasingly concerned, but wanted to trust her strength and the psychological importance of allowing this painful part of her childhood to emerge.

"Whoever it was behind me shoved me down the first step, and I had to reach out for the wall to stop myself from falling into Father Jonas. My fingers touched some sort of mildew, and I felt like screaming. It was so cold and slimy.

"Then Father Jonas stopped and reached into his back pocket. He took out a cloth and put it over his nose and mouth. There was a horrible musty smell coming from behind a door at the bottom of the stairs, and I kind of glanced behind me to see if the other men smelled it 'cause I thought it might be me and I felt ashamed. I thought maybe I'd wet my pants or something, but I couldn't tell because it was damp and I was kind of clammy. I'd never wet my pants before, but I felt so disgusting; I knew it was possible. I almost didn't blame them for the way they felt about me.

"When I looked behind me, I saw my father put on a mask too, and he and Father Jonas both put on these kind of thin gloves. I was wondering if they were cold or if I was just too disgusting to touch."

Although she seemed to be looking at me from a great distance, Anne studied me, as if to gauge whether I felt the same way. I was struggling to keep my boundaries. Everything in me wanted to wrap my arms around her and make it all go away. But, in retrospect, perhaps doing so would have been as much for my benefit as for hers, because I sensed that the story she was so dispassionately recounting had only just begun.

"Father Jonas looked back at my father," Anne continued. "It was my father who then put his own gloved hand on my shoulder and nudged me into the room after Father Jonas took a key out of his pocket and put it in the door. Father Jonas turned the key and pushed the door open with his boot. And, as he did so, a stench hit me, a smell so bad I could hardly breathe. It was like pig feces and rotting chicken innards, and for a second I thought, 'This is what Hell must smell like.' But at least I knew it wasn't me now."

I felt such pain and sadness for Anne in that moment, hearing how much she had internalized the horror and the abuse. As I watched her breathing and her face, she seemed disconnected but not distressed. So I let her continue.

"And it was so cold—like a tomb maybe. It was dark, too, but I could sort of see these shadowy shapes around us. And then I saw they were cages, like chicken cages. They were wood and about the size of the coops, so I thought maybe the elders thought I'd dropped some of the eggs on my rounds that morning, and they were teaching me a lesson for that. I hadn't dropped any eggs, but I knew that really wouldn't matter. Or maybe they thought I'd dirtied the laundry, so they were going to make me smell this really bad smell … I didn't know. All these thoughts were running through my head as to why they might be doing this."

She paused for a second and then added as an afterthought, or perhaps it was also a question, "I always tried to find a reason why, even though I usually couldn't."

It was almost as if Anne were in two places at once, one part of her in my office, observing me and commenting on her experiences, the other part far away. I suppose I was in a similar sort of state. Yet somewhere beneath the turmoil of my emotions, I registered that her attempt to find a reason for how the elders had treated her wasn't atypical. I knew that children assume fault for things outside their control just to have a sense of cause and effect, since this, at least in theory, allows for a semblance of control.

"The cages had doors on the top," Anne continued, interrupting my thought. "And I wondered if there had been a chicken in the cage and whether it had escaped. I kind of hoped it had, because it was horrible down there.

"But then, all of a sudden, Father Jonas and my father grabbed me and lifted me up. I was so surprised I started to struggle. But then I stopped right away, because I knew if I struggled I'd get hurt even worse than whatever it was they were going to do.

"They shoved me in the top of the cage and pushed my head down, so I had to sit with my knees bent. And then Father Jonas flipped the door closed and latched it. I could hear him slide the bolt shut, and then he took a chain off a hook on the wall and wrapped it around the cage twice and put a lock on that too."

We sat there in silence. I don't know where Anne went during that silence, but my mind was trying to catch up and understand the images that were clouded by my emotions. Taking notes wasn't an imaginable task, but I knew I could reconstruct her powerful story from memory after the session.

"After the elders left," Anne's story continued, "my eyes began to adjust to the small amount of light coming from two window slits at the top of one of the cellar walls. I could see other cages and the light waning as the hours passed.

"As far as I could tell, several hours had gone by before I heard footsteps. I had been sitting in an almost fetal position, unable to turn my body in any way. My back and sides ached, and I couldn't hold it anymore and I had urinated onto the floor of the cage. The urine had welled up underneath me, and I felt like one of the animals on the farm that shared a cage with its excrement.

"I had entered an almost hypnotic state, not comfortable enough to sleep, but detached from any awareness of myself and my physical environment. A couple of times I had actually found myself almost like looking down at my own crouched figure from somewhere above. It seemed like a dream, but I knew I hadn't really fallen asleep."

As she told me this, I must have come out of my temporarily stunned condition, because I remember thinking that sleep would have seemed inconceivable in light of such physical discomfort. She was looking at me again, but this time I suspected it was to check how I was taking what she'd told me, because she seemed to have returned fully to the present and had a relaxed smile on her face.

I realized then that, even from seasoned professionals—the police detectives, social workers, and lawyers who routinely conducted interviews into crime and abuse—Anne had seen numerous personal and emotional reactions to her descriptions of her history. I surmised that, in some way, she must have found solace in their amazement and horror, as it would have been the first sympathy and empathy she had ever experienced through all the pain and torture. I knew that, during this session, I too had been unable to suppress my personal reactions. I had periodically nodded my head back and forth, my lips curled slightly downward in sadness or pity. At this particular moment, I was at a loss for words.

I was still trying to recover my poise, and don't doubt that Anne realized this. But then I was able to refocus on my purpose at that moment—to understand and support her experience.

"Is this difficult for you to talk about?" I asked, momentarily wondering whether my question was motivated by her possible discomfort or my own.

"Some of it's hard to think about, but I've had to tell it to several people already," she answered somewhat apologetically, as if she had worried about disturbing them. "They always seem very bothered by it."

"Does what you're describing bother *you?*" I asked.

"Sort of, I guess, but not really. It's what I've been used to, and I accepted it as how my life was supposed to be."

This comment made me wonder why Anne would believe her life had been singled out for such misery. But then it occurred to me that maybe Anne wasn't the elders' only victim.

"Would you be the only one in the cages, Anne?" I asked.

"Usually there would be other girls, too, but not that first time. There were maybe fifteen to twenty of us who were put in the cages. They could stack the cages on top of one another, three high, to make room for more. It would be nice to have company there, because we could whisper to each other and play imaginary games, but it was horrible to be in the bottom cage."

Anne paused and looked downward.

"What was worse about the bottom cage?" I inquired, even though I suspected I knew. I couldn't tell if I was just using common sense or my thinking was gravitating toward the perversity and cruelty that had encompassed so much of her history so far.

"The bottom one would get all the crap and the vomit from the other two, and you couldn't do anything except sit there with it all over you. They would place us in the cages so that the person above you would have their rear end above your head. Since the cages were too small to actually turn around, you ended up with someone urinating or dropping their feces onto your head. The smell was so horrible that it was worse than being in the cage itself. And you couldn't move your arms enough to even push the crap off of you. When they took you from the cages, the elders got to wear scarves over their nose and mouth to avoid some of the smell. And they always wore gloves when they took you out and hosed you down."

Although I was losing my sense of incredulity, this imagery was still very disconcerting.

"How many times and for how long did you usually end up in the cages, Anne?" I asked.

"It could be three times a week or sometimes not for several weeks, and it began when I was seven and ended when I was about fifteen or sixteen. I could be left in there as much as twelve hours at a time. I really couldn't tell the time, but would sometimes know it had gone from early morning until nighttime, since the light from the little windows would go away or return. Living on a farm, you learned to tell the time just by the levels and types of lighting in the sky."

"What would you feel when you were put into the cages?"

"At first it was kind of a relief, because I knew they wouldn't hurt me or try to touch me for hours while I was in the cage, and I knew some of the other girls would usually be there. My whole body would become so stiff and it would ache, especially my back, and my muscles would sort of seize up, so I couldn't stand on my own or function for the first few minutes when they took me out. When I heard footsteps coming down the stairs, I knew they were coming for someone, but I never knew if it was my turn. So I would try to prepare myself."

"What do you mean by 'prepare yourself'?" I asked.

"I would do deep breathing and sometimes try to meditate, so I could focus on something else."

I found myself impressed with her ability to naturally use the very treatments we tried to teach in my profession. After a brief hiatus that provided us both a momentary relief, I asked, "Would you like to take a break, Anne?"

"Okay," she said, breathing a sigh.

I got up and went over to the small refrigerator in my office and took out two bottles of water. As I turned back toward my chair, I asked, "Would you like some water?"

"Yeah," Anne responded, with a grateful smile.

"Can you tell me what would happen when it was your turn?" I asked after I was seated.

"They would come to my cage and put on their gloves. They usually had cloths around their faces to deal with the smell in the room. They would take me out of the cage and have to sort of carry me, since my legs and body would be so cramped from hours just sitting crouched over and unable to move around. They would take me first to an adjacent bathroom and put me under a cold shower to clean me off. The water would be really cold, but it felt good to get cleaned off and just move around. At the same time, I would be very frightened, knowing they were going to hurt me soon.

"After the shower, they'd take me to either one of the prayer rooms or Father Jonas's office. They would often walk me naked through the church, which was very cold, especially in the winter since the building didn't have very good heat, and other church members would look at me with a sort of pity."

Anne paused again, a distressed look on her face.

"Is this uncomfortable to talk about, Anne?" I asked.

"Sometimes," she admitted.

"Would you like to continue, or do you want to talk about something else now?"

"It's cool. I can talk about it," she assured me.

I realized then that I had asked her at least twice if the subject was too uncomfortable to talk about, and her continual indication that it was okay led me to wonder if my own discomfort had motivated me to repeat myself. Hoping my motive had been more concern for her than for me, I continued. "Weren't the elders at all concerned that other church members would be suspicious or concerned that you were naked in their company?"

"I think they just saw it as part of the ritual of getting rid of sin, kind of like a baptism where the baby is naked and placed into the water by the minister or elders," she said.

"I guess I can understand how they might have connected these rituals, but I'm still amazed at the level of denial and how many in this community of hundreds of adults were accomplices," I remarked, finding her rationalization hard to accept.

"Most of the adults in the community never were aware of most of this as far as I knew," Anne said. "The people who would see me in the church when the elders took me from the cages were part of the inner circle, and they were very devoted to Father Jonas. Most of the other adults actually were only in the church when there were services or community activities."

"So, it seems like the elders and Father Jonas were smart enough to know that what they were doing would have been of concern to many of the adults in the community?"

"I guess so," Anne said somewhat sheepishly.

My question, I realized, had been a leading one, and it had steered Anne toward my desired conclusion. It was my impression that she knew this. But much as I wanted to help her see that what had been done to her was wrong, I knew that my personal beliefs and feelings shouldn't be directing her understanding of her life.

"Okay," I replied, equally sheepish.

"How many men usually participated in this, Anne?" I asked.

"Sometimes as many as six or seven, and I think always at least three," Anne said, lifting the corner of the area rug with her toe.

"What happened in the prayer room or Father Jonas's office?" I asked, bracing for a response that was certain to be difficult to absorb.

"They would lay me on a table or sometimes on the floor. They would be speaking in tongues, but sometimes their words were understandable and they talked about exorcising the sin and evil from my body. They would touch me and force their fingers inside me and sometimes would put other objects inside me, and one or sometimes several of them would get inside me. They were very rough sometimes. It would hurt a lot, and I would bleed, which they saw as a sign of the evil coming out from inside me. When they were done, someone would put a towel or sheet around me and take me home."

The casual way in which Anne ended her story seemed surreal juxtaposed with the near incomprehensibility of the entire episode. In all my years of practice, which included having worked with very impaired individuals and various forms of masochism and sadism, and having heard about almost every form of sexual deviation, I had encountered little that could catch me psychologically off guard. Yet, as I listened to Anne, without any outward and maybe with very little inward emotion, describe the atrocities she had endured as a young girl, I found myself not so much in disbelief, but stunned at how other humans could have behaved in the manner she had described, especially considering that their actions appeared to have been methodical and communal. I wondered how these men and I could actually be the same species—adult males raised in comparable cultures with fairly similar values and morals. This was one of those moments in Anne's psychotherapy where the only response I could find to begin closing the session was to say, "I'm so sorry this happened to you, Anne."

As was characteristic of her, Anne's response was to offer a slight smile, reflecting both an acknowledgement of my concern and her confusion about someone really caring for her pain.

After all, as a psychotherapist, part of my training had been to avoid interjecting my emotional experience into sessions. But, over time, I had learned that such rules had their place, and I would allow for my emotions, either as a way of overtly expressing empathy or, in this case, because my own feelings were so strong that they were evident anyway.

I had many more questions, but I realized we had passed our allotted time for the day. So I said, "I know this may not be a good time for us to stop, but we need to end in a few minutes. I'd be happy to try to find another time in the next couple of days to continue, if you'd like. I know this might bring up a lot of difficult feelings, getting back in touch with these memories."

But Anne merely said, "Thank you, but I'm okay. I can wait until next week."

Then, abruptly and eagerly changing the subject, she said, "Can I show you another quilt I made?"

"Sure, we've got a couple of minutes," I said, sharing her relief in talking about something else.

Anne unzipped her bulging backpack, which, for me, had come to represent the keeper of her creativity and expression. Pulling out a much larger quilt this time, she spread it across the floor, and we each leaned forward and unfolded it together, a ritual we would maintain over the years whenever she brought in a quilt to share with me.

As the cloth spilled across the floor, the image before me was spectacular in terms of both its artistry and the effort Anne must have put into it. It had a colorful background and another silhouette seeming to be in some sort of freefall.

"Wow, this is beautiful. So, what's it about?" I asked, knowing Anne felt awkward and shy about her creativity and, especially, about my amazement and respect for her artistry. However, she was growing to love showing them to me, and she looked pleased.

"It's a time machine," she said with rare animation. "And the person is falling back in time, like I do when I go back to my childhood to tell you about it."

I didn't say so, but I realized that, this time, her quilt was about our work together, and I felt a sense of pride in that moment, feeling I had become more important and safer to her.

As we folded up the quilt together, I asked Anne what she was going to do with it.

"I don't know. Probably give it to a homeless person," she said with a slight smile.

I felt a jolt and heard the word "No!" in my head, which I momentarily feared I'd spoken aloud. Her quilt was an expression of her life and our work together, and I believed that some day she would value it and experience it differently.

So I couldn't help but say, "Well, I think you should go somewhere and buy a blanket for the homeless, but keep this quilt. It's a work of art and a work of important emotional expression for you."

"Would *you* like to have it?" Anne asked to my surprise.

I struggled for a moment, wanting to think before I responded. I weighed the ethical importance of not accepting gifts of value from clients against what it might feel like for Anne if I declined. I knew these were really works of art and important to her life, and I wasn't comfortable for her to give them to me.

"I'd be willing to keep it here for now, and maybe we can talk further about it in the future," I said.

"That would be cool. I also have the one I showed you a few sessions ago. Would you keep that one as well?"

"Sure," I said. But then the conscientious side of me added, "But I'll hold them for you rather than keep them."

As Anne departed, her upright posture reflecting her confidence, I mused that, although our comfort with each other had vastly progressed over the months, I had felt decidedly uncomfortable during this session.

I again wondered if *I*, rather than Anne, had wanted to process this session further before a whole week went by. The juxtaposition of her lack of expression and my strong feelings made a lot of sense clinically, but it was quite unnerving at the same time. I had become more sensitive to my own psychological processes working with Anne, in part because of my heightened emotionality, but also because her own emotional expression was often absent.

As I pondered my feelings, I felt a little shaky regarding my boundaries, and I decided I would set up an appointment to talk with my former therapist. We hadn't worked together in a couple of years, but occasionally I would consult with her regarding important emotions or reactions that surfaced in me during my work with a client.

— CHAPTER SIXTEEN —

The annual ritual of heading out to just about the most eastern point in the United States, on the far end of a strip of land jutting into the cold, harsh North Atlantic, at the tail end of winter, to share a beach house with a group of friends, was something I cherished and found exhilarating. It was about afternoon walks with lifelong friends on some of the most beautiful beaches in the world, and a wonderful respite from the challenges of my work in the city.

But while a week on the tip of Cape Cod had renewed my energy for my work, my absence was sometimes difficult for my clients. And, as I was soon to find out, it hadn't been an easy time for Anne.

My first indication of the difficulty she'd experienced came from the tone of her voice as Anne greeted me my first day back. She was sitting in my waiting room, clearly more demure than she had been in our past few sessions, indicating either that she'd suffered some distress during the two-week interim or felt a greater distance from me due to the time I'd been on Cape Cod. As Anne entered my office, she remained unusually quiet, so I broke the silence.

"So, how are you this week?" I asked.

"Not so good," she said in a shaky voice. "I've been having really bad nightmares. Plus I haven't had any periods for maybe five or six months. Do you thing that's wrong?"

"What do you mean by the word 'wrong'?" I asked, looking puzzled.

"Do you think it's because I've done something wrong or it's bad or something?"

"I feel quite certain it has nothing to do with wrong or sin, but it might be something that is medically wrong. And I can't advise you more than that, but ..."

"But you can give me a doctor to talk to," Anne interrupted, her smile offering a touch of sarcasm.

"Yes, I could. Would you like that?" I asked.

"Is it someone you know?"

"It is someone I know well, and he's an ob-gyn and a very caring man."

"Could you tell him what's wrong before I see him so I don't have to tell him?"

"I'd be happy to tell him I'd referred you and what you have shared with me, but you'll have to tell him more details."

"Do you know if he keeps body parts in his freezer?" she asked, looking completely serious.

"I am sure he doesn't, but I'll tell you what. I'm going to his house this weekend and I'll look in the freezer, if you'd like, and then I can tell you for sure," I responded, confident I could do exactly this and answer her from a place of honest certainty.

"Okay, that would be cool. Can I ask one more question?" she inquired, demurely.

"Of course," I responded, pleased we were making headway in this area. Having no way to know what her symptoms indicated, I had to weigh the risk of delaying a medical evaluation a little longer against pressuring her to see him quickly and having the whole thing backfire. "I'll give you his name so you can make an appointment, and I'll call you after I look in his freezer, okay?"

"Yeah, that would be okay," she said, a slight smile on her face.

"So, tell me about the nightmares," I said, shifting our focus to her other area of difficulty.

"I've been having them since you went away on vacation."

It was interesting to me, and somewhat telling, that Anne referred to my being away, rather than time, as the parameter of her distress. But I deferred investigating that for the moment and asked, "What's happening in the nightmares?"

"I'm shouting at people, and I wake up crying and frightened."

"Do you know who these people are, and what do you understand about yourself in the dream?" I asked.

"They're adults. I think they're men. I'm always a child in them. I feel like I'm trying to win or something, but I never do. I wake up first."

"The word 'win' is interesting. Do you know what you're trying to win?"

"Not really, maybe to have them leave me alone. I feel like I'd be winning if I just could get rid of the nightmares," she added.

"That makes a lot of sense and might feel nicer, but sometimes nightmares are a way of releasing painful things that are inside."

"I'm also having nosebleeds."

This was one of Anne's fairly typical shifts from one topic to another. Sometimes the topics were somewhat related, and other times they were possible digressions from more uncomfortable material. I could at least see how stress might lead to nightmares and to nosebleeds, but they could also have been coincidental experiences.

"Sometimes I'm afraid to sleep, and I hate myself when I go to sleep," Anne continued.

"What is it that you're thinking about yourself that brings you to a place of hating yourself?" I asked.

"I just don't like what my life has been like, that I never got to have a normal childhood."

"I can certainly understand that you hate what's happened and not having a normal childhood, but you didn't create that. You know, it's logical to connect doing something wrong or behaving badly with being punished, and you seem to make the connection, too, but in reverse. Your logic is that if you're punished, you must have been bad."

Anne gave her typical response to one of my logical discourses, looking at me with a somewhat blank stare and softly uttering, "I guess so."

"Does what I just said make sense to you?"

"Yeah, it sort of makes sense, but I was a sinner according to God."

"Well, we could go down that path now, although you know we see that very differently. Or you could just think about something and consider if it might be worth trying. Maybe you could hate *what happened to you*, but not hate *you*."

Anne just sat there staring into space, not really looking at me. As best I could discern, she understood my words, but they couldn't begin to compete with the weight of her history and her pain. I could only hope that, given enough time and hearing enough alternative messages, they might have some impact.

As we sat there quietly for a few moments, each of us allowing our thoughts to absorb, I felt it might be an appropriate time to switch the topic.

I'd taken only one work-related call during my vacation; it had been from Nathan Cohen. Nathan and I had begun collaborating on Anne's case a few weeks before I went to Cape Cod, and it had been clear from that initial call that we shared great care and concern for our mutual client. Interestingly, when each of us had asked Anne about her comfort in releasing us to talk with each other, she appeared almost excited. Anne seemed happy to finally have people who seemed to both care for her and care about wanting to communicate about her welfare, much as two healthy parents might. In spite of her valiant attempts to get me to answer legal questions and get Nathan to provide psychological consultation, he and I managed to maintain good communication and preserve our professional boundaries.

Nathan had called to find out what I understood regarding Anne's first contact with Child Protective Services at the age of twelve. He had shared that

Anne had refused to talk and eventually had been returned to her community and more than a decade of further physical and sexual abuse, and he felt her past refusal to make any statement about the community might affect her legal claims.

I had been quite surprised and maybe a little embarrassed that I had no knowledge of this important part of her history. I had thanked Nathan for the information and promised to address it with Anne and get back to him, and I decided this was a good time to bring it up, hoping it might shed some light on her childhood and even connect to her present nightmares.

I told Anne about the events Nathan had briefly described and asked her if she felt comfortable to talk about what she and Nathan had discussed regarding that period in her life, when she had been taken into custody by social services.

Her response, however, was a bit surprising. "Nathan and I have never talked about this," she said. I was perplexed until Anne offered, "I think it was in my records with social services or something."

Relieved to have cleared up the confusion, I asked, "Would you be okay to talk with me about what happened at that time?"

"Yeah, that would be okay, I guess," she agreed, and she began reflecting upon her life as it had been fourteen years earlier.

"I was at home in the kitchen, helping my mother do the laundry," she began, "when I heard a knock on the door. I didn't answer it, since I knew it wasn't my place, but I heard voices, and a few seconds later, I heard footsteps coming toward the kitchen. I didn't know what to expect, and I was really surprised and frightened to see a policewoman come through the kitchen door with my mother. I'd never seen any police on the farm. They were part of the outside world, and the elders didn't want us to have anything to do with the outside world. The only policeman they'd speak with occasionally was the Deerbrook sheriff.

"Anyway, I hoped I hadn't done anything wrong. But the policewoman looked at me and said, 'Are you Anne?' and I heard my mother on the phone in the hall asking my father to come home immediately. She told him the police were there and wanted to take me away." Anne looked at me with wide eyes, as if to try to convey the incredulity and fear she'd felt at that moment. "Then, before I even knew what was happening or could talk to my mother, the policewoman said, 'Anne, I'm Deborah, and I need you to come with me. No one's going to hurt you, and you're not in any trouble. We just want to talk with you.' She touched my arm very gently, trying to nudge me toward the door."

I imagined how frightened Anne must have been at this moment, but how compliantly she would have obeyed the officer, since it was so engrained in her never to resist direction.

Anne recalled that the policewoman had then led her out the front door to a police car, one of two on the road in front of the house. She saw several neighbors out on their front porches, just staring toward her house and at her being led away by the policewoman. It sounded reminiscent of the way people had stared at her when the elders led her into the prayer room after keeping her in a cage, I mused privately, and, as if echoing my thoughts, Anne told me that, as they'd reached the police car, she'd seen the bars between the front and back seats and felt she was being placed in another cage. She'd instinctively pulled back, but Deborah had tightened her grip, opened the car door with her other hand, and helped Anne inside.

"I was certain I was going to be punished for something I must have done wrong, and the fact that I couldn't think of anything bad I'd done was irrelevant since I almost never could," Anne said, a dejected look on her face. "But then, something very strange happened," she said, perking up a little. "The policewoman got into the caged area with me. This had never happened when I'd been caged before, but I'd never been in a cage so large. It wasn't until later that I found out it wasn't a cage," she said.

"So, what was it like sitting in the caged area of the police car?" I asked, knowing I was being somewhat rhetorical.

"I kinda did what I always had. I curled up in the corner, against the far door, and didn't move."

Nathan had shared the police report with me, and I knew that, once inside the car, Anne had automatically reverted to her typical cage posture, curling herself into a fetal position and not moving. After sitting quietly for a few minutes, Deborah had asked, "Anne, do you remember my name?"

Anne's eyes had remained downcast, although she almost imperceptibly shook her head from side to side. Deborah softly reiterated her name, after which Anne cautiously asked, "Am I going to jail?" a look of defeat on her face.

Along with the police officer's report, Nathan had provided me with some history of the events leading up to Anne's removal from the community. Two days prior to the police officers arriving at the Martins' house, an anonymous caller had contacted the Medford Police regarding allegations of very serious child abuse within The Christian Movement. Knowing that the local Deerbrook police department would probably either ignore the call or, at best, be ill-equipped to assess the situation or intervene, the caller contacted the much larger police department in Medford.

Being the seat of Jackson County, the Medford police department retained jurisdiction for the overall county and, after receiving the anonymous tip, it had organized a team to go to two of the community's homes and remove the alleged victims. However, because the allegations were detailed and extensive, including a history of severe abuse dating back at least five years, priority was given to making certain that they followed protocol in every aspect, from obtaining legal authority to enter one or more of these homes and remove children to practicing the proper conduct that would maximize their ability to use any evidence found or information provided by the occupants. An anonymous tip did not imply evidence nor the right to invade private property. However, allegations involving child endangerment or abuse merited exceptions and allowed for police intervention.

Providing further corroboration regarding the legitimacy of the anonymous claim had been an unsolved mystery surrounding the discovery of a body on the community's farm a few months prior to the authorities removing Anne from her home. A twenty-two-year-old named David Hopkins had found his way to Deerbrook, where members had apparently befriended him and elders had recruited him into the community. After a period of time, he had become disenchanted with the community's "restrictions and rigidity" and wasn't faring well, either physically or emotionally, according to members who were subsequently interviewed.

One night, during a particularly harsh rain, David went missing. The next day, community members began a search of the farm and surrounding woods, but to no avail. By that evening, they decided to involve the local police, who, several days later, uncovered his body in a wooded area adjacent to the farm. Authorities determined he had died of exposure and ruled his death an accident, but remained concerned why a healthy young man wouldn't be able to survive to find his way back to the farm, only a half-hour walk away. They considered his death to be unresolved.

Nevertheless, the police department had conceded that, given the abuse allegations, it needed to deploy officers to intervene. And since the alleged victims were young females, the department believed it should utilize a female officer. There were only two female officers in the department at the time, however, and one was on vacation. That had left Deborah, brand new on the force and still in training, a period that dictated she participate only in observational roles. Yet, several officers planning the intervention concluded the situation constituted enough of an emergency to break with protocol and assign Deborah to the task.

"The officers gave me very simple and explicit instructions, to enter the house behind the sergeant, to locate and extricate the alleged victim as quickly as possible, and to take her to one of the police vehicles and sit with her in the back seat," Deborah had written in her self-evaluation. "All of these instructions I followed to the letter. However, I failed to provide adequate reassurance to Anne along with protection, an oversight I realized when Anne asked me if she was going to jail."

Realizing her mistake, Deborah had responded quickly to assuage Anne's fears. "Oh no, honey. You haven't done anything wrong," she'd said.

"Then why am I in a police car and having to leave here?" Anne had responded.

Deborah had been briefed not to discuss any details of the alleged abuse, nor to mention anything regarding her father being under suspicion, but she needed to respond to the question. "We want to talk to you more about your life here," she said. "We're going to take you to meet with a social worker who's very nice and will ask you some questions. I'm sure she'll call your mother when we get there, so that she knows you're all right."

Anne didn't understand, but she was too frightened to ask any more questions. "She tried to talk to me," Anne remembered. "She asked me if I had brothers and sisters and stuff like that. But I just didn't know whether I should talk to her about anything. I mean, she was on the outside. So we just sat there, and then one of the male officers came out of the house and got in the driver's seat and we drove away."

"What were you feeling as you drove away, Anne?" I asked.

"Well, I remember looking back toward the house, and I felt very frightened and sad. And there was still another police car parked out in front of the house, which worried me, because I didn't know if they knew that the elders and my father had hurt me and might take them to jail." Anne paused and then added, "because of me."

Having absolutely no concept of anything like "abuse," Anne couldn't have comprehended that the police might be investigating something illegal or wrong, unless it was something she had done wrong, I reflected. However, she said she'd instinctively wondered if the secrecy surrounding the elders' behavior might indicate that their actions would seem wrong to people outside the church. As she told me this, I recalled that she'd been taught it was Satan's goal to perpetuate evil and stop Father Jonas and the elders from cleansing the world.

Anne and the police had continued to drive for about fifteen minutes to Medford. She had only seen the town a few times, when the family had visited a restaurant to celebrate her brother's birthday. The family had never celebrated Anne's birthday other than to acknowledge it at the evening meal and include it in the prayers before eating. The police car pulled up to a red brick building with stairs leading up to a front door, with a sign above it that said Medford Family Services. Deborah got out of the car, and the policeman got out of the driver's seat and opened Anne's door, where Deborah had come around to her side. Anne got out of the car, and Deborah lightly touched her shoulder and directed her toward the building. They went up the steps and into a lobby where lots of people were sitting and waiting. Deborah stopped inside the door with Anne, and the policeman went up to a reception desk and spoke with the person on duty. A few minutes later, a woman entered the waiting room and, along with the policeman, came over and introduced herself.

"Hello. I assume you're Anne," she said in a pleasant tone. "My name is Julie Connors, and I'm a social worker here. I work with children, and I'd like you to come to my office so we can get to know each other a little. Would that be okay with you?"

Anne didn't know how to react. She could not recall ever having been asked whether anything was okay with her. So she remained quiet, and Deborah said, "Anne, I'm going to stay with you while you talk with Ms. Connors."

Having received no response from Anne, Deborah and Ms. Connors looked at each other, and Ms. Connors directed her eyes from Anne toward the door from which she had entered. She led the way, with Deborah following behind Anne. They entered into a hallway with several doors opening into small offices. About halfway down the hallway, they went into an office, where Ms. Connors directed Anne to a small sofa. Deborah took a seat on the sofa next to her, and Ms. Connors pulled up a chair to sit a little closer.

"How are you doing, Anne?" Ms. Connors began by asking.

Anne continued to look toward the floor, her only response being a shrug of her shoulders, indicating she didn't really have an answer.

"I'm sure you're wondering why you're here, Anne. I want you to know you have nothing to be afraid of, and no one will hurt you here. We're here to help you."

"Anne was worried she might be in trouble, and I tried to reassure her that she hadn't done anything wrong and there was no need to fear," Deborah interjected.

"That's a fairly common worry when someone from the police department comes to your house and asks you to go with them," Ms. Connors smiled. "But you're not in any trouble, Anne. We brought you here to see how you're doing and see if you need any help that we could provide." Although Anne hadn't looked up, both women were sure that she was listening. Ms. Connors then asked Anne, "Has anyone hit you or hurt you or touched you in any way that felt uncomfortable, Anne?"

But Anne gave no verbal response, nor any visible reaction.

"Do you have any physical pain right now, Anne?" Ms. Connors attempted.

Again, Anne didn't respond.

"Are you at all afraid to answer my questions, Anne?" Ms. Connors asked, leaning forward in her chair a little, trying to feel more supportive and prod her a little. Still Anne remained silent, hearing everything, but knowing, as deeply as she knew anything in life, that she couldn't tell anyone about the things that had happened to her. Also, knowing it was a sin to lie, she believed her only option was to remain completely silent.

As she had later noted in Anne's file, Ms. Connors had realized that Anne was either too frightened or too indoctrinated to speak and so had decided not to push her further at that time. Her primary goal was to build a relationship of trust and safety, and pressuring Anne would not have achieved that goal. Knowing that the plan was to keep Anne under the care of social services for a period of time, she knew there would be opportunity to build a relationship first and try to learn the facts later. So the next time she spoke, instead of addressing Anne, she turned toward Deborah and spoke to her, enabling Anne to listen without feeling pressured to respond.

"I don't think that this is the time to ask Anne any more questions," she said. "We'd like to have one of our nurses examine her to make sure she's okay. I assume you'd like to be with Anne during that time, Officer Peterson?"

As Deborah nodded her agreement, both women noticed that Anne's foot began to shake. This was the first physical reaction either of them had seen from Anne, and they realized that their last interchange had elicited some kind of anxious reaction. Ms. Connors looked back toward Anne and asked if something had just upset her. Anne looked up, and with the most energy either of the women had seen from her, she replied, "I won't see any doctors."

"Can you tell us why, Anne?" asked Ms. Connors.

"Because doctors are evil and dangerous, and they cut people up and keep the body parts," Anne said, her voice shaking.

Having heard speculation regarding The Christian Movement as a cultlike community, Ms. Connors wasn't shocked by Anne's statement. It mostly served to further her suspicions regarding the likelihood of physical and sexual abuse, insofar as keeping these children away from doctors would be a necessary protection for the perpetrators.

But keeping these thoughts to herself and hoping to calm some of Anne's fears, she merely responded, "I can understand that you're afraid of doctors, Anne, but I know our medical staff here very well, and they never hurt anyone and are very caring. We just want one of our nurses, Mrs. Jackson, to do an examination. No one is going to do anything to treat you unless you're ill or injured, and we would contact your mother to be here if that were the case. I promise that Deborah will stay with you the whole time to make sure you're safe and well cared for."

Anne gave no response and just looked downward again. It was clear to both women that she wasn't going to contest this any further, and her sinking posture indicated a sense of defeat or hopelessness. Both women felt very sad that this child was far too afraid and trained not to stand up against what she perceived as danger to herself. Ms. Connors wanted to move quickly with the exam and not subject Anne to any more time worrying, so she stood up and asked Anne and Deborah to go with her to meet Mrs. Jackson.

Anne rose very slowly, with a familiar sense of heading toward something that might be hurtful, but not daring to resist it. With Ms, Connors leading the way down the hall, Anne followed, her head lowered and her shoulders slumping. They came to a door that said Exam Room #2, and Ms. Connors opened the door and entered ahead of Anne. As Anne entered the room, she saw a woman in her mid fifties who reminded her of her mother. The woman smiled and said, "Hello. You must be Anne. I'm Mrs. Jackson, and I'm a nurse here. I want to take a little time to do a physical examination. I understand this might be frightening or uncomfortable for you, so I'll be very gentle and won't do anything that would cause any physical discomfort. I just need to see if you have any injuries, Anne."

Mrs. Jackson interpreted Anne's unresponsiveness as indicative of her extreme anxiety, and she realized that she would be performing her examination against the wishes of her patient. So she moved slowly toward Anne and put a hand gently on her shoulder to lead her toward a small changing room, showing her a dressing gown and a place to put her clothes, and explaining that she needed her to undress and put on the gown. Aware that an alleged history of abuse could generate a fear of being enclosed or feeling trapped, she left the door ajar.

As she moved away, she observed that Anne just stood there, but she wanted to give her a little time. And, a few minutes later, Anne opened the door very slightly, which Mrs. Jackson took as her cue to proceed. When she opened the door, Anne was standing there, facing the door and looking toward the floor. This time, Mrs. Jackson reached out, took hold of Anne's hand and led her into the examination room. Had Anne looked up, she would have noticed Ms. Connors was gone and that Deborah was standing next to some kind of bench or sofa that had a long white paper covering most of it. When Mrs. Jackson directed her to sit up on the bench, Anne complied, sitting with her head and shoulders slumped.

Mrs. Jackson began by asking Anne if she had any physical pain or discomfort. Anne shook her head slightly, and Mrs. Jackson proceeded with a series of standard examination procedures, taking Anne's temperature and checking her pulse and blood pressure, and other noninvasive procedures, such as examining her exposed limbs, checking for any bruises under her hair, and making sure Anne did not have any facial or other bone structural abnormalities. Several times during the course of the examination, she asked Anne how she was doing, to which Anne uttered a barely audible "Okay," although, on a couple of occasions, Anne whimpered almost inaudibly, "I want to go home."

"Don't worry, dear," Deborah said, trying to compensate for her previous insensitivity to Anne's fears. "You just need to stay with us for a few days, and then we'll talk about when you might go home." Anne merely continued to slump like a lifeless doll. "I think your mother might be able to come visit you in a couple of days," Deborah added, inwardly hoping she was accurate about this. But Anne, like a reluctant dog that had no choice other than to remain still while being bathed, seemed so sad and powerless that Mrs. Jackson felt as if Anne saw her as yet another adult doing what she chose with her.

After completing the less invasive parts of the exam, Mrs. Jackson put an arm around Anne's shoulder and asked her to lie back, gently directing her downward. At first Anne resisted, and Mrs. Jackson looked toward Deborah for help. Privately, they both wondered whether they might be recreating a familiar horrifying experience for the young girl. After Anne was lying on her back, Mrs. Jackson tilted Anne's knees upward, helping her to rest her feet on the end of the bench. Prior to meeting Anne, she had considered whether or not to do a vaginal examination. Now she decided against it. Her decision was partly influenced by how frightened Anne was, but she also knew that, following the exam, Ms. Connors would meet with Anne to do a thorough evaluation of any history of sexual trauma. If there was any basis to perform a more invasive examination, she could proceed then.

After completing the physical exam, Mrs. Jackson helped Anne sit up and steadied her as she stepped down to the floor. Directing Anne back to the dressing room, she said, "You've done beautifully, Anne. Thank you for cooperating. Please put your clothes on, and let me know when you're ready." As before, when Anne had done as she'd been asked, she cracked open the door to the dressing room and stood there limply, waiting to be told what to do next.

It was Deborah who stepped in then, accompanying Anne back to Ms. Connors's office, where she remained with her while Ms. Connors again attempted an assessment of Anne's psychological state and any history of abuse. But, other than responding "Okay" to Ms. Connors's inquiry as to how she was doing, Anne remained completely mute.

After about five minutes of light to moderate coaxing, Ms. Connors abandoned her inquiry and explained that she had arranged for Anne to stay with a very nice family with other children. "Their names are Mr. and Mrs. Lewis," she said gently, "and two of their four children are girls like you, who need a safe place to stay for a little while. I'll come over every day to visit you, Anne," Ms. Connors added, "and we'll talk about how to continue your schooling in the next couple of days."

"How did you feel at this point?" I asked Anne, as she sat in my office that day recounting the events that had uprooted her world fourteen years earlier.

"I was terrified," Anne admitted, "especially about the schooling. I was afraid they'd find out I hadn't gone to school, except for my dad teaching me to read a little from the Bible. But I hoped maybe I wouldn't be there long enough for them to find out."

"What happened then? Did you go straight to the Lewis's house?" I asked.

"Yeah. Ms. Connors told Deborah she would take me to the family's house. I guess she knew I wouldn't run away or anything. And Deborah gave me a card with her phone number. She said to call her in case I needed anything. But I was kind of in shock and didn't really know what was happening to me."

"So, what was the Lewis's house like?"

"It was a large, two-story house with a vegetable garden in front. That was kinda nice, 'cause we had one at home. The house was white with green shutters, and it had a white fence around the garden."

"So, what happened when you got there?"

"When we pulled into the driveway, a woman came out of the house onto the porch. She was kind of plump, and she wore an apron. But that's all I saw, because I was too afraid to look at her once we got out of the car. It wasn't until she walked over and said, 'Welcome to our home, Anne. I'm Suzanne,' that I looked at her face and saw she was smiling. She seemed nice. She said she hoped we could become friends and asked me to call her Suzanne. That was very strange, because I'd never called an adult by their first name."

"So, what happened after that?"

"We went inside, and she asked me what I liked to eat, and I told her I didn't know, because I only ate what I was told to. They both seemed surprised and kind of sad when I said that, but Mrs. Lewis just said to come in and we could get to know each other for a while before the children came home from school.

"After we'd had some tea and cookies, Ms. Connors told me that she'd told Mrs. Lewis that the police had taken me from the house without allowing time to retrieve any clothes, and Mrs. Lewis had replied that I was about her daughter Jeanne's size and I could share her clothes until my mother could bring my things. When I heard that, it seemed like I'd be there longer than a few days, and I also worried about how Jeanne would take sharing her clothes. But I was really happy to hear my mother was coming. I guess they must have noticed that, because they smiled at each other and that made me realize they were really kind."

"So, what was the house like?" I asked.

"It was really clean, and she said I could have the room next to her daughter Jeanne's room. Things weren't kept in near perfect order like my house, but the furniture looked more comfortable, and there was a really great kitchen and a television in the living room, something I'd rarely seen before, except in the windows of stores in Medford. Mrs. Lewis gave me a tour of the house. I was too scared to say anything, but she didn't seem to mind. She showed me my room, too. The whole day had been so strange, but, even though I just wanted to go home, a room to myself was such a wonderful relief, and she asked me if I'd like to take a nap. Once she was gone, it was really quiet and I fell asleep, but it didn't last long because, after probably about half an hour, there was a knock on the door."

Anne stopped, looking a little startled, like she would have felt being awoken by the knock at the door. "Who was it?" I asked.

"I was afraid to answer the door, so I just sat up in bed, and then a girl's voice came through the door. She said, 'Hi, I'm Jeanne, and I was a foster kid, too. Can I come in?'"

"Did you know what a foster kid was?"

"No, but I was afraid to ask," Anne said.

As transfixed as I had been by Anne's recollections, I realized we had reached the end of our time for the session and I had to interrupt her, but I had a couple of questions I wanted to ask her first. "Before we wind up…" I started, but, as I did so, Madison jumped up from the sofa and bounded toward the door. He'd learned what "wind up" meant and, for him, it meant "walk."

Anne and I both laughed, and our momentary shared amusement at Madison's antics made my next question seem all the more sobering. "Did you have any injuries or bruises that the nurse would have detected?" I asked.

"I had a few old bruises, but nothing that was really that visible. The elders were pretty careful not to do things that left visible marks. The nurse did stop and take a while looking at the fingers on my hands, though. I think maybe she could tell they had been broken before." Anne stopped talking, and I realized she had hit an emotional wall remembering something painful or traumatic.

But we were at the end of our time, and I chose not to investigate further without adequate opportunity to process the consequent feelings. By now, we both knew we'd come back to this later. So I merely said, "I know these are difficult memories for you, and I'd like to talk more about it next time if you feel all right to stop now."

"See you next week," she said, her tone upbeat. She looked relieved as she walked out the door.

I sat there thinking this had been a productive session, one that helped me to understand her life better. My thoughts then turned toward Madison, who was standing by the door eagerly awaiting our walk together.

— CHAPTER SEVENTEEN —

As I opened the door to my waiting room for our session the following week, I noticed that Anne seemed very jittery and distressed. "I'm feeling overwhelmed and feel all this stress building up, like energy that needs to be let out," she said, expressing her intense anxiety and depression before I'd even had a chance to take my seat.

"How long have you been feeling this way?" I asked, not really surprised since her emotions still vacillated from session to session.

"All week," she admitted.

"You seemed much calmer last week when you left my office," I remarked.

"Yeah, I was glad you were back, but then I got really worried again," she said.

"Do you know what has you so stressed and upset?"

"I'm worried about my health, and I finally made an appointment with Dr. Pearl, like I told you I would, and the future seems so confusing and uncertain, and I'm worried about how others are seeing me. I'm so different from everyone else. I'll never be normal," she said, looking very dejected.

"Wow, that's a lot to be facing at once," I agreed. "I'm not surprised you're feeling overwhelmed. Aside from being worried, how else is all of this affecting you?"

"I can't sleep, and I'm really worried and shaky a lot of the time," she said a little apologetically, as if she were sorry to be such a nuisance.

"When you say you can't sleep, are you falling asleep at all?" I asked.

"Maybe for an hour or so, but then I wake up and can't get back to sleep."

She seemed more tired, I thought, studying her face. "How long have you been sleeping that poorly?"

"For the past week, I guess," she sighed.

"Are you having more nightmares?" I asked, thinking that this might be why she wasn't sleeping well.

"Yeah," she said listlessly.

"What have they been about this week?"

"I'm hanging onto a piece of string that's slowly slipping through my hands, but it's the only thing preventing me from falling into a black hole. If I fall, it will mean certain death, so I'm trying to hold on as best I can. But I can't keep it from slipping, and I'm scared I'll let go or the string will run out and I'll fall."

It was a classic anxiety dream, and to gauge its intensity further I needed to know its frequency. So I asked Anne how often it recurred.

"It's a dream I've had several times, and it pretty much reflects how I feel about life at the moment. I have lots of different dreams. But it's worse when I know what I'm going to dream," she added.

"What do you mean?" I asked, sensing we were about to travel back to another powerful part of her childhood.

"Things set me off, and I know what's in store. If I'm in bed and see the bulge my feet make under the covers, then I know it will be a rough night. The trouble is, once you've seen something, you can't *unsee* it. I don't mean to look. The problem is when I see them by mistake. That's when I know what kind of night I'll have, and I try to stay awake. But it doesn't work, and the fear of going to sleep, knowing what's coming, is almost as bad as the dream itself."

"Does the bulge at your feet make any sense to you or connect to anything you can recall?" I asked.

"I remember my father coming into my room when my mom was asleep. I used to feel him lifting the covers by my feet while I pretended to be asleep, hoping he would go away but knowing he wouldn't. Then I'd feel his hands grab my ankles and pull my legs apart while I'd try to keep them tightly shut. But I was never strong enough, and I'd feel him start his journey up my legs. Sometimes he'd bite me, and sometimes he'd lick, slowly working his way around my legs and making this odd smacking sound with his lips as he went on. In my dream, I can feel the stickiness his saliva left behind on me and smell his aftershave. I knew that when his head reached the top of my legs, he'd pull himself up onto my body, penetrate me with his fingers, and bite my breasts at the same time. If he felt me tense up, he'd go harder and harder, laughing at me and smacking his lips together even louder."

She glanced at me to check my reaction. I had begun to think I was somewhat inured to these horrors now, after hearing about the cages, but I found myself disgusted listening to this description.

"Sometimes he would have anal sex with me through a hole in the sheets. I'm not even sure how the hole got put in the sheets, but he must have done it when I wasn't around or something. Sometimes my brother was allowed to watch and learn when my father did this to me."

"How do you feel remembering this, Anne?" I asked, wanting her to say "furious" or "disgusted."

"Just having to remember it is horrible. The shame doesn't go away. Waking up is hard. There's no good way to wake up from some dreams, and usually I'm crying. I feel like this huge failure, because I can't control parts of my life. I'm getting scared to go on more medication, and I worry that if I tell anyone how bad it gets they'll be mad at me, because I haven't said anything before now. Usually, I'm pretty good at hiding how I feel. I try to cover it up by making jokes and filling my day with stuff, but at the moment I'm scared."

Anne stopped and just sat there looking close to tears and staring downward, as she had been throughout most of the session. I wasn't surprised. Instead of anger or disgust, she felt shame, having internalized so much of the cruelty.

"I notice you're not really looking at me this morning, Anne. Can you tell me why?" I asked cautiously, for the first time really challenging her need to distance from me.

"I'm afraid you'll make me take more medications or get mad at me," she said, her voice subdued.

"I kind of thought so," I said. "Thanks for letting me know that's what's worrying you. Do you think you need to be on more medications?"

"I don't know," she said hopelessly.

"Okay, then I'll tell you what. I'm okay not to have an opinion on this. Let's help you figure out what you want, since that seems to be the question here. As for me being mad at you, you often think or wonder about that. So, do you think I'm mad at you right now?" I asked.

She glanced up momentarily. "I'm not sure," she said.

"Well, how can you tell if I'm mad?" I asked, concealing some mild disappointment I felt, since I'd hoped she'd gained more ground in trusting me.

"I don't know," she said again. "You'd be annoyed with me or not want to see me anymore."

"How would you be able to tell that?" I asked, hoping she'd refer to the exercise I'd given her in a previous session about looking for evidence to support her fears.

But her answer was still, "I don't know."

"Well, do you ever see or hear anything from me, like a facial expression, or words, that make you think I might be mad at you?" I prompted, momentarily wondering if my anger and disgust toward the people who abused her was detectable and could confuse her.

"Not really, although sometimes you look sad or maybe angry at something I tell you about my father or that's happened to me," she said.

It was a fair observation, and I was amazed at the occasional synchronicity we seemed to experience.

"I do have some of those feelings and probably reveal them," I admitted. "Does that make you think I'm mad at you?"

"Yeah, sometimes. I can't really tell. I never could tell when anyone was mad at me. Sometimes when they were hurting me or punishing me, they didn't even seem mad. They might even laugh or look happy."

With this comment, I felt chagrined. Her ability to perceive emotions and evidence to support her perceptions had been severely compromised, I reminded myself.

"Okay, so what you see or hear has been really confusing. Let's try to help you figure out a way to know if I'm mad at you. I could try to always tell you if I am, but I think it's so important, both for our relationship and so that you'll find comfort in being able to trust your judgment, for you to find your own way to know this, without me telling you. This is especially true because sometimes you leave here and think or wonder if I'm mad at you, and it takes a whole week to find out. So, how about this? I promise to always be honest about any negative feelings I have toward you, if I'm mad or annoyed or worried. If I don't say anything, then you can trust, or learn to trust, that I'm not upset and I feel okay. Can we try that?"

"Yeah, but you're my doctor, so you wouldn't really tell me if you were mad," she countered.

"That sounds like a catch-22," I said, but, seeing her completely perplexed gaze, I immediately realized my reference to such an idiom had made no sense to her.

"Sorry about that," I said. "You wouldn't know the term 'catch-22.' It means that no matter what you think or do, or what path you go down, you can't win."

"Welcome to my world," Anne quipped in a rare moment of sarcastic humor.

I returned her wry smile. "So, if you assume I'm mad at you and assume I won't be honest and tell you," I continued, "then there's nothing I can do or say to make you feel differently. Neither of us can win if you've set up a catch-22 in your mind."

Her eyes opened a little more brightly, and she said, "I guess that's kind of true, isn't it?"

I just smiled for a moment and then responded, "So, you developed this catch-22, and you're the only one who can change it. What could you do?"

"I don't know," she immediately responded.

I took a breath, feeling a little frustrated. "Well, you can start by not saying 'I don't know' before you even give yourself a chance to think about possible solutions. We both know you're really smart, and you need to let your brain, not your emotions, have a chance to have some power here," I added, wanting her to somehow feel enough trust in herself to make guesses and enough trust in me to feel safe if she guessed incorrectly. I have never been very tolerant of clients saying "I don't know." Right or wrong, I probably see it as lazy or overly cautious, and it creates a dead end to our process.

But, seeing her glance had turned slightly downward, I tried to assure her, "I'm *not* mad at you. I'm really interested in wanting you to find your way. I want to encourage and maybe sometimes push you, and it's okay for that to be a little stressful for me, or for us. okay?"

"Okay," she muttered sheepishly.

As Anne sat there, I felt like I'd given her too much of a lecture. Surely, I thought, she'll conclude she's done something wrong, and she'll see me as an annoyed adult/parent figure.

But then, to my surprise, she said, "I guess I could try not to think you wouldn't be honest with me, maybe to give you the benefit of the doubt."

"I think that's a wonderful solution to your catch-22," I said, relieved. "And you'd have to take a chance and just trust me, which is hugely important for you to feel anyway."

We both sat there looking at each other for a few moments. Something emotionally important had occurred between us, but I knew Anne was intimidated by it, while I saw it was valuable and indicative of her growth. Perhaps that's why I decided to ask the question that had remained in my mind since she'd told me about her dream. "So, I have a question," I started. "Was I one of those people in your dream, who would watch your father abuse you?"

"No," she said, her tone emphatic.

"Any thoughts on why not, since I'm one of the people in your life now?" I asked, feeling a little relieved.

"'Cause I don't think you'd just stand there and let it happen," she said, her voice a little tight, as though it pained her to acknowledge she believed I cared for her.

I felt a surge of emotion. I knew I had achieved maybe the most important goal in our relationship and work together. She had come to trust that she could count on me to protect her and not hurt her. We both knew what her response had meant, and neither of us needed to say anything further. I had one of my momentary pangs of confusion about how much Anne moved me emotionally, especially because she did not emanate tangible or discernable emotions herself. Of course, I also knew that was why I had such strong feelings, and I knew we were both growing.

It was an intense moment, and it was growing uncomfortable, at least for me, so, moving forward, I commented, "Just the sleep deprivation alone is probably contributing significantly to your anxiety and feelings of being overwhelmed, and we may need to get you some help, at least to stabilize your sleep."

Anne looked stricken. "Get me some help?' she asked. "What do you mean?"

I searched for the most gentle and convincing wording I could think of.

"Well, you know I'm a psychologist, which means I have a doctorate in psychology. But do you know what a psychiatrist is?" I asked, realizing I was treading on very thin ice given her fear of physicians.

Anne looked puzzled for a moment and said, "I guess I thought it was maybe the same thing."

"We're both doctors in mental health, but psychiatrists are able to provide medications. They don't really treat the physical body like physicians normally do, but they have medical training. I have a really good friend who's a psychiatrist. He's very warm, and he's also a gay man," I said, realizing I was revealing more about a colleague than I normally would. "So I'm sure you'd feel safe with him, like you're beginning to feel with me and with Nathan."

"Would I have to go to a hospital or some kind of health clinic?" she asked.

"No, he has an office a few blocks from here and sees people privately, just like I do."

"Why can't *you* just give me the medications?"

"Because in Massachusetts, psychologists aren't licensed to prescribe them."

"Would he have to know everything about me? I don't want to have to talk to someone else about all the things I've told you."

"No, he would need to know about your symptoms and any kinds of thoughts or emotions that might be causing them now and, at least, understand there is a history of physical abuse. But he wouldn't need to know all the details of your whole history. However, I think it would be very valuable and help him to provide the most accurate medications if you would share more of the details. Your history is very much connected to everything you're experiencing now."

"Could I just see him and tell him about my sleeping and being nervous and depressed and not talk about my life at all?"

"In truth, my best guess is that, unless one of us provides a reasonable amount of information, he might be hesitant to provide medications, since he might not be able to accurately understand what you need. It would be like going to a doctor, which I know you don't want to do, and telling him you're in pain, but not where it hurts."

Anne thought about this for a moment. "Okay," she said finally. "Well, if you'd call him and tell him whatever he needs to know before I see him. You're sure he's really nice and won't get mad or yell if I say something wrong?"

Realizing the depth of Anne's fear, I felt bad for her, knowing she was going to be very frightened following through with this. I found myself saying what her friends had told her to get her to see me initially.

"I promise he won't get mad or yell and will be incredibly caring and kind. I would never, in any way, knowingly, put you at risk to be hurt by someone, Anne."

"Okay," she said uncertainly.

"I'll call him today and make sure he can see you soon, and then I'll call you to set up an appointment. His name is Dr. Howard." There was a pause as we sat there looking at each other waiting for some direction.

Then, suddenly, Anne made one of her abrupt transitions.

"I met this woman named Nicole, and she put her hand on my hand while we were at a movie. Is this considered the beginning of sex?"

Wondering how much this event might be contributing to her anxiety, I responded, "Well, I can't really speak for what Nicole might want or feel, but it's often a gesture of affection that might mean she feels attracted or connected and would want to have more of a physical or sexual relationship. How would that feel for you if it was a prelude to more physical touch or sex?"

"I wouldn't want to have sex," she answered quickly.

"Do you feel you would never want to have sex with her?"

"I don't know. It would seem really weird and horrible."

I hesitated for a moment, wondering how to proceed. Then, one of those crucial questions that could prove overwhelming, revealing, helpful, or maybe all three came to mind.

"Have you ever had sex, Anne?" I ventured. It would have been easy for me to assume that Anne would not consider the sexual abuse she'd suffered as "having sex," but that was an assumption I wasn't willing to make. Her interpretation of that part of her history was crucial to her identity and to her ability to ever explore or enjoy sexuality.

She looked at me with a strange expression, both perplexed and confused.

"What do you mean?" she asked, the question mark obvious on her face.

"I want to know how you understand what's happened in your life in terms of sexual experiences. It's something important you'll need to figure out eventually, and I guess I'm concerned this is going to come up as an issue before you may be emotionally prepared to deal with it. Sex is a natural part of dating for most women."

"Does that mean if I date someone I have to have sex?" Anne asked apprehensively.

"It doesn't mean you have to do anything," I responded, feeling like a parent talking with a shy sixteen-year-old daughter. "It means it's likely to come up eventually. You're concerned it may be surfacing already."

"So, what should I do? I don't really know what having sex with another woman would mean. I mean, Mickie and her friends make jokes and talk about it all the time, but I don't even listen, 'cause I don't know some of the things they're talking about. I feel really stupid. I'm so different from everyone else, and I don't fit into this place."

"I know this may be hard to take on faith, but in time you'll also feel real familiarity with this world and will find ways to fit in. But it won't happen nearly as quickly as you might want. I truly believe you'll do well at finding your way, but I also believe it will take time."

Anne shifted her glance from me downward and just looked sad. I knew that what I'd said was easier said than done, and that she knew it would be a lonely, scary, and painful time. After a pause, I asked, "Would you be willing to try to answer my earlier question, since that's what took us down this path about having to deal with so much that's confusing?"

Anne looked puzzled. "You mean about whether I've ever had sex?" she asked, looking annoyed.

"Yes," I said, nodding.

"You know they had sex with me many times, so why do you ask that?"

"I want to know how you've come to view it, whether you saw it ..."

I stopped in mid-sentence, not wanting to lead her answer. She needed to form a response herself or maybe not at all. So I continued, "I want you to just answer however you want."

"Well, I didn't feel like I was having sex. I didn't even know what sex was or that it was something called sex. I thought it was how the elders got rid of sin and punished me. But when Mickie and her friends talk about sex, they seem to like it and say it feels really good. It was always painful for me, and I didn't like it. So I don't know. Do you think I've had sex?"

"Well, it sounds like it was more about something being done to you than as something you chose to express. I guess I want you to at least be open to the belief that a sexual relationship would be something completely different from what you've experienced. That doesn't mean it's something you ever have to choose to do, but I don't want you to never have sex just because you fear it would be anything like what you've endured."

"Well, what would I have to do if I had sex with someone?" she asked.

I thought about the naïveté in this question and wondered about whether it was appropriate, being a man, to help her understand women's sexuality. My gut gave me the answer. "You know, not being a woman, I don't think I'm the person to help you know more about what women do with each other sexually. How would you feel maybe asking Mickie the question you asked me?" I asked, a slight hesitance in my voice.

I felt conflicted between my uncertainty that Mickie could handle this with enough sensitivity, and whether to throw another therapist, albeit a woman, into the mix. This just felt like too much for Anne to grasp and endure.

"Why can't you just tell me?" she pleaded.

"Because I'd be guessing, and I don't see that as right or necessarily helpful," I responded, feeling less certain about my directional choice.

I was about to offer the idea of speaking with a lesbian colleague when Anne said, "Well, Mickie loves to talk about sex, so I guess I could ask her." It was almost as if she was rescuing me, or both of us, from the dilemma.

"Just see how that goes, and we can figure it out from there," I said, relieved to have worked through the impasse, at least momentarily.

"Okay," she agreed.

Then, abruptly changing direction again, she said, "Can I show you a couple of things I brought in?"

"Sure, but we're almost out of time for today. Is it something I can read before our next session?"

"No, it's a picture of me as a child that my mother sent me last week and a quilt I made last night."

Even before she took the photo out of her backpack, I was immensely curious to see what the child Anne, who had endured incredible pain and survived, would look like. But when Anne handed me the photo, I was struck by how typical looking she had been. I had no idea what I'd expected, but I guess a part of me had thought she'd look distinctive in some way, perhaps miserable or malnourished or bruised, all stereotypes I held regarding abused children. However, when I thought about it, Anne's perpetrators were very committed to hiding their maltreatment of children, at least in any way that would be discernable to outsiders or members of The Christian Movement who weren't aware of what was happening to Anne and other children.

My reaction, I think, was motivated by a vestige of denial still lurking inside me, denial that my species could treat its young so cruelly. Then, as I was looking at the photo, Anne startled me again. "This is the first time I've ever seen a picture of myself as a child," she said. "I'm surprised it was even taken, since I don't ever really remember a picture being taken of me. I remember some pictures being taken of my brother and one time of my parents, but not any of me. We didn't have any mirrors, since they were considered to be about self-absorption, and we weren't supposed to focus on our appearance. So, the only images I ever had were reflections from a window or the pond on the farm, but they didn't really let me see what I looked like, not like a photo does."

"So, what are your thoughts when you see this picture of yourself?" I asked.

"I don't know. I'm not smiling or anything, and I look kind of sad. My clothes look weird. They don't really seem to fit. I kind of don't really look cared for, but that was what the kids were dressed like, I guess. Now, though, I see people dress their kids really cool for photos, but I don't know if that means they care more about them or just want them to look good for others."

"I think that's the thing I see as well, a little girl who's shut down. But you and I know this little girl had lots of feelings and thoughts, but had to put them away. As for the clothing, I assume you were given hand-me-downs from other families?"

"Yeah, that's true, but they could have given me ones that fit a little better," she said.

"They could have done a lot of things a whole lot better," I allowed myself to comment, loving, as I did, our moments of accord.

Anne simply smiled, knowing by now that I liked getting in a shot at her family and the church once in a while.

"So, can I show you the quilt?" she asked.

"Sure, but we may have to talk about it more next week," I said, checking my watch.

Anne reached into her little backpack of expression again and extracted a really beautiful quilt that was large enough to cover a king-sized bed. It was multihued, with a heart in the center in which she'd sewn in the rainbow colors.

"It's about myself, and the heart represents my sexuality," she said, her eyes shining. There were silhouettes around the heart that she described as her new community of friends and people helping her and angels that were looking out for her for the first time in her life. The cuts of fabric were more haphazard than symmetrical, representing confusion about her spirituality, she told me.

As usual, I was enchanted and stared at it for several minutes, before I realized the time.

"Wow, we have to stop right now," I exclaimed. "I have a client in about two minutes."

Anne gave Madison her usual hug and stood up, turning to me with a smile. It felt like we had traversed another rocky path fairly well.

— CHAPTER EIGHTEEN —

During our session the following week, Anne was in generally good spirits. I was more attuned to the yo-yo–like pattern in her emotional state, which traversed from more upbeat and relaxed to heightened anxiety and depression. She had called during the week to confirm she had set up an appointment with Dr. Howard, but she had not seen him yet. I wondered if her markedly improved emotional state reflected either a desire to avoid medications or relief after having let out some powerful and painful secrets about her childhood, including her father's role in the abuse.

Anne interrupted our usual opening silence as Madison performed his ritual of turning in circles on the sofa and then plopping his big head in her lap. "He's so cool," she said. "You know I have nine cats, but Madison is so different. He's like my friend, and I can't wait to see him every week." Madison's ears perked up and his tailed wag, hearing his name.

I simply loved having my four-legged co-therapist in the office, and I knew he offered her an immediate comfort that probably enabled her to hang in there during the early months when she was still frightened of me. "Yeah, he's really pretty cool," I agreed. "And I think he really likes you," I said, taken aback by the "nine cats." "How did you end up with nine cats?" I then asked.

"I've kind of rescued them. At first, there were just two, but after I started leaving milk and food out, more of them started hanging out. So, now I kind of have all nine of them living around my place. I've named all of them and can't tell if they actually have other homes or were abandoned."

As much as the number of cats surprised me, her care for them didn't at all. "I realize how important animals are to your life and you feel comfortable with them."

"Yeah, I kinda think so," she said, her smile reflecting her awareness that we both knew this was something she couldn't feel with humans. After that, our traditional quiet ensued.

"So, is there anything you wanted to talk about today?" I asked, silently hoping we could return to something I wanted to ask about from our previous session.

"Not really," she replied, her meek tone reflecting her trepidation about what I might want to talk about.

This wasn't lost on me, but I had begun to feel that talking about the abuse, as painful as it was to do, was also helping to decrease her anxiety and depression. "When you talked last time about the nurse who examined you when you were taken from your home, you said she may have noticed your fingers had been broken before. Can you talk about this today?"

"I figured you were going to ask me to talk about that," Anne said.

"When I was nine, I was learning to play the piano and could pick out tunes quite easily. I started trying to work out what other notes to play, and my dad became really angry. He said I was better than my brother, Jacob, and that it was wrong and not God's order for me to be better than a boy. He then slammed the piano lid shut on my hands, getting all four fingers on each hand. It was an old, really heavy wooden piano, and it broke several of my fingers. I don't remember how many, but my mom had to wrap them up, and someone on the farm did something to make sure they healed properly. Eventually, they got better, and they don't even bother me anymore."

I felt myself sink a little, as I had before a couple of times when I listened to what had happened to her. I just gave her a look of sadness, which Anne always seemed to notice. She smiled slightly, mirroring my expression.

"That must have hurt incredibly," I said. "Did you cry when it happened?" I asked, wanting to know how she reacted to that level of pain in front of her father.

"No, I never really cried when anyone was around. I'm pretty sure I screamed for a few seconds. It hurt really badly for weeks. I wasn't allowed to have anything for the pain, but the pain eventually got better. I remember my mother, one of the two times I ever remember, looked at my father with a how-could-you look when she came running into the room, saw the piano lid on my fingers, and lifted it. She knew he did things to me and sometimes punished me to get rid of sin and do the work of God, but I kind of think this was beyond that, since it had seriously injured me and I was still her child."

"So, care to tell me about the only other time she seemed perturbed by one of his abusive behaviors?" I asked, bracing my stomach and my mind for the next example.

"Well, the other one wasn't really abusive. My mom and I called it 'The Christmas Cake Incident.' One Christmas when I was probably about ten, my mom made this Christmas cake with a really cool snow scene, with Santa and a sleigh and some trees and two kids. One was a boy for my brother, and the other a girl for me. We were made of marzipan, and I think this was one of the few ways she could kind of give us a little Christmas, since my father wouldn't allow any presents or a tree or anything.

"When she brought it to the table, my dad took a toothpick and stuck it through the little girl, making it look like she'd been stabbed. My mom gave him that look then, but it may have been mostly because he had ruined her cake and Christmas scene. He started laughing about stabbing me and carried a big knife around with him the rest of the night."

Anne and I both sat there for about thirty seconds, me absorbing what I had heard and Anne probably doing what she did to disconnect from the emotional power of this moment in her history. I didn't have her defenses, and it was all so new to me and so outside my understanding of human capacity—both her father's capacity to inflict such harm on a child, and hers to survive and put it away somewhere. Inside I was thinking "What a sadistic bastard," but I managed to contain myself and try to stay where Anne was.

I thought for a moment that maybe a true survivor is that rare person who has a strength that is somehow equal to or greater than the strength of evil possessed by a perpetrator. Each of their strengths was way out on the continuum of typical human capacity. Anne didn't indicate any interest or desire to talk about this incident further, however, and I was okay to let her guide us, so I asked if we might talk more about her time in the Lewis's home.

"Okay," she said agreeably. "But I can't remember where we left off."

"You told me you took a nap in your room," I reminded her, "and that Mrs. Lewis's daughter had knocked on your door and told you that she was a foster child too."

Anne smiled, remembering. "Yeah, Jeanne was nice, and she gave me a teddy bear," she said. "And I spent most of the next six weeks lying in bed, hugging it and crying, except when Mrs. Lewis asked me to join them for meals. I also started homeschooling with a tutor Ms. Connors, the social worker, had provided."

"Did you do anything else with the family, Anne?" I asked.

"Yeah, I went to church with them on Sundays, but I didn't like it. They'd asked me if I'd go, though, and I didn't want to offend them. Plus, I was scared to offend God. But I was also scared to go to a church outside the farm, 'cause God probably wouldn't like that either," she said.

"Kind of a catch-22, I guess." I smiled.

She grinned, remembering the term and, I hoped, feeling good that she was just one step closer to being "in the know," since she was so afraid she wouldn't fit in to life outside the farm.

"Yeah, it was hard to know what to do, 'cause I didn't know what the rules were," she said. "I sometimes played with the other kids at the house, but I didn't know the games either. So my favorite thing was to watch television.

That was nice 'cause we could just sit there together and watch, but we didn't have to talk or do anything."

On her third day at the family's home, her mother had visited, accompanied by Ms. Connors. Anne was glad to see her mother but showed no affection when she arrived, having learned to hide all of her emotionality around her family and almost anywhere else. They'd sat in the living room for about thirty minutes, and her mother had asked basic questions about how she was doing and how she was being treated.

Each time she'd asked, Anne had answered softly only "Okay." Ms. Connors had done her best to facilitate the discussion, encouraging Anne to talk about her schooling, meals, or anything else she could think to bring up. When the conversation still seemed to hit a dead end, she'd tried to be encouraging, indicating that it was often difficult to have a visitor and know what to do. Anne learned subsequently, from talking with one of the other kids, that her mother's visit had been supervised. One of the older, more experienced kids had explained that supervision during parental visits was common in child-abuse situations, to protect the children and to observe how they were treated by their parents.

The words "child abuse" alarmed and confused Anne, who believed that her father's behavior had been for her own good. She also didn't know how anyone would know about how he'd treated her and, after learning her visits with her mother were being supervised, she worried that people believed it was her mother who had hurt her.

Abuse was a word that Anne heard Ms. Connors use, too. Ms. Connors had arranged for Anne to talk to a psychologist while she was at the Lewis' house, a woman she'd met with a number of times. Anne told me that the psychologist had asked her to play with dolls as a way of sharing things that might have happened to her. Sometimes she'd also asked Anne to draw pictures with pencils or crayons.

"What did you draw?" I asked Anne, curious to know if the creativity she demonstrated so beautifully in her quilts had been apparent in her drawing, too.

"Oh, pictures of myself, my family, the trees and animals on the farm, and my house," Anne said. "Sometimes the psychologist gave me tests, too. I had to play with blocks and construct puzzles."

"What was that like?" I asked.

"I guess I was always afraid I was betraying God or my family by even talking to them, but I was afraid not to do what they said. So I just followed instructions, but didn't talk much," Anne replied.

"So, if you didn't talk, what happened?" I asked Anne.

"Well, they kept saying things like, 'Anne, we know people have hurt you, and we need you to tell us about these experiences.' But I wondered how they knew, and, if they knew, then why were they asking me?" Anne said. "They didn't hit me or anything to get me to answer, but I could tell they were annoyed. But I was more afraid of the elders than of them. The elders could cast a spell on me if I told anything, so I kept quiet."

Indeed, it seemed that Ms. Connors and the psychologist had been stymied as to how to reach Anne. Ms. Connors noted approximately six weeks after Anne had arrived at the Lewis's home that, during the sessions with the psychologist, Anne simply "sat and rocked back and forth, possibly as a means of soothing herself.... Without further corroboration," the report concluded, "we were obligated to return Anne to her parents' custody and close the case."

It hadn't been long after Ms. Connors submitted that report that Mrs. Lewis had knocked on Anne's bedroom door, as she customarily did when Anne had visitors. This time, however, not only was Anne's mother there with Ms. Connors, but her father was also standing in the living room.

"Anne tensed up," Ms. Connors had reported of the encounter.

Reading her report, I'd felt, or perhaps read into it, the distress I imagined the social worker had felt at that moment. Ms. Connors's experience had trained her to recognize abused children, and so she would have been near certain that, despite the lack of evidence to corroborate the tip police had received, Anne had been violated. But she'd had no choice other than to release Anne to the custody of her parents.

"I did not provide Anne with my phone number or suggest that she call me if necessary in the future," Ms. Connors had concluded, "as I suspected that doing so could increase the probability of retribution."

It was not only Ms. Connors who had needed to demonstrate restraint at this moment. Anne's response to her parents' arrival had been equally reserved, especially given the tumultuous mixture of feelings Anne recalled having experienced, seeing them both in the Lewis's living room.

"As I entered the room, Ms. Connors stood up and explained that my parents had come to take me home. I remember I had mixed feelings. I was relieved knowing I could go home and my father wouldn't think I was sinning or betraying the church anymore, and I was afraid I'd be severely punished for having been taken away. But, it was kind of funny when I looked up at my father for a minute. His face was calm, and that was really unusual. I sort of knew he was happy I hadn't said anything to hurt the church or him in all that time."

Anne's recollections of that time were further corroborated by Ms. Connors's report. "Mr. Martin rather abruptly asked if they were free to take 'our child home.' He then turned to Mrs. Martin and said, 'Let's go, Mother,' and Mrs. Martin stood, took Anne's arm, and, in a very hushed voice, said, 'Thank you' to Mrs. Lewis. I had the impression that she was being very careful to hide even this sentiment of appreciation from one mother to another from her husband."

"What about Mrs. Lewis?" I asked Anne. "How did she react to your sudden departure?"

"She seemed kind of sad," Anne said, "and she gave me a hug. I wanted to hug her back, but I didn't want my father to think I'd been disloyal in my feelings to my family, so I just stood there. I think Ms. Connors understood why I couldn't show any affection, 'cause she didn't try to hug me."

As they had driven away, Anne told me, her father had asked her what she had said about their family, the elders, or life on the farm. She had responded that she had said "nothing," and her father had not interrogated her further, which, Anne thought, seemed to indicate he might have believed her. After all, they were allowing her to go home, and that said a lot about what they could have learned.

She had not been at all certain, however, that, once at home, life would return to normal. But she told me that, for the next six months, she had not been subjected to any further abuse.

This hadn't relieved her fear, however. Unable to discern if the reprieve was some kind of reward for her behavior or if Father Jonas and the elders feared the authorities might still be investigating The Christian Movement, she remained constantly vigilant when any of them approached her and fearful that any day they would resume their abuse.

As the time of the hiatus lengthened, however, she allowed herself to vacillate between hope that having been investigated provided her safety, and increased anxiety that, as time decreased their fear of further investigation, they'd be more likely to hurt her again.

Before winding up for the session, I had one last question. "Why do you think social services took you away at that time, Anne?"

"Well, I didn't know then, but I later heard that a family that had recently moved away and was angry with the church may have called them or called the police or something. They'd had a falling out with Father Jonas about church teachings or beliefs. I kind of know this, because my mom told me she was asked about her relationship with the mother of this family. So, I think she was pretty sure that was why this happened at the time."

As Anne left that day, I felt especially satisfied with our session. I had learned a great deal about why she had not cooperated with the authorities when they'd intervened on her behalf, and I looked forward to sharing the information with Nathan, since he'd been so concerned that this aspect of

Anne's history could hinder her case. As the door closed, I picked up the phone and dialed his office in Portland.

— CHAPTER NINETEEN —

The next morning Anne had woken early, feeling both excited and nervous about her journey for the day. She'd looked forward to going into the city but had been intimidated by it. She'd also had some fear that members of the church might be able to find her there. Officers at the safe house had given her numerous assurances that the safe house was well hidden and protected, but had made no such assertions regarding other places.

But Anne had reminded herself that it had been her own request that this meeting take place at Nathan Cohen's office, an appeal based on her desire to venture beyond the safe house. She hadn't stepped foot off the small property since arriving there, except to go out into the backyard, which was fenced and secluded.

So, despite her apprehension, Anne had gone downstairs for her usual breakfast of oatmeal, toast and coffee. Being a creature of habit, who was unfamiliar with the concept of choices, she'd eaten the same thing every day at the safe house.

It had been arranged for her favorite police guard to accompany her to meet with Nathan. Mike, as Anne had come to call him, was the one male officer with whom she felt comfortable. "I had no idea why he felt safe, but he had from the beginning. He was kind, and he didn't look at me the way most men look at women," Anne told me.

Officer Mike was also black, and no black person had ever harmed her. In truth, she hadn't seen many black people, except for a rare kid recruiters brought to the farm to help find God and overcome his sinning ways. Mike also liked to laugh and be playful, and they would play cards together and hang out on the back porch on occasion, just shooting the breeze.

Mike had become a comforting friendly face to Anne. The nights he'd been on duty, he'd sit in her room for a few minutes to ask how she was doing and if there was anything she needed. If Anne could have trusted anyone to be close to her, it would have been Mike.

"We need to get going, Miss Anne," Officer Mike said, coming into the kitchen as Anne was finishing her breakfast.

A few minutes later they were headed toward downtown Portland in a car that, Anne had later told me, "looked just like the type the police drove, but it didn't have the usual blue and white colors with all the words that identified it as a police car. It didn't have a siren on top either, but there was one sitting inside the car."

Mike had noticed her staring at it. "Do you know what that is?" he'd asked.

Anne had become comfortable enough with Mike to respond normally to questions, not hesitantly or in a hushed voice. It was okay for him to see her ignorance, and he was gently helping her to learn about the normal world.

"It looks like the ones on police cars," she'd said. "Did it fall off?"

Mike had smiled, but even after having known Anne only a short time, he'd understood that she was sensitive regarding her naïveté about much of the world. So he explained that he could attach the siren to the car's roof with a strong magnet.

"It's only for use in emergencies, though," he'd added.

Otherwise, the car had been unidentifiable as a police car. This had made sense to Anne but still seemed somewhat strange, since Mike was wearing a police uniform and was, therefore, anything but anonymous. But she'd felt far from being safe enough to challenge anyone, even Mike.

"So, how are you feeling today, Ms. Anne?" Mike had asked as they'd driven down the freeway heading into downtown Portland. He'd often called her that. It was odd, Anne had thought, but she kind of liked it. She'd had absolutely no cultural or interracial experience to make any meaning of what Mike had intended as an expression of affection and respect for her strength.

"I'm kind of scared," she'd said truthfully.

"What might you be afraid of this morning?" Mike had asked kindly.

"I don't know. I've never really been in a big city."

"I can understand this isn't familiar, but I'll be there with you. If you feel too uncomfortable with something, you look at me and wink, okay?"

"Yeah, that would be okay," Anne responded, smiling at Mike appreciatively.

"It's kind of our secret language for today, Miss Anne," Mike said.

Anne had thought that was "really cool." Making things lighter or playful had been one of her means of emotional and psychological survival her whole life.

As they'd exited the freeway, Anne had been somewhat overwhelmed by the tall buildings and all the cars and people. It had been like arriving in a foreign land, full of customs and sights that were both exciting and unpredictable, each of which produced a rush, some good and some not so good. She could have been in Paris or Moscow for all she'd understood around her.

CHAPTER TWENTY

After completing a review of his notes from his last meeting with Anne, Nathan opened the door to the waiting room that served the attorneys representing victims of crime in the state of Oregon.

As he did so, he reflected upon the thought, sensitivity, and considerable personal funds he had committed to its design. He'd placed the comfortable loveseats and club chairs far enough apart to provide boundaries between the clients occupying them. And the colors were mauve and pale green, chosen on the advice of an interior designer who consulted with psychiatric hospitals in developing appropriately soothing and sensitive décor.

The décor, he thought, expensive yet welcoming, reflected his personal taste and his commitment to go beyond the typically drab and limited offerings provided by public agencies. He observed that Anne, who was engaged in conversation with the officer who had accompanied her, appeared to be quite anxious, and Nathan's impression was that the policeman was trying to distract her from her anxiety.

"Hello, Anne," Nathan said, walking toward them and also briefly introducing himself to the officer.

"Pleased to meet you. I'm Mike Jones," the affable-looking policeman said, extending a beefy hand.

"Welcome to my office. We'll need about two hours, officer," he said, assuming the policeman would wait. But then, seeing Anne's fearful look, he asked her, "Would you be more comfortable if Officer Jones remained outside or joined us? That is, Officer Jones, if you're available?"

"I'd feel better if he could stay," Anne said with a pleading look.

"Of course, Miss Anne," Mike smiled. "Please call me 'Mike,'" he added, directing himself to Nathan.

"Then, how about if we all go into my office," Nathan said. He felt it would help alleviate some of Anne's trepidation if he immediately took charge of structuring their meeting.

Anne and Mike stood up and walked toward the door, and Nathan gestured to one of the two maroon leather lounge chairs on one side of a mahogany coffee table.

"How about if you sit in this chair, Anne, and Mike, maybe you could sit next to Anne here," Nathan invited. Then, walking around to the other side of the coffee table, he said, "I'll sit over here."

Either out of politeness or some uncertainty, Anne and Mike waited for Nathan to reach his chair and then sat down almost simultaneously.

"So, how are you doing today, Anne?" Nathan began.

"Okay," came the barely audible reply.

"You seem more anxious or uncomfortable today," Nathan observed.

"Yeah, I am. This is a big building, bigger than any building I've ever been in, and the elevator was very scary."

"Was there a problem with the elevator, or do you get claustrophobic?" he asked, realizing that even a simple mechanical glitch could set her back.

"What does that mean?" she asked, looking a little embarrassed.

"Oh, I'm sorry, it means you get frightened when you're in small or enclosed spaces, like an elevator," he answered.

"Yeah, that's really scary. It reminds me of my past …" Anne said, her words trailing off.

"What are you referring to in your past?" Nathan asked, taking the reference as a cue.

After a pause, Anne mumbled, "being kept in the cages," looking down toward the floor.

Nathan and Mike looked surprised, although Mike almost instantly realized this must have been why she'd been afraid of the elevator door closing. As for Nathan, he'd certainly encountered cases of children being caged and restrained, but he hadn't known of any such abuse being perpetrated against Anne.

"What do you mean by 'the cages'?" he asked, alert for any new information that could help her case.

But Anne had withdrawn again. "Can we talk about this another time?" she asked.

She'd aroused Nathan's curiosity, and he felt frustrated. But he simply replied, "Absolutely. I assume it doesn't have any connection to Mr. Jenkins?"

"No, he was never a part of any of that as far as I know."

"Well, how about if we go ahead and talk for a while, and when we're finished, maybe I'll walk with you down the stairs and show you around the building," he coaxed. He hoped giving her a tour of the building would help prepare her to deal with the legal world, a public trial, and the adversarial circumstances she would inevitably face, from which he could only protect her to a limited degree. He knew that, ironically, she had faced far more adversarial circumstances, but this was a horse of a different color.

"That would be neat," Anne said, perking up a little. "Actually, this building is pretty cool. Until today, though, I've never been in a building taller than two floors, not counting the basement. How tall is this building?"

"Actually, it's seven stories, not counting the garage levels," Nathan told her, pleased to have engaged her interest.

"What's a story?" she asked, and, once again, he remembered how much her sheltered history had precluded awareness of so many basic things in the world.

"A story is another word for a floor. I think it may have its origin from long ago, when windows of buildings had words and stories on them, either in stained glass or etchings," he said, congratulating himself for having information at the ready to keep the conversation progressing, even if unsure about the veracity.

"Oh, that's cool. I've seen that in churches," she said, seeming genuinely interested and easily able to relate to a religious reference.

"My guess is that it began with church windows, since churches were usually the most ornate and important buildings in communities, and the stories of the Bible are often depicted on church windows," Nathan continued, hoping the conversation would somehow circle back around to Anne's experience.

"We didn't have that on our church windows. The only windows were too high up to be able to see pictures anyways," Anne said with a shrug.

Nathan wasn't surprised. Anne's church and community had a lot to keep hidden, he thought, wondering if that had been the architect's actual intent or a convenient coincidence for Jonas Smith.

"So, do you feel okay to try to talk some more about the church today?" he asked, directing the conversation back to his objective for their meeting.

"Yeah, I guess so," Anne said somewhat hesitantly.

"Good. Because I wanted to ask some questions that you might be able to help me understand," he said, trying to impart the sense that she could help him, since he knew that helping people was one of her primary motivators.

"Okay, I'll try," she said, rising to the task.

Nathan glanced at Mike, whose smile offered encouragement. "I wanted to ask what you might know about other children who were hurt or treated like you were," he said.

"What do you want to know?"

"Well, first of all, how many others might have been part of the abuse?"

Anne didn't answer right away, so Nathan realized that he had used a term she might not be fully in agreement with. So he continued, "I realize I'm using the word 'abuse,' and you might view it as something else, but that's the term the law and social services use to describe the things that have happened to you and, I assume, to other girls."

"Okay," Anne said meekly. "I'm not sure, but I think maybe fifteen to twenty."

"Were they all girls?"

"Yes, as far as I know. The only ones I ever knew about or saw in the cages or coming out from Father Jonas's office were always girls. The elders believed girls were bearers of sin and needed to be saved."

"Just out of curiosity, do you believe that, Anne?" Nathan asked, wary of disrupting the progression of his questions, but unable to resist asking. He also knew the damage inflicted by the brainwashing could impact both any civil litigation as well as her credibility.

"I guess I do," Anne said quietly, fearing that Nathan, like everyone else, would see her thinking as wrong and maybe be annoyed with her.

Then, cautiously, she asked, "Are you mad at me?"

"Why would you think that?" Nathan asked, feigning surprise as though the idea were unthinkable, although it was a familiar fear among his abused clients.

"Because you think I'm wrong."

"Wow. Well, I don't think you're wrong, but I think you've learned to see the world a certain way, and you've been taught to believe what you believe, just as I've been taught to believe things I believe, and they're different beliefs from mine, but I'm not at all annoyed or mad."

"Okay," Anne said, seeming to believe him.

"So, do you know the names of most of these other girls, Anne?"

"Some of them. But some of them were older or from families we didn't really know much."

"Were they from fifteen or twenty different families?"

"No, maybe about ten families."

"So, that means that in some families more than one girl was abused?"

"Yeah, I guess so," she said, wondering why that would matter.

"Did everyone in the church know what was going on?"

"No, only some of the adults, the elders, and probably the parents of the other girls."

"How many elders are there?"

"Well, between the elders and deacons, I think about fifteen— maybe six elders and nine or ten deacons," Anne answered. But then she seemed to realize the reason for his question, because she sat up straighter and asked, "Will I have to see these people in court or something?"

"I don't know that now, and it depends on a lot of things. If they're arrested and charged with crimes, and if they were to fight the charges and go to trial, you might have to testify. But that's months away, at least. It's also possible you might be asked to identify some of them in a lineup, but they wouldn't be able to see you or know you're there."

"What's a lineup?" Anne asked.

"It's a procedure for a witness or a victim to be able to pick someone out from a group of people who stand in a line, to identify someone as the person who committed a crime. You would pick the person out of the group, and if this fit with other evidence, it would become a powerful tool in our eventual prosecution." Seeing her posture stiffen, Nathan added, "But you wouldn't be in the same room, actually. You'd be looking at them behind a glass wall, and they wouldn't be able to see or hear you."

"Do I have to do that, pick someone out of a lineup? And do I have to testify?"

"That's a very complicated question, Anne. A judge could require that you testify, but you couldn't be forced to identify someone in a lineup. However, you might still be required to take the stand as a witness in court and be required to identify a person there."

Then, since she was obviously extremely apprehensive, Nathan added, "What does the idea of doing these things feel like for you, Anne?"

"Very uncomfortable and very scary," she said nervously.

"I can understand your discomfort, but what scares you the most?" he asked with a sympathetic tone.

"That they'll attack me," Anne responded, bringing her arms up to her body in a protective stance.

"Anywhere you might have to testify or identify anyone, you'll have police officers with you. And I'll also always be there to protect your rights," Nathan assured her.

"Okay, that would be good, I guess. Can Mike be there?" she asked, glancing toward Mike and offering a smile.

"Well, I don't know for sure, since it would need to work with his schedule, but we could certainly try to provide enough notice for him to see if he could arrange to be there. That is, assuming Mike's okay with that?" he said, turning toward the officer.

"I'd be more than happy to be there with you, Miss Anne, and, usually, with a little notice, that can be arranged," Mike offered with a warm smile.

"Cool!" was Anne's reply, sounding more boisterous.

For the second time, Nathan observed the camaraderie and sense of safety Anne felt with Mike. This kind of anchor might be crucial in providing enough of a sense of security for her to face strenuous cross-examination, he thought.

The meeting continued, with Nathan asking a lot of questions, in part to better understand Anne's history and in part to both assess Anne for the rigors of and familiarize her with the process she would face when opposing counsel attempted to discredit her testimony. As their time neared its end, Nathan said, "Anne, I have a couple of final and very important questions, and I need you to give me your honest answers, even if it's your best guess. Do you know of or believe there are any other children besides Amanda who might currently be being abused or be having sexual contact with members of the church?"

"Not that I know of," Anne responded, a hesitancy in her voice.

"How about in the past six months or year?"

"No one that I know of, but I haven't been babysitting for any other families for quite a while. I've been doing accounting for the church mostly, and only was helping out a few afternoons a week with Amanda and Eric."

"Okay, one last question for today, and then we'll stop. Are you at all afraid to talk to me or answer my questions or tell the truth or give me information about people at the church?"

"I'm kind of afraid," she answered truthfully. "But," she added, "I'm cool to answer the questions and will be honest, if that's what you mean. I'd never lie, because I'd be punished by God if I lied."

"I know you believe that, Anne," Nathan said, realizing, at that moment, that her fear of God would become vital in establishing her credibility with a jury. She would simply need to tell the jury what she'd just said. He took a moment to notate the exact words she had used, so that he could refer to them when eliciting her testimony in a courtroom. He knew that it would be ideal if Anne would speak spontaneously, but having a previously noted quote to fall back upon was probably the next best thing.

"Okay, then let's go find the stairs. I'll show you some of this building, and we can drive over to the courthouse, which is another building kind of like this one," he suggested, not wanting to take any chances with her safety by walking the short distance.

— CHAPTER TWENTY-ONE —

Three weeks had elapsed since Nathan's meeting with Anne at his office, and he had received notice of a court date for the trial of James Jenkins. The District Attorney had charged Mr. Jenkins with numerous counts of child abuse, rape, sexual acts with a minor, assault with the intent to commit bodily harm, including the injuries inflicted upon Anne, and withholding information regarding a criminal investigation. The trial was set to begin in two months in Portland. A grand jury had taken little time in handing down the charges after being provided a synopsis of testimony and physical evidence resulting from the police investigation.

The accused had refused a plea bargain, which didn't surprise Nathan, since all of the evidence was either circumstantial or statements provided by a child, either of which could be substantially challenged. There was no physical evidence, and Anne was only a witness to what she perceived as a sexual act, and Amanda's older brother, Eric, was a very limited witness, since his hiding under the bed prevented any eyewitness accounting and no words had been spoken.

In spite of widespread speculation regarding a much larger pattern of abuse within The Christian Movement, Nathan had presented Anne's case completely on its own merits, without reference to allegations and rumors regarding the community, including several past investigations and convictions.

Mr. Jenkins served as an administrator in the movement, but was not an elder, and thus, the church itself and the community might not be able to be held responsible for his actions. The movement had hired a very strong legal team, which had threatened a lawsuit if any such references in any way slandered the "good name and reputation of this upstanding Christian community, upon whom many people depended for faith, salvation, and survival," as the defense team had put it. Somewhat in conflict with the effort to disavow themselves of any connection to these crimes, the movement was covering Mr. Jenkins's substantial legal costs.

Soon after receiving notice of the court date, Nathan had contacted Anne at the safe house to invite her to come to his office so they could begin to discuss her eventual testimony. Nathan also knew that Anne would be the first witness and that this experience could set the stage for her comfort, credibility, and ability to provide testimony in ensuing trials, because even though defense attorneys in subsequent trials would be barred from bringing up her own history of abuse to diminish her credibility, they would be free to refer to her statements and actions in previous trials. He needed to protect Anne and simultaneously support the prosecution's ability to convict the perpetrators.

Anne arrived with Mike again serving as her escort, which pleased Nathan since Mike was already serving as a safety anchor. But she was nervous nonetheless, which he had anticipated and hoped considerable preparation would alleviate to some degree.

His plan to prepare Anne consisted of rehearsing what she would experience by creating a mock courtroom and using colleagues portraying opposing attorneys to question her so that she could practice testifying. Since the preparation would be very detailed and time-consuming, and because he was sensitive to Anne's comfort with this approach, Nathan caringly suggested, "Anne, I was wondering if maybe it would be nice for Mike to be able to have some free time for a couple of hours, since it's certainly safe here and we need to spend time just going over lots of details and history."

Anne shifted in her seat and began picking at the skin on one of her fingers, but responded, her voice shaking, "Yeah, that would be okay, I guess. Are you sure no one could find us here?"

"I'll tell you what. After Mike leaves, I'll lock the door to my office, and no one can enter without us knowing. And how about if we give Mike a secret knock so we know it's him. Does that sound okay?" Nathan asked, smiling a little.

Anne's face brightened at the prospect of increased safety and the idea of sharing a secret code. "Yeah, that would be cool. What will you use for a secret code?" she asked.

"How about if you think of a secret knock that only we three would know," Nathan suggested, wanting Anne to feel a role in her own safety.

"How about three knocks three times for the three of us?" Anne suggested, smiling.

Mike looked toward Nathan with a slight smile, enough to acknowledge his understanding of his intent, but not so much as to make Anne feel he was making fun of her in any way.

"Okay, that's cool, then I'll go wander for a while," he said, getting out of his seat. "I'll see you in a while, Miss Anne. You'll be safe here. This guy seems pretty careful about things," he added, ambling out. As soon as the door closed, Nathan visibly turned the lock, to assure Anne even further.

Anne sank a little further into her chair after Mike left, showing her heightened vulnerability. Nathan knew that the next thing he had to say wasn't going to lessen those feelings, but he had no choice.

Taking the chair across from Anne, he began. "We just received notice that a court date has been set for Mr. Jenkins's trial, and it's eight weeks from tomorrow. So that gives you and me almost two months to get you to a comfortable place testifying."

Noticing her glance shift downward, Nathan tried to offer some comfort. "I know this seems sudden and is very scary to hear, but you'll be in a much better place after we work together and prepare. You'll know me much better and have lots of practice." Then, realizing any further assurances would be redundant, he said, "So, tell me your thoughts and feelings hearing about the court date."

"I don't know if I can do it," Anne said, her voice quivering.

"You know what, that's okay. You don't need to know if you can do it. You just need to know you can do lots of practicing with me, and after all that practicing, you can then see how you're feeling."

"Does that mean if I don't think I can do it, I don't have to testify?"

"No, you will still have to testify, because you've witnessed a serious crime, and the court would issue you a subpoena and order you to testify."

"Yeah, but I already told them several times what I saw, so why do I have to tell people again? Isn't that what *you're* supposed to do, since you're a lawyer and it's a legal thing?"

"The law says that an accused person has the right to face his accusers, and that includes witnesses. Even though we know Mr. Jenkins is guilty and did very bad things, the way the law works is that he remains innocent until proven guilty in a courtroom. This is a case in which you're the only adult witness, and without your testimony he might not get convicted," Nathan said, his tone sounding more like a lecture. Quickly catching himself, he softened his tone and added, "I know that doesn't make this easier for you."

"I just don't want to have to see the elders, and I'm really afraid I'll screw it all up," Anne said, looking frightened.

"Remember, I want you to not focus on being in court right now and just pretend and role-play with me. You have to believe me when I say that this, like most things, gets better and easier with practice. So, can we at least start and see where it goes?"

"I guess so," Anne replied meekly.

"Well, let's get started. What I'd like to do today is have you go through the history with me, just as I'll ask you to do when you testify. First, let me ask if you've ever seen a trial or courtroom testimony anywhere?"

"No."

"How about on television or in a movie?"

"No, I've never really seen a movie except for a few films we saw in Sunday school," she said.

Nathan ventured a guess that these hadn't been films that would have involved a courtroom. At least he was working with a blank slate, he thought, so she wouldn't have negative images of witnesses being grilled or attacked by opposing attorneys or defendants losing control and attacking witnesses, as films occasionally depicted.

"Let me tell you a little about what the courtroom will look like then, Anne, since you've never seen one," Nathan began, reminding Anne of one of the courtrooms they had briefly viewed during their tour of the building a few weeks previously. "First, you'll walk up to the witness stand and be sworn in," he continued, explaining also the roles of the judge and jury and where everyone would be sitting.

It was a level of preparation that Nathan was accustomed to providing to child witnesses. He told Anne he'd like her to role-play a "first run-through," as he put it, of his questions to her. If she became nervous just knowing she'd have to participate in this safe and private setting, he would know they had a lot of work in front of them.

"Okay, Anne, I'm going to have you sit here and pretend you're in the witness box," he said, pointing.

"Do I really have to sit in a box?" Anne resisted.

"Well, it really is a box with a door that you go through and close behind you," Nathan replied, but even as he spoke, he realized he'd re-created the image of a cage. Not sure how to retreat, he decided instead to be real.

"I just now realized what that might sound like to you, like a cage from your childhood," he admitted softly.

"Yeah, that's what I was thinking. Do I have to be in a box?" Anne asked again, her frightened look returning.

Realizing how much he was asking her to just trust him, Nathan instead felt like another adult forcing Anne into something. "It's not really a box, actually," he said, backtracking some. "There is no top on the box. You'd be sitting in a chair, like you are now, and the sides of the box come around you, maybe up to your stomach, but there's nothing around you above that, and again there's no top. And it isn't locked. The door is just latched so that it stays in place, and you could unlatch it at any time and walk out. However, it would be important to try to stay there while you're testifying."

"Why do they have you sit in a box?" inquired Anne.

Nathan knew that question was coming even before the words came out. He was becoming familiar with Anne's combination of curiosity and seeking knowledge as a means of protection, or maybe even deflecting them from something uncomfortable. "Well, when you think of a courtroom, the judge sits in a box, and the jury sits in a long box. The witness box is slightly below the elevation of the judge, but higher than the box the jury sits in. Even the audience is sort of in its own large, boxed-in area, and it's at the lowest level, on the floor of the courtroom. I guess courtrooms box people into their roles, and maybe the heights of the boxes even define the importance of their respective roles in the courtroom."

Anne furrowed her eyebrows, indicating, Nathan thought, that she understood and agreed with his logic. In the very least, his explanation appeared to have diminished her sense of being the only person in a box. So he continued.

"Now, with all that said, there might be some other provision that could be made under the circumstances of your history, and I'll talk with the judge about it. Maybe there would be a way to keep the door open. I promise I'll ask, and we'll talk more about a comfortable way to do this. I'm really sorry I didn't think about the similarities with the cages," Nathan said, his words and tone showing care and support.

"That's cool. I know you weren't thinking of that," Anne assured him, her tone equally caring.

Nathan thought that in some ways this was an important event, made more so by their ability to work through it. It wouldn't be the last time he wasn't sensitive enough to the many things that could confuse or threaten her.

"So let's do this today, just sitting like we normally do, and not with me standing," he said.

"Will you have to stand when I testify?" Anne asked.

"Whenever an attorney is questioning a witness, he or she stands and asks the questions. The witness gets to sit and be more comfortable, however," Nathan said, smiling.

"Okay," replied Anne, with an amused look on her face. They both knew her being comfortable wasn't too likely.

"So, let's start. I'm going to ask you the kinds of questions I would ask in court."

"Okay," replied Anne again.

"Good morning. Would you state your full name for the court?" Nathan asked.

But when Anne just sat there, looking perplexed, he said, "Go ahead. I want you to answer the questions."

"Oh, okay. I wasn't sure if I was supposed to do that," Anne said, looking confused.

"Let's try again. Would you state your full name for the court?"

"Anne Martin."

"Please tell the court your date of birth, Ms. Martin."

"March 15, 1975."

"Ms. Martin, can you recall the date of Friday, December 4, 1998?"

"What do you mean?" Anne asked, making Nathan realize he hadn't been specific enough.

"Do you remember the events that happened on that particular day?" He tried again, feeling a little frustrated.

"Do you mean when I called the police?"

"Yes, that's the day I'm referring to."

"Yes, I remember that day."

"Would you please tell the court what happened that day?"

"Do you want me to tell you what happened the whole day, or when I called the police?"

Her questions, Nathan realized, showed how concrete her thinking was, and he wondered how this might frustrate the defense attorney. He also realized it might annoy a judge and jury. He tried to ignore a niggling sense of pressure. They had a lot of work to do considering that this was by far the easiest task she would face.

"I'd like you to describe the events that happened beginning when you arrived at the Jenkins' home that day."

As Anne began recounting the story, she seemed to relax, and Nathan found himself somewhat relieved, thinking that this part of her testimony might go relatively smoothly.

After she finished, he asked a couple of clarifying questions, and she seemed to respond without much difficulty. He considered going further and asking her a few questions that would serve to establish her credibility and commitment to telling the truth, but he knew she might construe this as a challenge and become too uncomfortable. So he wound up the session and set up a time for them to meet again the following week.

His goal in the first few weeks was to familiarize her with the types of questions she would face and with the overall type of proceedings and dialogue that typically occur in court. He also hoped to take her to the courthouse and familiarize her with mock testifying in the actual setting, and he knew it would be vital to further educate her regarding the role of the defense attorney. He hoped Anne could view her part as being like a role in a play, and learn to take things less personally.

But Nathan knew this was far easier said than done for most people, especially victims of abuse or rape, since personal attacks were among defense attorneys' most effective tactics to damage witnesses' credibility.

Still, in spite of her intense fears and fragility, he knew that Anne had great fortitude, a very good memory, and the inherent skills and ability to survive being under attack. However, he also knew her primary defenses were to withdraw and shut down rather than to fight, so he would need to help her find an alternative approach.

Just as he was contemplating this, Mike knocked at the door the prescribed nine times, calling out his name to identify himself. Nevertheless, Anne froze with fear.

Reminded once again of the depth of her fear, Nathan asked, "Are you okay if we open the door, since it's Mike?"

"How do you know it's really him?" Anne asked, looking frightened and wrapping her arms tightly around her chest.

"Well, it certainly sounds like him, and do you think anyone else would know both his name and the secret code we made up in here?"

"I guess not," Anne responded, feeling admonished.

"I have an idea," Nathan said, thankful for the inspiration. "Can you think of something only you and Mike would know about and ask him a question regarding that?"

Anne thought for a moment, too intimidated to venture a guess.

"Mike, Anne wants to be sure it's you, so she's thinking of a question she wants to ask you," Nathan called out.

"That's fine, Miss Anne. You ask whatever you'd like," the officer called back.

Hearing his voice, Anne looked up. "It's cool," she smiled. "Only Mike calls me 'Miss Anne' like that."

With that, Nathan opened the door. Anne smiled with obvious relief as she saw Mike standing there, and easily walked out the door into the world—as if Mike could single-handedly protect her from an onslaught of assailants.

Her trust was both powerful and inaccurate in terms of real danger, Nathan thought. It seemed that once she trusted someone, she inverted the magnified mistrust she carried for most people. Maybe there's a powerful natural desire to find a way to feel safe even in the midst of tremendous evidence to the contrary, he mused. If so, it might explain why people who have been hurt continue to trust again in their lives.

— CHAPTER TWENTY-TWO —

It was a beautiful day in early June. The air was warm, somewhere in the lower eighties, and wonderfully dry. It was one of those days I wanted to head over to the Charles River, put down a towel, watch the sailboats, and read myself to sleep. This was a play-hooky day for lots of people, I thought, but I had the kind of job where the impact of playing hooky was disconcerting for my clients, so off I went to work.

Arriving at the office, Anne, sporting bright green hair, immediately greeted me at the front door. I couldn't help but smile, and my reaction was not lost on her as she offered a somewhat strained smile in return.

This, plus the fact that she was fifteen minutes early for our appointment, indicated that something was up, so I chose to not address her fashion statement.

As I approached her, she looked somewhat contrite but didn't say anything. She gave me a worried look, and I debated asking if she was okay, but I decided not to initiate the session outside the boundaries and privacy of my office. I instead merely said hello and opened the door, whereupon Madison bounded into the waiting room, pulling me in before I could even extract the key.

"Just give me a few minutes, Anne," I said while I recovered my balance.

"Can Madison wait with me?" she asked.

"Why don't you ask him?" I smiled.

Anne gave me a whimsical look and immediately crouched on the floor, confident that Madison would join her, which he gladly did.

I disappeared into my office, where, after reviewing my schedule for the day, I opened the door. Anne stood up slowly, walked inside, and took her seat on the sofa, her pal promptly joining her.

We sat for a few moments in silence, as we usually did. But on this occasion, her silence was very loud and told me she had a lot to say.

"So, what's going on?" I asked.

"How do you know something's going on?" Anne asked, seeming pleased that I did know, but not entirely surprised.

"You're unusually quiet, and that tends to mean you're upset," I said, sharing her smile. Occasionally I sensed that Anne was holding back verbalizing what her facial expressions and body posture revealed, so that I might interpret her feeling, thus confirming that I was really connected. As much as she had gained trust in me, it was still somewhat fragile and she needed a lot of confirmation.

"I guess I am," she conceded. "Do you know we've been meeting for a year almost? Do you think I'm getting better? Sometimes, I wonder." She paused and, with a slight look of defiance, waited for a response from me.

As often happened when I heard that question or concern from a client, my stomach tightened a little. I guess it evoked that inner fear that's always back there somewhere, a fear that ultimately I haven't been helping someone.

But it was a question that naturally arose periodically, and could represent various underlying issues. I also always had to consider that just not getting worse could be the value of our work together.

"I'm aware that we're approaching a year," I said carefully. "But I think that more important than whether *I* think you're getting better is *you* wondering if you are. Would you like to talk about that first or tell me what in particular is upsetting you?"

"I don't know. I'm just really upset," she said petulantly.

"Can you tell me what's bothering you?"

"I called my mom, and my father got on the phone. He told me he was using my inheritance to visit my brother in the Philippines. I don't know why he's doing that to me. It's the first time in months that he's said or written anything mean to me. I thought maybe things were better after I told him that wasn't okay," Anne said, looking defeated.

I thought for a second and then said, "Well, progress is often two steps forward and one step back. The fact that it's been several months since he's written one of his mean notes may mean your willingness to confront him and set limits has had some effect. I guess that we have to keep in mind that he's eighty-four years old, and his ability to change, or maybe even remember you setting limits, may be very limited. It may take several approaches to have an ongoing impact. So, what hurts the most about what he said?"

"That he just wants to upset me or hurt me. I don't really understand why he would want to use my inheritance. He has the money to travel and doesn't need to use the inheritance. Nathan says that if I ever want to press charges or provide evidence against my father, we could also go after a civil settlement against his assets. I'm not really sure exactly what that means."

Her response contained so many pieces of information that I needed to decide on a direction for our discussion. Perhaps inspired by my belief in justice and my intense dislike of her father, I asked, "So, what keeps you from pressing charges, since your father was one of the perpetrators?" I asked.

"I could never do that. It would destroy my mother, and I can't do that to her. And he was only doing what he knew God was telling him to do. He believed he was punishing a sinner, and that's what our church believed. I'd like to stop him from giving away or using my inheritance, though. He's always said that I would never see any of his money, and that it's only going to his son and real child. So it's kind of strange that he's even acting like I was ever going to inherit anything."

"Well, it's pretty hard to tell what the reality is here," I said. "He may have never planned to leave you money and may just be trying to upset you. How does this affect how you feel about your father?"

Anne hesitated. "Sometimes I don't like him and he isn't nice to me," she said after a moment. As incredible as that understatement was, she was shifting toward a more accurate view of her father's actions and treatment of her.

"Okay, do you think he's being mean when he tries to hurt or upset you?" I asked, trying to encourage her to shift a little further. I strongly believed that until she saw his behavior as wrong and cruel, she wouldn't be able to see herself as innocent and good.

"Yeah, but that's what he's always been like."

"So, we agree he isn't a nice man and is hurtful to you. Do you think he can be a mean man?" I asked, feeling like I was taking on Nathan's role as an interrogator.

"He's very stern, but he's only mean to me and sometimes sort of to my mom," Anne said, her skeptical expression revealing that she knew I was leading her to view her father less charitably than she had done previously.

"Do you still believe you deserve to be treated this way, to have him deny you any inheritance and to say things to hurt you?" I asked.

Anne didn't respond, and, after a long pause, I asked, "Are you a little less certain that you deserve to have been treated the way you've been?"

"I think I'm more confused," she allowed.

"What's making you more confused, Anne?"

"I don't know. Everyone, including you, is always saying that this was wrong, and, I guess, as I feel a little better about myself at times, I don't think I did anything wrong or deserved to be treated this way," she said, although her lack of any visible anger conflicted with this statement.

Although I had an intuitive sense that she was progressing, along with moments of actually seeing evidence that she felt better, this was tangible feedback that indicated something was beginning to shift internally for her. Solid self-esteem wouldn't tolerate any sense of deserving to be abused or treated the way her father had treated her. We were taking those two steps forward, maybe even three, I thought.

"That's a fair answer, and I believe that someday you and I will look at what's happened in very similar ways. We'll both believe what was done to you was very wrong."

Anne looked at me, her expression impassive, as if she didn't want to hurt my feelings by contesting what I'd said but she couldn't really believe it either.

"So, what do you think you might need, besides resolution regarding the inheritance, that might allow you to be more at peace now?" I continued.

With a certainty in her tone, indicating this was something she had given a lot of thought to, Anne responded, "I want them to apologize and take responsibility. And I want my father to acknowledge he loves me and give me credit for how I'm doing now."

I heard her shift to "them" instead of "him," but I truly believed Anne's feelings were really about her father. So I chose to stay focused there.

"I can understand that," I said, "but I also really wonder if he's in any way capable of doing that, even if he feels it. That isn't who he's ever been at all. You know, underneath everything, you're a good, caring person, and that isn't going to change through your life. He is something quite the opposite, and I doubt it will change through his life. My fear is you want him to do something you need to do."

"What do you mean?"

"Well, in some ways it's about forgiveness, and I sort of see forgiveness as letting go of the negative feelings, the hurt, the anger, the sense of betrayal—and that doesn't mean letting go of believing someone was wrong. It means not carrying the pain with you everywhere you go, but you can still always know they were wrong. I don't even think it's important to communicate forgiveness to someone. It's something that needs to go on inside of us. For you, it may mean knowing you are absolutely a loveable person and he was wrong to abuse you. And you are worthy of all the credit imaginable to be where you are now. It's all about believing it inside yourself, irrespective of what he communicates. I know, like many of my pieces of advice, it's easier said than done. But it's still something to work toward."

"How do I do it?" Anne asked, her eyes glazed from having to process my speech.

"Well, I guess you begin by looking at what you truly believe. Do you believe it was wrong to abuse you and hurt you the way he did?"

"Yeah, I think I sometimes see it as wrong," she admitted softly.

"Do you see yourself as moving toward your own recovery and goals?"

"Yeah, sometimes," she said, her tone reflecting hesitancy.

"Well, that's the process I'm talking about, maybe slowly seeing yourself and things in a good light, and telling that to yourself every day. The research says that if you consistently tell yourself something positive, over time you may begin to believe it. Of course, the reverse can happen, and that's what happened throughout your childhood. You repeatedly heard you were a sinner and wrong and simply learned to accept it. This is about countering that message now. You didn't have the tools or the ability to do it then, not with all that was challenging you, but you do now. So, how about if you commit to saying one thing every day that addresses the needs you have from your father? I honestly think you feel your mom loved you and that she was almost as trapped as you were, so this is mostly about your dad. Could you try that?"

"I guess so," she said, seeming a little exhausted from the effort of coming to terms with all we'd discussed. I had definitely surpassed her stamina and ability to absorb my lectures today.

"That's fair, and I'll remember to check in with you about how it's going," I added.

My intense feelings about how wrong the abuse toward Anne was may have been instrumental in her progress so far. I just needed to remain aware of their presence and role in our work together.

We sat for a few moments, quietly looking at each other, smiling slightly in response to the awkwardness, and then Anne said, "I saw Dr. Pearl, and it was really horrible."

Having spoken with Dr. Pearl during the week, I knew that it had been very difficult for Anne. Dr. Pearl had shared that he found himself somewhat anxious, knowing he was intensifying Anne's terror, even if trying to help her. He also had indicated that his greatest concern was that he might find sexually transmitted diseases and physical damage, since she had been the victim of many years of unprotected sex and likely injurious events. He had chosen to not share this concern with Anne, unless there were adverse findings.

I had chosen to refer Anne to Dr. Pearl, a prominent OB/GYN, to assess Anne for several reasons. I certainly found him to be competent and conscientious, and I viewed him as compassionate and affable. He was also a good friend, and this gave me greater confidence that he would be even more sensitive to Anne's psychological distress and needs. Anne had stipulated the last criteria for selecting Dr. Pearl, however, insisting that he be a gay man.

"Do you want to talk about it a little?" I asked in a soft tone.

"I had a panic attack the morning of the appointment," Anne said matter-of-factly.

"What were you thinking about that morning?" I asked, hoping to help her better understand the connection between her history and her emotional response.

"I was thinking about letting a strange man touch me and put his hand and things inside me."

"How did you even know what to expect?" I asked, probably knowing the answer.

"Mickie told me what would happen, and she was really reassuring, but it didn't help that much. It was like reliving all the men in the church abusing me. I know he's a doctor and someone I should trust, but that was true of my dad and the elders," Anne said, looking downward.

"What happened during the examination?" I asked, struggling with whether delving further into this was helpful or just another painful intrusion.

"The whole thing probably lasted a minute or so, but it seemed like a long time. I was shaking, and I'm sure he knew I was terrified. He was really nice, but I think I did that disassociating thing and just stared at the ceiling. He tried to explain what he was doing, but I don't even think I heard anything he was saying."

"Maybe that's okay, and it's how you got through a really difficult experience again," I said, very caringly. "Did he share any thoughts about you not having periods for this long?"

Anne's posture relaxed as we shifted from her memory of the exam to a more informational place. "Yeah, he thinks it's probably due to all the stress I've had to deal with. He said that the only other reason this could happen to a woman my age was pregnancy and some rare disorders, all of which he felt confident about ruling out," Anne said, smiling slightly.

"Well, that's very important for us to talk more about since this is your body telling you that the stress is just too much."

"Yeah, I figured you'd say that," Anne said with a hint of sarcasm.

Looking at the clock, I realized our time was winding up for the session, and I wanted to ask her a question that had been on my mind for a couple of weeks. I had wanted to give her emotions the time to bring it forward, but that hadn't happened. "When you talked about your dream a couple of weeks ago and then about your brother sometimes watching your father with you, I wondered if your brother ever participated in these experiences," I asked.

Anne's silence loudly answered my question and, simultaneously, indicated she wasn't comfortable talking about the subject. So I backtracked.

"We don't have to talk about this now," I said. "I think I have the answer, but if you feel like writing about it or talking about it another time, maybe we could do that."

"Okay," she said meekly.

"So, we didn't really finish talking about your concerns with whether you're making progress. Do you want to talk more about that today?"

Back on more comfortable ground, Anne responded easily. "I know I'm moving forward, and I feel calmer in my life most of the time, but it all just seems so hard sometimes."

"I know that. And your father continues to have a real impact on you, although he has so little control over your day-to-day life now. I have no doubt in my mind that you're progressing all the time, but that doesn't necessarily make things easier. I often find as people get better and stronger, they challenge themselves at much higher levels, so they still feel like they're heading uphill and struggling."

"I'm working on a quilt about Dr. Pearl," she said then, in one of her quick changes of subject. "Would you like to see it when it's done?"

I answered, "Yes," and took this as a cue to leave the difficult stuff alone. I suggested we wind up. Her response was to brighten considerably, in part out of relief and maybe in part from knowing that I had learned to sense her limits better.

"So, aren't you going to ask about my hair?" Anne asked, realizing we were almost out of time.

"I figured you'd tell me about it if you wanted to."

"Isn't it the coolest green? It's environmentally friendly. I've been learning about global warming and some of the people whose villages and lives are being destroyed by it."

"Well, I think both the sentiment and the color are fabulous," I said, wondering if that sounded just too gay. "You've come in with different hair colors before, but today is the first time you've told me they have a particular meaning."

"Oh, they all do. The blue and purple days are the days when I'm feeling more down, but the hair color shocks people, so that makes me feel a little better."

"And the red hair?" I asked, feeling we were on a roll.

"Those are my angry days," she responded, quite surprisingly, since I'd never seen her express anger.

"I wonder why we've never talked about these important feelings?" I asked, regretting that I knew the answer. I had been missing her way of telling me what she couldn't express with words.

"I don't know. I guess it's easier to just color my hair than talk about feelings sometimes."

"My guess is that you're actually talking about the red days mostly, since you do talk about sadness but never about anger," I remarked. But, on this pensive note, I indicated we needed to stop and suggested that maybe we could talk more about the red days in the future. Anne said nothing, leaned over and gave Madison a hug, and walked out, smiling.

After Anne departed, I sat down on the sofa where my clients always sat and contemplated a book I'd read dealing with the concept of resilience. It discussed what characteristics were inherent in women who didn't just survive abuse and trauma, but thrived later in their lives.

Most inspiring to me was their strength, resilience, and dedication to have a good and seemingly normal adult life.

In many ways, Anne fit the book's description of someone who has great inner reserves. The authors had made it far easier for me to ascertain why Anne had survived, when most of her peers weren't even capable of testifying, let alone having viable lives.

One of those characteristics involves finding a meaning regarding why the abuse happened, and I had begun to believe that the powerful question of "why" was just beginning to surface for Anne.

— CHAPTER TWENTY-THREE —

When Anne and I met two weeks later, she seemed in a better space than she had the previous few weeks, even smiling slightly when I opened the door to my waiting room to invite her into my office.

Once she was settled, without saying anything, she took out a piece of paper and handed it to me. "I gather you'd like me to read this," I said.

She nodded. So I began to read.

LESSONS

"Look into her eyes. Look straight into her eyes, then push from your hips. Push for heaven's sake. How will she know who's in charge if you don't push?" I lay down on my bed, face up, trying not to move, as my brother attempted to follow directions. Eventually, my father lost patience and pulled him off.

"Watch—like this," he said, as he climbed on top and pinned my arms behind my back, pushing in and explaining what he was doing as he did it. Finally, he got off and stuck his clenched fist under my butt, so my hips were up in the air. "Try now," he said, and my brother got back on top of me. After what seemed like an eternity, the lesson ended, and I watched him hug my brother and tell him how well he'd done for a first try.

The "lessons" started when I was nine years old. "Timing is crucial," my father said. "Once she comes of an age, her sin will manifest itself as bleeding, and then there's a whole set of new problems. You must learn while she's still free of it." My brother tried hard, and his clumsy eleven-year-old attempts were not so much painful as uncomfortable and embarrassing. Occasionally, my mom would stick her head 'round the door and make comments like "Tea's in five minutes" or "Keep the noise down," but she never intervened.

As time went by, my brother's techniques improved. He could pin me down, undress me, and be finished in less than fifteen minutes. It also seemed like the older he got, the more he enjoyed it, but whatever the case, he called it his "duty." My father was obviously proud of his progress, but kept reminding him that soon the bleeding would start. I was hopeful that once it did, my brother would stop— that somehow the risk of contamination from my "sin" would be too great.

I was happy the first time I bled and wasted no time telling my father. I was convinced this would be the end of the lessons, but he had other ideas. It was essential that my brother perform his now "perfected" routine every day that I was bleeding, as this was the only sure way to protect the family from me and my sin.

I was around twelve, and my brother was seventeen. Even though we didn't have a normal brother/sister relationship, neither of us enjoyed the next few years. My father warned my brother about the danger of doing it when I wasn't bleeding, and he would constantly remind me that my "sin" had taken all the fun out of it. Occasionally, my father or the church elders would watch to make sure he was doing it right, and sometimes my brother would perform the "duty," but usually it was just him in the bedroom.

After a while, my periods became irregular and unpredictable, something of a relief for both of us. When he eventually left home, no one took over, but the thought of bleeding made me panic.

Once I left the church, I thought the fear of bleeding would go away, that it would be a part of the healing process, but my periods got more and more erratic, and the fear and panic intensified. Sometimes I had out-of-control bleeding that went on and on and on. It was scary, as I didn't understand why, and I wanted it to stop.

They say that the things that keep us together are our shared memories, but for my brother and me, our shared memories have torn us apart and created a rift that neither of us can mend. He says he was as much a victim as I was, the difference being that he can never seek help by having others understand. He says public opinion is against people like him, and that he would be hated and misunderstood. When I reflect back on it now, it's like we were trained animals.

For me, I think my brother needs his own lessons. I hope that one day he's in a situation where he has to trust someone when it's really hard, and I hope that when that happens, his lesson is that he can feel as unsafe as I did.

I sat there for a moment and felt a tear in my eye. My professional neutrality was fading, and my emotions were surfacing. My urge was to quickly block the visible emotion, but I couldn't. I looked up at Anne and realized she was watching me closely. A calm came over her. As inconspicuously as possible, which was not at all, since she was sitting six feet away looking right at me, I gently wiped the tear away.

I knew we were both avoiding the elephant in the room—the tear falling down my cheek and my brushing it away. I debated whether to address it if she didn't—although I didn't expect her to be that forward. One of my concerns was her proclivity to interpret my behaviors negatively until proven otherwise, and I knew she might construe the tear as an indication that I felt hurt or negative.

Deciding to address my response, I said, my voice somewhat shaky, "I'm very moved by your story, and I felt real sadness together with such respect for your strength."

A slight smile crossed her face. "Cool," she said softly, an expression of her care in that moment. It was also her way of telling me we were fine, and I almost wanted to keep crying from relief.

What had affected me the most as I listened to this portrayal of her role as a surrogate of sorts, I thought, was that it didn't shock me the way it would have a year earlier. I also realized that, maybe for the first time, she had reflected upon one of the horrendous experiences perpetrated upon her, and, without hearing how I or others viewed it, had come to understand how wrong and cruel it had been and had seen the perpetrators with such a perspective.

Over the fourteen months we had been working together, I had struggled with whether the men who had abused Anne and the other girls might truly view themselves as fulfilling God's mandate or whether they were sadists practicing intentional cruelty. Anne was clearly experiencing a parallel struggle now as we each, in our own way, tried to understand why the elders had treated girls this way.

So there was really little I needed to say. My sense was that my silence and the expression on my face told her I shared her sadness and confusion, at least as much as an observer could.

Deciding or needing to shift the topic, Anne said, "I'm having a really hard time with school." In her typical character, she didn't offer any further details, seemingly wanting me to ask questions that would direct our focus. I threw the ball back in her court.

"What's happening at school?" I asked.

"I can't go to two of my classes this week," she said.

"How come?" I asked, no longer very surprised by the abruptness of her segue ways.

"In my film class, the professor's showing *Silence of the Lambs*, and when I looked it up on the Internet, I knew I just couldn't watch it. And in my American history class, they were discussing slavery, and I got shaky and overwhelmed. We're supposed to read about it for this week, and I tried. But it's really upsetting. I'm worried I'll get in trouble and I won't pass."

"Have you talked with your professors about what you're feeling?"

"No, do you think I should do that?" she asked.

"How do you feel about talking with them about why this is difficult for you?"

"I don't know. Maybe they'll think I'm really weird or messed up or something," Anne said, glancing downward.

"Do you think they might be caring and compassionate?" I asked, offering a gentle smile.

"I don't know. One of them, my film professor, seems like she would."

"So, how about starting with her and seeing how that goes, since it seems safer? If that goes okay, then talk with your other teacher," I suggested, nodding my head to offer encouragement.

But Anne was still squeamish. "Couldn't you just write a note to get me out of the class, like a doctor's note or something?"

"Well, I have two thoughts. One is that you're going to face things throughout your life that are difficult and trigger painful memories, and you can't avoid them all. But, what you *can* do is learn to express your needs and your feelings at the time, whenever you can. If I wrote a note for you, then you wouldn't learn to feel okay protecting yourself. My other thought is that, well, you know I'm a professor, and if one of my students came to me and shared that she had a history of abuse or something really painful and the material was triggering issues, I'd listen very carefully, take it seriously, and respect her needs. And maybe we'd be able to work out some alternative."

"Yeah, but you're a psychologist, so you're supposed to be really sensitive about these things," she countered, her look of skepticism giving challenge to my obvious encouragement.

"Well, I know a lot of teachers and professors who aren't psychologists, and they care about their students. I guess, like many things, you are at some level taking a chance. But I truly believe the odds are in your favor."

Anne simply nodded. I had learned this represented an agreement of sorts, one with an asterisk that implied reluctance.

We were silent for a little while, and I wanted to take any further pressure off of her, so I asked, "So, you haven't talked much about your friend Mickie lately. Are things going okay with the friendship?"

Obviously relieved by the shift in subject, she seemed more energized as she responded. "Well, she and her girlfriend are having more trouble, so she's kind of been preoccupied. But we're going camping in two weeks with some of Mickie's friends. And we're supposed to go canoeing, too."

I smiled. "Well, you're officially a lesbian now," I teased her.

"Why do you say that?" she asked, looking perplexed.

"Because you're going camping. Gay men stay in hotels with fabulous mirrors and designer sheets, and lesbians go camping. Oh, you still have so much to learn," I teased.

Anne smiled, and that felt so good inside for me. I spent so much time taking her or going with her to really painful places, that it felt good to be able to make her smile. I think I was also feeling more relaxed about not having to always be serious out of fear of confusing her. And that felt good, because humor was such an important part of my life.

But our moment of playfulness ended abruptly when Anne said, "My mom called me yesterday and told me that my father was arrested last week, but only for a little while. They found the bodies of two girls. The police think they were around ten when they died. They're apparently fairly certain the girls were murdered, and they would have been around my age now."

"Do you think you know who they were?" I asked.

"I'm not really sure, but I think my dad was probably either involved or knew about it, and that's why they arrested him. My mom said my dad is really frightened I'll talk, and they're both really frightened I'll be asked to testify. I actually don't know anything, although I haven't told them that."

A part of me was incredibly proud of Anne in that moment, because, perhaps for the first time in her life, she held some kind of power or control over her father. The irony, I thought, was that her power was all based upon his perceptions rather than on anything tangible.

"That's really cool," I said, in her vernacular, knowing that she'd guessed I knew what she was thinking.

She looked at me with a somewhat perplexed gaze and asked, "Why do you say that?"

"What's your guess?" I said playfully.

She didn't even need to ponder this. "That I kind of have some leverage for the first time in my life with him," she said, her smile reflecting her pride.

"Yep, and that's really 'cool,' to put it in your words. To put it more in mine, it's 'karma.'"

Anne had enough of a holistic view of life by now to understand my meaning of the word karma, but had a questioning look.

"What goes around, comes around," I offered, nodding my head gently. "Do you have any idea why they may have suspected him in particular?" I continued.

"Not really. My mom said my dad gave them information that led them to the bodies but denied having anything to do with it. I talked to Nathan this morning, and he said that it's highly unlikely they will attempt to prosecute my father, because it would be hard to prove twenty years later and because he's eighty-four, and they don't want to have to deal with housing and caring for him."

I understood the logic, but I couldn't move beyond my feeling that this man, who had participated for years in the ritual molestation of one of his daughters and had knowledge or involvement in the death of two other girls, personified true evil. Anne's composure and apparent calm with the outcome she had described agitated my frustration and anger, and I doubt I hid my feelings, although I did hold my tongue. But that was the best I could do, and I think we both accepted that.

— CHAPTER TWENTY-FOUR —

A month had elapsed since Nathan had begun preparing Anne to testify in court, and he had been able to get her to successfully respond to questions that he anticipated from the opposing counsel. They had visited the courtroom several times and practiced having her approach and sit in the witness box. Nathan had her envision the jury and the people in the courtroom, and talked about where she might direct her eyes and how to respond to the judge.

They'd also worked out a plan for her to look at Nathan or Mike when she felt confused or needed to feel she had support in the room. Nathan had not yet alluded to the presence of the defendant nor to the possibility that other members of the church would be in the courtroom, knowing this would be very intimidating, if not outright threatening, to Anne.

Further, to date, Nathan had posed his questions gently, and he had been her only interrogator. However, today, for the first time, he was bringing in other attorneys to engage her in a more challenging cross-examination. With only a few weeks to go, he needed to expose her to increasingly realistic circumstances that more accurately reflected what she would be facing.

Rounding up two of his colleagues who most typically served in roles as public defenders hadn't been too difficult. Since Anne was only testifying as a witness, they understood the parameters didn't include delving into her own history and also knew to tread closely to the edge of this boundary as a way of preparing her and Nathan for their upcoming roles. However, knowing he had only this one day with his colleagues present, Nathan felt that they should meet in the actual courtroom for the upcoming trial, allowing Anne to experience the most accurate mock circumstances he could provide. He had rounded up a group of friends and associates to sit in the courtroom, including a close friend who was a former judge, to create even more realistic circumstances. He had thoroughly explained to Anne that all of these people were in her camp, even though they were to play roles that at times felt adversarial.

Nathan realized he was going to greater lengths than he normally might for witness preparation, but the circumstances were extenuating. Anne was not only facing the intimidation of opposing counsel and the defendant, but she would be testifying in front of the elders, who viewed her as a traitor and a child of Satan.

Since Anne also at times still viewed herself this way, testifying put her burgeoning sense of self-worth in fragile territory, a danger compounded by the fact that she could never return to the only world she had known, having been, in essence, excommunicated. Also, this was only the first of several anticipated trials, as she was the primary, if not the sole, witness to a twenty-five-year ring of atrocities and abuse.

Also, Anne had become very special to Nathan, sort of an adopted daughter whom he was committed to protecting. There was something about her mixture of great sadness and pain coexisting with great strength and bravery that had captured Nathan at the outset. Apart from Anne's particular situation or his feelings about her, it was completely legitimate and prudent to rehearse and prepare witnesses to testify, Nathan thought, as long as you didn't unduly alter their perceptions or their factual presentation.

Each side began with a brief set of presenting arguments, with the judge presiding and even someone acting as a bailiff. At the end of the presenting arguments, the judge called Anne to the witness box, and Nathan undertook an abridged version of questioning his witness. She seemed calm during this process, and Nathan felt hopeful that she would remain so when the opposition began its interrogation.

He had enlisted two opposing attorneys: David Borden, who played the good cop, and Susan Horowitz, one of Nathan's closest friends and a tough defense attorney, who played the adversarial role. While the questioning from David went smoothly, with Anne remaining calm as he took her through the chronology of events and questioned her regarding her perceptions of Mr. Jenkins, the questioning from Susan Horowitz did not.

From the outset, Susan, as her role required, was less than friendly, showing disdain for the witness and the prosecution's case. And as soon as Susan stepped toward the witness box, Anne's posture became rigid and she averted her glance downward.

After all, in spite of all their practice, she had little reason to feel safe among strangers, let alone people who were truly out to diminish her or harm her, Nathan thought. She was going to be highly anxious and outright fearful in the witness box regardless of how much they rehearsed, he realized.

Susan challenged Anne's memory and tried to confuse her several times, and Anne appeared to be extremely fearful. Yet, Nathan was pleased to see that, overall, Anne remained committed to what she remembered. On several occasions, she even became angry when Susan asked her about her feelings toward Mr. Jenkins.

At one point, Nathan chose to check in with Anne regarding her understanding of the intent of the questioning. Her response indicated she knew this was a "play kind of thing" but still didn't think this woman needed to be so hard. He asked Susan to keep that in mind and simultaneously asked Anne to hang in there and trust the process, even if it felt uncomfortable. He even joked that they could maybe find a picture of Ms. Horowitz and practice their dart-throwing after the mock trial ended. Anne's response was a smile and a single word, "cool." Susan looked at Nathan and gave a smile that said "touché."

When everyone else had departed, Nathan congratulated Anne on her performance.

"Do you have any questions, Anne?" he asked.

"Yeah," she said. "Where will Mr. Jenkins sit?"

Nathan showed her. "You'll only have to look at him to identify him as the man you saw on top of Amanda," he said quickly, noticing her begin to shake.

"He'll try to attack me," Anne said in a choked voice.

"I swear to you, Anne, that there will be so many police here, he won't even think of it. I promise you that if he so much as squeaks, police will remove him and charge him with contempt of court."

Anne seemed unconvinced. She stayed silent, but her expression said, "You don't know these people."

— CHAPTER TWENTY-FIVE —

When Anne heard Officer Mike knocking on her door at 7 a.m., she had already been awake for five hours. For the previous several nights, she'd been unable to sleep. Today she had been awake since shortly after midnight with worries about being in a courtroom racing incessantly through her mind.

"Good morning, Miss Anne. Rise and shine," Mike called from outside the door. "We're gonna knock 'em dead in there today."

Anne could not have imagined someone like Mike when she was a child, or even until the past year, she thought, hearing his voice. Not only was he her cheerleader, but she knew he would never try to hurt her and would not simply stand by while others did. However, Anne felt far from confident that either she or Mike could "knock 'em dead." At best, she hoped she didn't completely fall apart in the witness box.

But she couldn't keep Mike waiting, no matter her trepidation, so she called, "I'm awake, Mike."

"How'd you sleep?" the big officer asked when she opened the door.

"I didn't sleep very much," Anne grumbled.

"Well, I've got some breakfast ready, and we need to get going soon, so we can be there in plenty of time to get good seats."

Anne cast him a quizzical look. That sounded kind of strange, she thought, since she already knew where she'd be sitting, right behind Nathan and next to Mike. Nathan had promised he'd arrange that. But then, seeing Mike's grin, she realized this was one of his many jokes, and, grimacing acknowledgment at his attempt at humor, she got up and started getting ready for her day in court.

Dressing in the pants and matching jacket that she'd agreed to wear, she felt strange. Nathan had explained the necessity to wear them, using the analogy of how the church had required her to wear fatigues. This was the type of uniform the court required, he'd said. Since she'd fought his request to wear a dress, this was a compromise, she reminded herself. Anyway, Nathan had explained that he would be wearing a suit and tie, something he rarely wore when they met casually, so she wouldn't be the only one feeling strange.

"Well, Miss Anne, for not having enough sleep, you sure look nice," Mike said when she joined him in the kitchen for breakfast. But then, realizing how quiet she was, he stopped trying to bolster her with cheer.

"No sleep, no appetite?" he said kindly, when he noticed Anne picking at her cereal. "I can understand, but you just have to remember all the things you've learned with Nathan, and remember that I'm there and totally on your side. I'll have your back today, Miss Anne."

Anne had started to smile when he'd said he was on her side, but then her expression grew perplexed. Mike realized that he'd used another unfamiliar expression.

"Somehow, I have a feeling you don't know the expression 'I'll have your back,'" he said.

"No, I don't," Anne admitted, although without her usual defensiveness, since it was a joke now between them that she knew so few of the cultural expressions everyone else was familiar with.

"It means, I'll be looking out for you and be there to protect you—watching out to protect you against the things you can't see," he explained.

But Anne's fear and tendency to think concretely had the better of her. "Who will be sitting behind me?" she asked.

"Hey, Miss Anne, it's only an expression meaning I'm there for you and will be on your side. No one will be able to hurt you," Mike said, although he knew that the opposing attorneys would do everything they could get away with to attack her sanity and credibility. In fact, one of them was a female attorney. Being able to get away with more than a male attorney attacking a fragile female witness/victim, she had a reputation for often escalating her attacks.

They were quiet during the drive into town. As they arrived at the courthouse and pulled into an underground garage, Anne could see numerous television trucks with antennae jutting into the sky. Nathan had assured her that none of the cameras would be permitted into the courtroom, but the sight unnerved her. They drove down one level and pulled into a parking space designated for official vehicles. Before Anne could even open her door, four police officers approached the car.

Along with three male officers was Officer Nancy, her other strong support at the safe house. After the three other officers introduced themselves, Nancy put a hand gently on Anne's shoulder and said, "Even though this was to be my day off, I so believe in what you're doing that I had to be here to support you."

Such gestures of support and genuine caring were so unfamiliar that she didn't know how to acknowledge them. So she merely met Nancy's gaze for a moment and hoped the tough, stern-looking officer understood that she acknowledged her gentleness.

What Anne couldn't yet comprehend was that, in Nancy's eyes, they were sisters, not the kind related by blood or family of origin, but the kind who stood determinedly by each other in the face of oppression. And Anne would have been astounded to realize that Nancy saw her as possessing real strength and toughness.

As they prepared for the walk to the courtroom, Anne noted apprehensively that the police were certainly taking her protection seriously this time, since there were so many officers. It struck her again that she was a key witness to a lengthy history of illegal and abusive behaviors on the part of not only church members but also the leader they devoutly followed. She felt a mix of relief and awkwardness at being the object of this level of security.

Along with assuaging her fears, the increased security served to heighten her awareness of danger. As protective and dedicated as the police were, she knew the elders were intensely committed to protecting their church and Jonas Smith. She also knew they would risk their own safety in their devotion to their beliefs and protecting the secrecy that had endured for more than twenty years.

Yet, in spite of her fears, the walk into the courthouse and to the courtroom was uneventful. As they headed into the building, the policeman in the lead bypassed the elevators and headed to a stairwell. Was this part of their security measures, or had Mike told them about her fear of elevators, she wondered.

As if reading her mind, Mike whispered, "No, Miss Anne, they don't know you're afraid of elevators. We're using the stairs for security. You know how you feel an elevator is too enclosed and almost feel trapped? Well, when you think about security, it is. With stairs, you can easily turn around and go back down, or even up, if you need to. But with an elevator there's nowhere to turn."

Anne, by now having trouble speaking, nodded her understanding.

They climbed two flights of stairs to the third floor. As they stepped into the broad marble hallway, Nathan, who'd been waiting there, came toward them, gently putting his arm around her.

"How are you, Anne?" he asked, a deep sense of protectiveness arising in him.

"Okay, I guess," she managed to mumble.

As they entered the courtroom, two of the police officers took up positions at the back of the courtroom to have a good view of everyone in attendance. Nathan led Anne to the second row, and Nancy and Mike took seats on each side of her.

They had only been seated for about five minutes when the bailiff spoke.

"All rise," he announced as the judge entered the chambers.

Unknown to Anne in the second row, the courtroom was completely packed with reporters, a group from her community, and a large contingent of law students for whom Nathan had managed to gain access, in part to take up seats that members of The Christian Movement might otherwise occupy. He had done this both for their benefit as law students and because he knew they were dedicated to him as a champion of victims' rights. Just their loyal presence and their reactions could impact the jury, Nathan knew, similar to the way an audience stacked with an actor's friends and relatives influences critics. He had long ago learned that the expression "life is a stage" was also apt in the courtroom.

Anne and Nathan had agreed that she would be present for the opposing attorneys' opening remarks, and these took about an hour. Then Anne heard the bailiff say, "The prosecution calls its first witness, Anne Martin." Later, she would reflect that it had been strange to hear her name called, never having attended school or any event dedicated to anything other than to inflict pain or abuse upon her. But at that moment, there was nothing in her mind other than all her rehearsals with Nathan. As she heard her name, she rose on cue, stepped past him, and slowly walked toward the witness box, not looking at anyone else in the room except the judge, as Nathan had instructed.

As Anne approached the witness box, the bailiff walked toward her. She turned toward him, as rehearsed, and put her hand up to take the oath that swore her to tell the truth.

Nathan was officially designated as a member of the prosecuting team to enable him to interview Anne as a witness. As she stepped into the witness box and the bailiff closed the door, he stepped forward to begin what he knew would be the easiest part of her day.

"Would you please state your full name for the court?" he said.

"Anne Martin," she replied, looking directly at him, as they had rehearsed.

"Ms. Martin, can you recall the afternoon of December 4, 1998, and the incidents that have brought us to this courtroom today?"

"Yes."

"Would you please describe, in your own words, what happened that day?"

Anne felt herself relax just a little. Recounting the history felt easy, and she found herself unexpectedly calm. She was able to go back to the place and time and to visualize herself in the situation. She told the story without emotion and in great detail, watching the events unfold in her mind, as if viewing a film or play, as she always did. In this case, however, she had told her story so many times that she felt almost like the narrator of a movie, visualizing the story yet knowing it was rehearsed.

All the while, she looked directly at Nathan, occasionally glancing toward Mike, whose smile continually comforted and encouraged her. As she finished, she calmly stopped and looked to Nathan for further direction.

"Ms. Martin, is Mr. Jenkins, the man you are referring to, in this courtroom?" Nathan promptly asked. He had been waiting for this moment for a long time, he thought with satisfaction.

"Yes."

"Would you point to him?"

Anne felt herself tense up as she looked toward the defense table, where Mr. Jenkins sat calmly, staring directly at her, almost as if he was staring her down. She slowly raised her right hand and pointed her finger at him.

"For the record, let it be noted that the witness is pointing directly at the defendant. That is all I have for this witness. Thank you for your testimony, Ms. Martin," Nathan concluded.

The next voice Anne heard was the judge's. "Does the defense wish to cross-examine this witness?" she vaguely heard him say.

Anne continued to look toward Nathan and saw a slight smile on his face, a smile she knew was his best attempt to calm the anxiety he anticipated from her. They both knew the moment had arrived.

Then she heard another voice, that of a woman, say, "Yes, your honor."

Footsteps approached.

Anne's heart beat faster. Her breathing grew shallow.

A sense of wanting to shut down and disconnect from everything around her, her lifelong coping mechanism, threatened to overwhelm her, but she quickly focused on Nathan, using him as a cue to recall her responses to the defense attorney's questions.

The defense attorney's voice cut through the courtroom. "Ms. Martin, how long were you in the church?" she asked.

The voice, stern and judgmental, reminded Anne of the way the elders had spoken to her, and she had trouble breathing. She took a slow, deep breath, as Nathan had taught her. "I grew up in the church, since my parents were part of it," she said faintly.

Nathan dug a hole in his legal pad with his pen. Anne's response had deviated from the simpler answer they had rehearsed. He didn't want her providing any kind of new, unrehearsed path for the defense to travel down.

"You don't like Mr. Jenkins, do you, Ms. Martin?" the defense attorney continued. "May I call you Anne?"

Anne felt confused, having two questions to answer, and she didn't like it.

"Which question would you like me to answer first?" she said testily, surprising not only herself, but also Nathan and the defense attorney.

"Why don't you choose?" came the reply.

"He's okay, and I never disliked him," Anne said, easily remembering their rehearsal of this question.

"Thank you. And may I call you Anne?"

"I don't care," Anne said indifferently.

She couldn't understand the reason for this question, and it wasn't one they had rehearsed. Nathan, however, fully understood that it was an attempt to make her feel more comfortable and safer with opposing counsel.

"So, would it be fair to say you don't particularly like him?"

Nathan stood. "I object," he said. "The witness has already responded to this question, your honor."

The judge looked at the defense attorney. "I believe that was asked and answered already, Ms. Perkins. Do you have a purpose in re-asking the question?"

"Your honor, I am trying to establish that the witness actually may have had a negative opinion or feeling regarding my client, and this might, therefore, affect her credibility as an accurate and objective witness."

"I'll allow the witness to respond, but please don't waste the court's time trying to establish nuances each time you wish to make a point," the judge said, turning toward Anne and instructing her to answer the question.

"I'm not exactly sure what the question was now," replied Anne.

"So, would it be fair to say you don't particularly like him?" Ms. Perkins resumed.

"I guess so," Anne said uncertainly.

"You've got it in for him, don't you, Anne?" the defense attorney continued, taking short, clipped steps around the witness box, so that Anne had to follow her with her eyes.

"What do you mean?" Anne asked, seeming uneasy. She would have liked to look at Nathan, but she felt compelled to keep looking at Ms. Perkins when being spoken to.

"You would like to see him punished, wouldn't you?"

"I think he should be punished if he is found guilty," Anne answered truthfully.

"Is that why you're here testifying?"

"I guess so," Anne said, warily, sensing that Ms. Perkins was leading her into one of the traps Nathan had warned her about.

"So, your primary motive here is to punish Mr. Jenkins?"

Nathan realized that this line of inquiry was leading Anne into a trap, but it was within the bounds of permissible cross-examination.

"No, I'm here to tell what happened," Anne said simply.

"Touché," Nathan whispered to himself.

"Let me ask you a hypothetical question, Anne," Ms. Perkins continued in a softer voice. "If a person didn't like another person and thought they deserved punishment, do you think that person might ever be tempted to try to paint a worse or more damaging picture in order for justice to be served?"

Nathan rose to object, but before he could, Anne asked, "What does 'hypothetical' mean?"

So he decided to allow the defense attorney to clarify the meaning in order to see how this might confuse the direction of inquiry. He considered that Anne's limited vocabulary might offer an occasional advantage in frustrating the defense counsel.

"A hypothetical situation assumes that something akin to a real-life situation exists. I am asking you to just think about how another person might respond in a situation similar to yours."

"What other person?" the genuinely flummoxed Anne asked.

Ms. Perkins spoke more slowly, almost as if addressing an impaired person. "It isn't a *particular* person. It's just an *imaginary* person. I want to know if you could *imagine* that someone else might be influenced by their feelings of anger or wrong to try to present another person in a worse light. I'm not talking about lying, only about trying to present the picture more strongly to ensure that justice prevails."

Anne looked at a loss. "Can I make it someone I know?" she ventured finally. "That would make more sense to me."

Someone in the jury box snickered. The sound heartened Nathan. It meant at least one of the jurists felt for the poor, naïve witness as she endured the high-powered attorney's attempt to make a point.

Ms. Perkins straightened the cuffs on her tailored jacket and turned to the judge. "I withdraw the question, your honor," she said.

It was a small victory, but Nathan was pleased. He was beginning to see a rebellious side of Anne, the part of her makeup that had allowed her to survive so much.

When she resumed, Ms. Perkins adjusted her voice to sound caring and gentle, in view of the jury's potentially more sympathetic view of the witness.

"Anne, I know this is difficult to talk about, but I realize that you too may have been hurt or treated wrongly by men like Mr. Jenkins," she said, trying to make her voice sound gentle and caring.

Nathan rose immediately.

"Your honor, I strongly object. The witness's history is not relevant to this trial, and any inquiry into her history could have irreparably damaging effects on her in this kind of setting. In no way should she be subjected to anything like this question simply because she is serving as a witness."

No one in the courtroom missed the concern in Nathan's voice at that moment, and the impassioned way he had jumped to his feet.

"Okay, Mr. Cohen, I get your point," the judge said. "The objection is sustained, Ms. Perkins. You are not to ask any questions of this witness in regard to her own life and history that are not directly related to this defendant and actions that occurred in his home or with his family."

"I understand, your honor. However, I am greatly concerned that the witness's own history might have a very strong impact on how she perceived the events in question. It goes to the heart of her credibility as an accurate or objective source of information."

"Ms. Perkins, you have my ruling on this. Now proceed with your next question," the judge concluded.

Ms. Perkins had run into two consecutive roadblocks, one from Anne and now one from the judge. She again had to switch her direction.

"Ms. Martin, would you like to punish Mr. Jenkins?" she continued in a neutral tone.

Anne stiffened. She knew her response would feed into the prosecutor's hand. "Yeah, but they have evidence and found his semen on her, so he should be punished," she answered, flustered.

Knowing that this dramatic statement would lead to a strong reaction from the opposing counsel, Nathan waited.

"Your honor, this statement is completely out of line and inadmissible from this witness. I request that you address this," Ms. Perkins snapped.

"The jury is instructed to completely ignore the last statement from the witness. This is hearsay, something she was not at all a witness to, and she is not a reliable source regarding the scientific evidence related to this trial in any way. Ms. Martin, you must only answer questions asked of you and may not provide statements or opinions regarding anything else. Can you understand that?" the judge said, turning to Nathan to solicit his assistance in counseling his client.

But before he could utter the words, Nathan spoke. "Your honor, I would like a few minutes with my client to help her understand this concern and your instructions," he said.

Still rattled, Ms. Perkins jumped in. "Your honor, may counsel approach the bench?"

"Yes, I would like both attorneys to approach the bench," the judge agreed.

As the two attorneys approached the bench, Anne felt anxious and confused. Had she done something wrong? The rules of the courtroom, in spite of all her preparation, were hard to understand at times; and when she felt frightened or upset, it was even harder to make sense of the rules.

Then, in a voice clearly intended to be heard by the jury, Ms. Perkins said, "Your honor, this is a very damning statement to have come forward in this way, and it is highly likely to influence the jury's perspective at a very inappropriate time. It is virtually impossible to ignore such a statement sitting in front of them, even with your request to do so."

"I understand your concerns, Ms. Perkins, but the legal system depends upon the belief that a jury is capable of listening to the instructions of a judge and of putting such a statement in perspective."

"Your honor," Ms. Perkins began again, nearly interrupting the judge, "this is serious enough to warrant consideration of a mistrial. My client's life could be irreparably damaged by this event."

"I am not granting a new trial, Ms. Perkins. Your objection and request are noted, however. I will reiterate my instructions to the jury, and we will proceed after a fifteen-minute recess."

Knowing that Anne was more distraught by now, Nathan was grateful for the chance to reassure her. He walked the few steps to the witness box, where Anne awaited his approach with eyes anxious for his approval.

"Hey there," he said gently as he approached the box.

Anne felt teary with relief just to be able to talk to him personally again.

"I know this isn't easy. How about if we take a walk for a little bit?" Nathan said.

Stepping out of the witness box was like an unexpected breath of fresh air. Anne hadn't felt claustrophobic in the box, as she'd rehearsed there so many times, but she hadn't expected to be released so soon. As she headed out the front door of the courtroom with Nathan beside her and four police officers unobtrusively trailing them by about ten feet, a sense of exhilaration took her by surprise. It was the last thing she would have expected to feel on this day, a feeling, she would later realize, that had been born of her first taste of standing up for herself in public to seek justice.

As soon as they'd gained enough distance in the wide hallway to assure some privacy, Nathan congratulated her again. "Wow. You're doing so well, Anne! I'm so proud of you. Just remember, only answer the question asked, okay?"

"Okay," Anne beamed, near giddy with relief that he thought she'd done well.

Nathan intentionally chose not to address her feistiness, since it could easily play in a positive direction.

Instead, he touched her arm very briefly and lightly and leaned close as if to tell her a secret. "I'm taking you to a great seafood place on the water for lunch," he said.

For the first time that day, Anne smiled.

When they returned to the courtroom, Nathan directed Anne back to the witness stand, where it seemed, almost with the intent of giving Anne no room to take a breath, Ms. Perkins immediately arose and approached her, asking a question en route.

"Ms. Martin, how long had you been babysitting the Jenkins children, Amanda and Eric?"

"I think for about four years," Anne said.

"Were you paid for your babysitting services?" Ms. Perkins asked.

"No."

"No. Then how come you would babysit for free? You must have really liked being with these children."

This last sentence smelled like a rat to Nathan, but there was nothing to which he could object at this juncture.

"It was my service in the community. I had sat for families before. Everyone provided different kinds of services for the community. I loved being with the children, but that isn't really why I wasn't paid," Anne answered calmly.

"I imagine that your love of the children may have, at times, made you wish you could have children of your own to love?"

Anne looked perplexed. "I guess so," she said.

"Is it also true that you felt jealous of Mrs. Jenkins and wanted to be in her shoes?"

The rat Nathan had anticipated was out. But before he could object to Ms. Perkins's question, Anne erupted, looking at Ms. Perkins with an anger Nathan had never seen before. "You're a big fat liar!" she yelled, her face flushed with anger.

Through his shock, Nathan registered how childlike Anne's response had been. It also had, he chuckled, been entirely incongruous, since Ms. Perkins had, in his view, the body of an overworked anorexic.

"Ms. Martin, you are not allowed to make any statements about Ms. Perkins or insult any of the attorneys here," the judge said, turning his impassive gaze on Anne. "You must confine your statements to the questions asked. If you disagree, just say so."

"I insulted her because she insulted me by accusing me of things that are lies," Anne said, her voice shaking and tears cascading down her cheeks.

Anne had played right into the hands of the defense at this point, and Ms. Perkins didn't waste a moment capitalizing on it.

"Your honor, this witness is clearly demonstrating emotional instability, and I think the court needs to consider her ability to even testify, let alone provide an accurate account of a history that is so emotional for her."

"I am aware that the witness has some very strong feelings, Ms. Perkins, but that doesn't necessarily diminish her credibility," the judge said levelly. "I am also aware that you are treading on very precarious waters with your line of questions, which are more statements than questions."

His tone had indicated he would not tolerate any nonsense from the defense attorney. But he softened as he turned to Anne. "Ms. Martin, I'm going to ask you to do something a little unusual here. If you hear a question or a statement that really upsets you, I would like you to turn to me rather than respond in any way and tell me how you're feeling. If any question seems too painful or unfair, you and I can decide what to do with it. How does that sound?"

"That sounds okay," Anne responded to the judge, but then, under her breath, she added, "Idiot. She doesn't know what she's talking about."

The judge had to have heard at least part of this but chose not to intervene further, hoping Anne's emotional release would enable them to proceed without further incident.

If Nathan had been a cat, he would have been calmly licking the last of the milk off his lips and purring. The judge had aligned himself with the witness to try to maintain decorum in his courtroom. At the very least, this couldn't bode well for the jury's perception of the defense attorney and her approach. After all, Ms. Perkins had already planted the notion that the witness herself may have been the victim of abuse. To have established that possibility and then to be perceived as attacking her wasn't a good formula for support from the jury.

He gave a satisfied sigh, reflecting that, having centered his concerns around Anne's ability to handle the pressure, he hadn't even considered that somehow the opposing counsel might lose control of the setting. And, if he hadn't been so concerned with his client's well-being, he might have actually been amused at his legal adversary's loss of ground.

Ms. Perkins was not perturbed for long, however. When she continued, her manner and tone were almost indifferent, as she attempted to portray the greater poise and maturity between clearly defined adversaries.

"Ms. Martin, when you walked into the Jenkins' house on the day in question, did you hear any sounds?"

"No, I didn't hear the children anywhere."

"Does that mean you heard no sound coming from anywhere in the house?"

"I didn't hear anything."

"When you went upstairs, before you opened the door to Amanda's room, did you hear any sounds at all?"

"No."

"If Mr. Jenkins was actually engaged in some kind of activity with Amanda, even just wrestling around on the bed with her, wouldn't you have heard some kind of sound coming from the room?"

"I don't know. I didn't hear anything."

"I understand you didn't hear anything, but don't you think you might have heard them moving, or the sound of the sheets moving, or some kind of sound coming from the room?"

"Maybe, I'm not really sure."

"So, it is quite possible that you might have heard a sound," Ms. Perkins concluded with convoluted logic.

"Your honor, the witness has answered to the best of her ability. Ms. Perkins reached a conclusion that the witness didn't provide," Nathan said, barely rising from his seat before the judge indicated with a rise of his hand for him to sit down.

"Objection sustained. Ms. Perkins, you will please refrain from making conclusive statements that are other than the direct testimony provided by the witness," he said wearily.

"When you opened the door, Ms. Martin, what did you observe?" Ms. Perkins continued, undeterred.

"I saw Mr. Jenkins lying on top of Amanda."

"Did you see him moving his body or touching her in any way that was inappropriate?"

"He had his hand over her mouth."

"But that is the only thing you saw him doing with his hands, correct?"

"Yes."

"So, you never saw him engage in any sexual behavior or touch her inappropriately?"

"He was lying on top of her, and that didn't seem right. I mean, what else could it have been?" Anne asked, her tone more abrasive.

"Could they just have been having fun doing something that wasn't sexual or inappropriate?"

"Then, why did he have his hand over her mouth?" Anne asked, this time with a little more confidence, enjoying throwing questions back.

"Please just answer the question, Ms. Martin. Is it possible they were just playing?"

"I guess so," Anne responded, sounding a little more defeated.

"You also testified you saw Eric's foot protruding from under the bed, is that correct?"

"Yes."

"What did you think that meant?"

Anne hesitated and looked perplexed. "That he was under the bed," she said with a hint of sarcasm. Another snicker came from the jury box.

"I understand that, but why did you think he was under the bed?"

"Because he was scared and hiding."

"Did you see his face or his body?"

"No, just his foot."

"But you concluded he was scared and hiding."

"Why else would he have been under the bed?"

"Is it possible that he might have also been playing with his father and sister, maybe some kind of hiding game?"

Anne hesitated. "I guess so," she said after a moment.

"So, Anne, you have testified that you saw nothing that looked sexual, other than that Mr. Jenkins was on top of Amanda. You have also testified that you saw nothing that would tell you that the three of them weren't playing some kind of game. Yet you concluded that Mr. Jenkins was touching Amanda inappropriately, having seen nothing to indicate that, and you concluded Eric was scared, having never seen anything to tell you that."

Anne sat there, not sure if she was supposed to respond.

"Would you please respond, Ms. Martin," Ms. Perkins prompted, with a glance toward the jury as if to show what patience she was demonstrating with a foolish child.

"Oh, I thought you were just saying that, and I didn't realize it was a question," Anne said apologetically, upstaging Ms. Martin again with the jury.

Nathan was both fascinated and very proud and impressed with how well Anne was engaging in this chess match. She was stepping outside the parameters of his coaching, but it seemed to be working very effectively.

"I am asking you if you would agree or disagree with that statement."

"But why would he be lying on top of her?"

"Please just answer the question," the defense attorney said in a long-suffering tone.

"Could you repeat it?" Anne asked, looking bewildered and slightly amused at the same time.

Ms. Perkins raised her eyebrows in frustration. "You testified that you saw nothing of a sexual nature, yet you concluded that sexual activity took place between Mr. Jenkins and Amanda. Is that correct?"

"Yeah, I guess so," Anne said, looking at Nathan in confusion.

"Thank you, Ms. Martin," the defense attorney concluded, aborting her cross-examination on a victorious note. "That is all I have for this witness, your honor," she said, aware that she had run into more roadblocks than successes and didn't want to encounter another.

"Do you have a rebuttal or further questions for your witness, Mr. Cohen?" the judge asked, addressing Nathan.

"I just have a couple of questions, your honor," Nathan said, standing to approach the witness box.

As he moved toward her, his gait and smile told Anne she'd done well and, although her stoic and defensive posture didn't change, she smiled back.

"Ms. Martin, is there any doubt in your mind that the defendant was the man on top of the little girl, Amanda?" he asked, with an air of dismissing Ms. Perkins's cross-examination as having been euphemistic at best.

"No."

"Did it appear to you that he and Amanda were having fun? In other words, did you hear any laughter or, in your opinion, did it look like they were playing?"

"No."

"I have one last area of questioning, Ms. Martin. Have you at any time during questioning or a deposition regarding this case, or testifying today, ever told anything other than the truth?"

"No."

"Can you tell the court why you would never lie?"

"Lying is a sin, and God punishes you."

"Thank you, Ms. Martin. That is all, your honor."

"Court is recessed until 1:30. I will remind the jury you are not to discuss this case or anything you have heard in this courtroom today with anyone," the judge pronounced, pushing back his chair and lumbering toward his chambers.

Nathan stepped forward and opened the door to the witness box, holding out his hand. Anne did likewise, as if she were a princess stepping down from her coach.

"Lunch, Madame?" he asked, offering her an arm, which Anne accepted graciously.

— CHAPTER TWENTY-SIX —

At the beginning of the week, Anne had called me to say she had been injured on her camping trip. As she entered my office for our session this week, I asked her how she was doing.

"Okay, I guess," she said, sounding ambivalent.

"So, tell me what happened."

"Well, we were canoeing, Mickie and I and her friends, and we got caught in some rapids. I fell out of the canoe and almost drowned. I've never been a good swimmer, but I had a life vest on, so it kept my head up. I broke my wrist when the rapids threw me into some rocks, and I tried to protect myself. I have lots of bruises, and they remind me of the bruises I had as a child. The worst part was that it took nine hours for any medical help to arrive. The rafting company apparently wasn't very prepared to handle an emergency."

I knew she knew I cared and it was okay to kid around with her, so I said, "Well, now you're more like a gay man. Lesbians usually stay in the raft, and we gay men are the ones who fall overboard. But we usually drown, because we can't wear life jackets. That orange just never goes with anything," I added, grinning.

Anne actually laughed, but then she grabbed her rib area, and it was obvious that doing so was painful. I hadn't realized she had bruised ribs as well. "Oh, I'm really sorry. I didn't know it would hurt for you to laugh," I apologized.

But she just smiled a little, mostly to put me at ease, and said, "Yeah, I bruised a few ribs on my right side, but it's okay. Overall, I'm having an okay week, but I'm sort of more depressed."

"Well, that doesn't exactly go together, but maybe you can tell me more about it."

"I met with Dr. Pearl and may need to go on birth control pills, which seems really weird since I'm not having sex with anyone."

"I gather that might seem rather odd," I agreed. "But I assume it's related to things going on medically for you?"

"He wasn't sure, but said that, considering my history and how I'm doing emotionally, he thinks it could be stress," she responded, looking defeated.

"So, how does that feel for you if it's caused by stress?"

"I don't know. I don't really care if I'm not having periods—unless it's a bad thing. Do you think it is?"

"I think you know I'm not the person to answer the medical questions, but it's another indication of your body telling you that you're far too stressed. But, at least, that's ultimately something over which you have a fair amount of power."

"Yeah, I guess so," Anne said tentatively.

"Would you be okay if Dr. Pearl and I spoke, to make sure we're on the same page?"

"Sure," she said, her momentary enthusiasm again telling me that it felt good that people care enough to communicate about her.

"So, tell me more about what makes you say you're more depressed."

"I've been crying three or four times a day and seem to react almost immediately to so many things. And I'm really restless and fidgety."

"You're actually describing what sounds like a mixture of agitation and depression, where you feel a lot of restlessness and irritability, rather than shutting down. Are you also nervous or worrying more lately?"

"Seeing Dr. Pearl made me realize what has happened to my life, and I'm more angry about …," Anne paused, exasperated. "How could they have done all these things to me? I get really upset when he wants to examine me, and I get so frightened."

"I know this is a frightening and uncomfortable thing for you to go through. I think most women feel some discomfort and awkwardness, but probably not the fear you feel. Are you at all afraid he might do something to hurt you?"

"Not really. I know he's doing what he's supposed to do, but it's just another person touching me there, and it brings up all those memories. I don't want to remember all that stuff. How can I forget about it? Someone told me hypnosis might work," she said, looking worried I might disagree.

"Well, in truth, I'd have some reservations about you undergoing any type of hypnosis. It might help you not focus on some of the memories, but it has the potential to trigger other memories, and that concerns me. In some ways, I see you as too vulnerable to that happening, and your emotions feel so fragile right now that I would rather try to help you cope with the memories and pain than have you tread into unpredictable territory. When do you see Dr. Pearl next?"

"In a month."

"Do you think the memories and your emotions are likely to calm down if you don't see him for a month?"

"Maybe," Anne responded, her tone uncertain.

"Well, how about if we see where that goes, because whenever there's a specific trigger and we can remove that trigger, that's the simplest and least threatening means of treatment. That trigger will be gone for a month at least. Maybe, over the next couple of sessions, we can work on some relaxation techniques," I said, trying to offer something that would give her some control.

"A friend of mine told me I was really courageous to get through everything I got through. Am I courageous?" she asked, looking slightly hopeful.

"Wow, I think that's a good question, but one you really need to come to your own conclusion about."

"Okay, but do *you* think of me as courageous?"

"In all honesty, I think of you as incredibly courageous, even courageous to talk about all of this with me and come to terms with so much pain and confusion about the truth. That takes a hell of a lot of courage."

Buoyed with new confidence, Anne started talking about a couple with whom she had become very close. They'd had a foster child who had been removed from his drug-addicted mother, a single parent. The couple had thrown a party to celebrate his sixth birthday. Along with her joy, Anne had found herself aware of the stark contrast with her own childhood.

After describing the elaborate plans the couple had made for a clown and a balloon maker, she asked me, "Why didn't my family want me to be part of anything or celebrate my birthdays?" This was one of her "Why" questions that left me feeling sad and perplexed as to how to respond.

"Maybe we'll never understand that, but we can talk about our theories," I said.

"I miss that I never got to have a real childhood and never felt loved or special," Anne said, looking defeated. As always, there was no hint of anger.

"So, what does this feel like as you think about it now?" I asked gently.

"It makes me kind of sad," she replied, the flatness of her words confirming her emotions.

I wondered whether she also felt angry, even though it remained unexpressed, but I refrained from asking, since I knew the question arose from my own belief that she should feel anger. I was also aware that the experience of anger might be more stressful than relieving to her. Then, as if reading my mind, she continued, "I don't really feel angry, just sad."

"Do you know whether the other girls who were your friends in the church, especially the other girls who were also abused, had similar experiences?"

"I don't remember any of them having parties or ever going to any celebrations, and I don't remember any of them ever talking about presents they got. We weren't supposed to celebrate, since we were burdens rather than blessings from God, like the boys were supposed to be."

"So, one thing you're saying that might help answer why this happened to you is that this was about how girls were treated, rather than only about you or about whether you were loved or not."

"Yeah, but how do you know you're loved when no one ever says it, and you're never hugged and no one ever celebrates your birthday or gives you any presents?"

Realizing the depth of sadness in her question, I responded, "I'm not sure you do know. One might just feel loved without someone saying anything or acting in supposedly loving ways, but it would be awfully hard for a child to feel this. Let me ask you a question. If you take out the word 'love' and, instead, use the word 'care,' can you imagine that there were people who cared about you?"

"Yeah, there were these two ladies, and I used to hang out at their house a lot. They were really nice to me," Anne said, her smile reflecting a happier memory.

My sense and experience told me that when a child grows up in a highly destructive environment and is still capable of functioning relatively well, then there has been someone who really cared and modeled psychological health somewhere. These women were the only possible source Anne had ever mentioned.

"Can you tell me about your relationship with them?" I asked, feeling some kind of relief that someone, somewhere had been there for this little girl.

"Yeah, they were Winnie and Nellie, two old ladies who were maybe in their seventies. They both had gray hair and wore old-lady dresses with aprons on them. They were probably in Deerbrook before the church even began to settle there. I used to spend a lot of time around them. It was a safe place. I never thought of it then, but I kind of wonder now if maybe they were partners. That wasn't even a concept then, but they were like a couple and kind of adopted me a little.

"Winnie and Nellie ran the dairy. It was a small shop that sold milk and butter and some other food things. They weren't really part of the church, although they did come to church services sometimes. We sold them milk and butter from the cows on the farm, and they sold it in their shop in town. We were mostly a crop farm and didn't have many cows, so the church community used up most of our dairy, but there was enough left to make a little money selling the rest to them.

"Five or six days a week, my mom and I would deliver milk to them, so I got to see them a lot. When I was little, I remember that I used to run in the store ahead of my mom, and when they saw me, one of them would hide and jump out at me to make me laugh. No one ever tried to make me laugh or be happy like that, other than a couple of my friends. Winnie and Nellie were always kind to me. They would sneak me sweets or a piece of fruit when they saw me and would always ask how I was.

"They ran the dairy until I was around ten, and then it closed. I assume they retired. I remember one time my mom let me spend the whole day with them on the understanding that I would witness to them and get them to come to the church. So, when I got there that day, I told them right at the start that I was secretly supposed to do that. I was maybe seven or eight, and I remember one of them saying, 'How about we just agree that we'll come to church with you this Sunday? That way we can have fun today.' My mom was really pleased with me, since they didn't attend very often.

"When they retired, they moved away, and I never saw them again. I think I maybe felt like people do when they lose their grandparents." Her look of nostalgia told me she had come to peace with their passing out of her life, much as I had done with the loss of my grandparents.

I pondered for a moment and then said, "It sounds like life knew you deserved love, and this is how it was given to you. Do you think they had any idea about the abuse?"

"They would see bruises on me sometimes, but I think they knew that if they said anything or intervened, it would be really bad for me, and they'd never see me again. I'm sure they had no idea about the sexual abuse or the cages or anything like that."

Absent any segue, as was not unusual for Anne, she said, "I sent an e-mail to my father, and I brought up training my brother to have sex with me, and his only comment was to ask if I had shown it to anyone else."

"So, what are your thoughts about his response?" I asked.

"Well, part of me was angry that he didn't even acknowledge that it happened or apologize in some way, but I can't get really angry at him," she said, her tone softening.

"When you say you can't, do you mean you don't really have that level of feeling, or are you saying it wouldn't be right or something?"

"Maybe a little of both, but I think I'm more afraid I'd get out of control."

"What would that look or sound like?"

"I don't know, but I think it would stress me out more than it would help, and I'd end up getting sick from all the stress."

I found myself grappling with two very different trains of thought. One was wondering if feeling anger would ultimately release stress or heighten it. The other was to realize how much she was gaining insight, being able to attach emotional and psychological stress to her physical health. "It sounds like part of you wants to tell him what all this is like, and another part sees the effort as more stressful than beneficial," I said.

"Yeah, that's kinda what I was thinking. Do you think I should get mad at him?"

"Well, that question could be asking one of two very different things—or both. What do you think I might answer here?" I challenged.

"Aren't you supposed to be working to help me understand what I should feel?" she asked.

Smiling and playing really dumb, I said, "I don't know, but if you can guess what I would say, it might tell us something important. Go on, take a guess."

"That I don't really need to ask if I already know what you think," she responded, mimicking my tone quite well.

"Yeah, that's one part of it. But I also think it says we're now thinking more alike regarding what happened to you and about your father's role. So, I already told you I view your question being about two different things. What do you think they are?"

"What I actually feel and whether I should tell him."

"Bingo!" I blurted out.

Anne gave me one of her more sarcastic smiles, probably to match my own, and sat there with a smug look, obviously choosing not to say anything at this juncture.

It felt like a game of tag. I was willing to concede, but really wanted her to express whatever insight, or lack thereof, she had at this point. So I asked, "So, rather than this be about what either of us believes, what do you feel like here?"

"I feel like telling him how sick and horrible this was, not just to me, but also for my brother and for my brother's and my relationship. Sometimes I wonder if one of his goals was to keep us distant so that we would never team up against him."

Having never really contemplated this myself, I was really impressed with her response. "You know, as you say that, it isn't something that I had really considered, maybe because I don't give your father credit for being that sophisticated. But in truth, it makes sense, and the fact that it comes from you is more powerful, because it may be coming from a place of simple truth rather than just being a theory on my part," I offered as encouragement, wanting to maintain the momentum.

I paused a moment and then asked, "So, since the answer to the question of why all this abuse happened to you is not necessarily as simple as 'God's will,' what are some of the other reasons that it might have happened?"

"I don't really know," she said, her retraction reflected in her hesitant tone.

"That's fine, and this isn't something you need to know, like a fact. I want us both to just share our ideas, because someday I think you'll find whatever meaning and reasons you choose to accept. So, give me any thoughts that come to mind."

Anne paused for a few moments and then said, "Well, I guess I could have just had bad luck and been in the wrong place at the wrong time." She then stopped.

"Any other images come to mind for you?"

"Well, maybe they were just really mean people and liked being hurtful."

"Can you think of any others?"

"Not really. You said you would share some ideas, too," she challenged.

I smiled. "Very clever! Okay, well, your two ideas are maybe the two I would have considered above all. A few others I've considered include something called 'group think,' where a whole group of people develop a strong belief that can easily be very wrong, but they reinforce each other just being part of a group. This is a more powerful likelihood when there is fear in challenging the leader. Another thought is that Jonas Smith was extremely powerful in his leadership and influence, and that is something we usually see in cults, like the one led by Jim Jones."

Seeing a perplexed look on Anne's face, I responded, "You don't know who that is, do you?"

"No," she replied, looking a little embarrassed.

"He was a very powerful cult leader who convinced his followers, about nine hundred of them, to commit a mass suicide. I think for the first time it told the world how powerful and dangerous cults can be, but I don't know that it led to any real changes.

"Another one of my theories is that women went along with all of this and, in the very least, didn't discourage the men from controlling and subjugating them. Compared with the children, who didn't have any real choice, adult women may have had some choices.

"So, those are my other thoughts. Any comments on them?" I asked, feeling a little tentative throwing out my pronouncements.

"Well, I don't know how I feel about the women. I don't think they had any real choices."

"I can understand that, and that's a pretty complicated question of when and how we have choices, but these are only images or theories to consider. And I'm also aware you struggle with your feelings of safety or trust with women sometimes. So, I haven't been sure how you viewed their sense of choice," I added upon reflection.

"Yeah, it's pretty confusing to me, I guess," Anne said, nodding her head.

After a brief pause, Anne continued, "I've also had two bad dreams lately. One of them was triggered by Oprah. She had a show on abuse and rape and women who were coping with it. I can't understand why just one rape would be so overwhelming, and I kind of think they should just get over it."

As stunned as I was by her statement, when I put it in the context of her background, it was entirely understandable. In some ways, I saw it as incredibly insensitive, but told myself that her insensitivity was the result of tremendous desensitization, and certainly not a reflection of who Anne was overall. In that moment, I realized how important it was to find a context that helped me to not misjudge her.

"I feel like I've gone through so many rapes and so much abuse that I can't see that being raped only once could still be really painful," Anne offered, confirming my own thoughts.

A part of me was relieved by her insight, and I searched for the right words to support her. "It's about having learned to tolerate so much pain, and you become numb to further pain, maybe even others' pain, just to survive. What is really good, though, Anne, is that you can now see that your own experience could cloud your perspective. That's what insight and self-awareness are all about."

Anne simply nodded in what seemed like an acknowledgement of my attempt to support her and make her feel okay, but her silence showed that this was pretty complicated for her.

"So, what was the other dream about?" I asked, hoping I wasn't opening some larger issue since we had to wind up soon.

"Oh, in the other dream, I was diving to get barnacles off the bottom of a boat, and people kept pulling me under when I'd come up for air. You and Dr. Pearl were trying to pull me up into the boat. The people pulling me down were my mother and father and some of the people in the church. And my brother was pulling me both ways, which seemed really strange."

For me, nothing about this dream was strange at all. It was a perfect metaphor for the journey she was traveling. "Does it make sense to you, though?" I asked.

"Yeah, you and Dr. Pearl are the ones trying to help me and get me away from the people who hurt me."

"That's how I understand it. What about your brother? What do you understand about his role in it?"

"I think my brother was caught in the middle like me, and sometimes he tried to help me and sometimes he hurt me. I've never known what to feel about him."

"It's a great dream. That doesn't mean it's comfortable, but it's about what you're feeling and going through, and sometimes that can help feelings to surface and help you figure things out. Well, we need to stop, so I'll see you next week, okay?"

"Okay," Anne said. She then leaned over and gave Madison a gentle and loving hug, stood up slowly, reflecting her physical discomfort, and departed.

CHAPTER TWENTY-SEVEN

Noticing that Anne had been holding some papers on her lap since we'd begun our session, I asked, "So, is that something you wanted us to talk about today?"

"Yeah, it's what I did for a creative writing project for my midterm," she said, handing them to me.

"Do you want me to read this now?" I asked.

"Yes, if that's okay," Anne responded quietly.

Until this moment, I thought I had learned of, and endured, the most shocking experiences of Anne's childhood, but I was wrong. I began reading.

"Child, are you climbing that tree again in your Sunday best? Get down and come inside before your father sees you, and we all suffer for your foolishness," Shauna's mother yelled.

Shauna dropped to the ground and ran indoors. She hadn't really been climbing the tree, more kind of sitting in it thinking. But she knew her mother was right, and she didn't want to catch it when her father got home. As she sprinted upstairs, she passed Joshua, her brother, playing with his new Hot Wheels car. He looked up, annoyed.

"Watch out!" he yelled. "Do you have to be so clumsy?" By the time his last words were out, Shauna had run through her parents' room and into the walk-in closet that was her bedroom.

Considering its size, it wasn't a bad bedroom. It was exactly six feet wide, and her father had built a wall-to-wall wooden platform at the furthest end away from the door. It was solidly constructed, with pullout drawers underneath and an old, comfy mattress nestled on top. There was a small, wooden chair and table on the left-hand side of the room next to the bed, and, on the right, one part of the original closet had been boxed off to create a small wardrobe for Shauna to hang her clothes. Next to the wardrobe was a mini chest of drawers, only about twelve inches in width, but tall, with eight deep drawers. It was covered with cutoffs of wallpaper from the dining room and had a small mirror precariously fastened to the top.

Shauna loved her chest of drawers. They had bought it for two dollars at a church rummage sale a couple of years ago, and with her mother's help, she had spent a happy afternoon scrubbing it clean and lining the drawers with white paper. The following morning when Shauna woke up, the first thing she had seen was her new chest of drawers, wrapped up like a gift, in cream wallpaper with little pink rosebuds and proudly showing off a mirror framed with the same paper.

She opened and closed each drawer carefully, and she pulled out a shiny purple bead, just like the one she admired so often on her mother's dressing table. Shauna's eyes had filled with tears as she'd clutched her new treasure. Then she heard her mother's softly chuckling voice. "Every little girl needs a hiding place and something special to go in it."

Although she was quite content with her bedroom, Shauna had often wondered why she had to sleep there. After all, Joshua had a big bedroom all to himself, and he was two years younger. It wasn't as if they didn't have room to spare. There was an empty guest room, as her mother called it, but they had never had any guests who stayed overnight. Shauna just couldn't understand why she couldn't have that room for her bedroom. She had asked her mother once, but her mother at first looked surprised at the question. She had quickly composed herself, though, and had said, "Your father wants his women close by in case he needs comfort in the night. I can't always give him the comfort he needs, so you need to be close by."

It was true that the older she became, the more comfort she seemed to be forced to provide. Even so, why couldn't she still have her own room, she wondered.

Shauna then asked, "Is it because comfort can be noisy? Because Joshua sleeps through just about anything."

Her mother's stern look and tone of voice made it clear that there would be no more questions and no further discussion.

"It's just how it is. Don't be asking your father, or we'll never hear the end of it."

As I finished reading Anne's story, I found myself most affected by two things: the use of the actual name of her mysterious sister, whom we had never talked about, and the strange circumstances of Shauna's bedroom being in her parents' closet—so her father could have "all his women close by."

Just the use of the word "women" to describe a little girl was ominous. I had sensed for a long time that something very strange and foreboding had occurred regarding Anne's sister, and I was hoping we might finally talk about it. Was that the clinical me or the curious me? I didn't know. Anne's history was so fascinating and powerful that I think those two natures in me often overlapped in their desire to dig deeper.

"I'm struck by how much this is probably about your life, and I doubt you used Shauna's name by coincidence," I remarked. Anne gave me a barely perceptible smile.

"Do you think you're ready to tell me about your sister?" I asked, feeling wary and bracing for what I might hear.

Anne nodded. "This is so painful for me to talk about. It's the first thing in my childhood that I can remember."

I could see a depth of sadness in her eyes that I'd never seen, even through all that she had shared with me. It can be very difficult knowing I am encouraging someone to address something that is very painful to express. I sometimes envision my role as being akin to a surgeon's, generating significant short-term pain with the sincere belief that the person's quality of life will be better in the long run.

We sat in silence for about a minute, one of those minutes that seemed much longer. I knew that Anne was awaiting a cue from me, but I wanted her to share this in whatever way she chose, so I simply said, "This is one of those times you're caught between the pain of reliving a memory and wanting me to know about it. So, let your heart decide where to travel. You may not be ready to talk about it yet."

Seeming relieved by the permission to not talk about it, Anne began. "I don't really know anything about what happened earlier that day, but I remember walking up the hill," she said. "There was this hill on the farm, and the community would gather there for ceremonies or sometimes celebrations. It was a very misty day, not quite rainy, but very gray."

Anne's face took on a similarly ashen tone as she reflected. "I was five, and Shauna was seven," she continued. "According to my father and the elders, Shauna was 'Satan's child,' conceived out of sin.

"It was November 5, 1980, a date I learned years later, a date my mom has said meant nothing to her, but one she nevertheless referred to every year as 'the day we lost Shauna's soul.'"

Anne's eyes grew glazed.

"My mom and I walked up the hill together with some other people, maybe about thirty in all. Jonas Smith and the elders and some of their families had gathered at the top of the hill. They had formed a circle around the clearing, as we would for ceremonies. In the center was an unlit bonfire, and everyone was singing and praising God. But I was watching Father Jonas and my father walk up from the path into the clearing with my sister, Shauna, between them, wearing only her vest and underwear.

"Shauna's face was bloodied and bruised and pale, and she kept her eyes firmly fixed on the ground as they walked toward us. My mom held my hand, and she held it so hard that it was hurting me. I noticed she was shaking, and I wanted to ask her if she was okay, but I knew I was forbidden to speak there."

Transfixed, I felt myself shaking a little as I experienced the emotions that Anne was expressing. As hidden as Shauna had been from me, her life was now very vivid.

Anne calmly continued. "The assembled group stopped singing and became silent, almost as if they knew what was going to happen. Then my father and Jonas picked up Shauna and stuffed her into a small wooden cage, tying the top down firmly with rope, praying in tongues and asking God to forgive her and save her soul. Then I saw some of the elders bring pieces of wood and put them around the cage. My father and Jonas Smith weren't doing that, but they were swaying in a trance and speaking in tongues.

"I couldn't understand much, but I heard some of the elders saying things like 'God have mercy on this evil soul.' I think it was about then that I realized they were starting to light a fire and thought they were trying to scare Shauna and punish her for something she had done."

An incredible sadness washed over Anne's face, and her body slumped as she reached this moment in the story.

"They picked up the cage and set it on top of the fire, and then there was fire all around the cage, and I heard Shauna begin to scream—a horrible and terrifying scream, like when an animal has been terribly wounded and just needs to die.

"Everyone started praying in tongues and chanting louder and louder, with such intensity that I felt my stomach start to turn. Father Jonas stood back and raised his hands up, thanking God loudly for giving him the wisdom to deal with sin.

"Then I saw my father beckon to some of the boys, among them my brother, and they gathered around, throwing branches on top of the cage. I watched my sister scrunched up in her wooden coffin, no longer screaming or showing any fear or struggling to get out, just still.

"I don't have any idea how long we stood there, and I remember kind of disappearing. And then everything was quiet except for the crackling of the fire. At first, it had seemed like the fire took forever to start, and I was sure that any minute they'd put it out and drag Shauna back to the basement, satisfied they had punished her enough. But then I heard her screams, they were so intense, and I knew this was for real.

"I couldn't look back toward Shauna, and it took everything in me to not cry. I knew this would appear as feeling sorry for her, and that the elders would interpret my tears as judgment of them, which would get me punished afterward.

"I felt my mom grab my hand, gripping it so tightly that it hurt. I looked at her, and she wasn't there. I just saw this stone face reacting to nothing anymore."

Ironically, Anne could have been describing her own behavior in that moment, but the parallel seemed lost on her.

"I was staring at the fire and caught a few glimpses of Shauna behind the flames, but then everything disappeared. After a while, I was aware we were still there watching the fire, still crackling but burning down until it was mostly embers and ashes left."

Anne's head slumped downward, as if still looking at the ashes on the ground.

"As we turned to walk down the hill, my mom started talking about what we were going to have for dinner, and I realized that she had put this moment, the death of her child, away, very far away somewhere. I know now that this is how she survived, and she couldn't have done anything else.

"The only other thing I remember is, much later on, as our family sat around the kitchen table eating sausages, my father turned to me and said, 'Those are your sister's fingers we cooked up for you.' I started to gag as my older brother laughed hysterically, and my father told me I'd regret it if I threw up on the table. I became allergic to meat after that," she added, looking at me, knowing I'd find this clinically interesting.

"Still today, I can close my eyes and see Shauna, trapped and burning, engulfed in fire, and I can smell the burned flesh and feel my mother's grip tightening on my hand.

"At that moment, as my sister's life ended, my life also changed. I was too young to really understand exactly what had happened, but that day I caught a glimpse of my own future, a future filled with men who hurt me and women who wouldn't protect me, a future governed by a God who was out to get me. I was still a child, but I knew I could never feel safe again. It was a moment in time that shaped who I am now, and a moment I still often think about, especially when I'm under stress.

"From then on, every time I was put in a cage and left to think about my sins, I was terrified I'd end up on a bonfire. And every time I was raped, beaten, or abused, I was consumed with a mixture of fear, guilt, and confusion—fear of what was to come, guilt that I had survived, and confusion as to why God seemed to make it so impossible to ever do the right thing.

"Sometimes, the guilt still floods through me in an uncontrollable wave, often when I least expect it. It masquerades as anger, anger at what I had to deal with, anger I can't remember what Shauna looked like, and anger that she left me.

"But how can I be angry at a seven-year-old girl for something that wasn't her fault?" Anne asked.

Her remark seemed mostly rhetorical, so I chose not to respond.

"Each day, as I struggle to make sense of my life and find myself thinking about the sister I hardly remember, I wonder if she would have been a good sister—if I would have been a good sister. I wonder if her death scared my parents and prevented the same thing from happening to me, and I wonder if I will ever be able to move on with my life, unhindered by the past."

Listening intently and powerfully moved, I remained quiet. Finally, feeling a need to say something supportive and caring, I said, "There are some things we never get to know, but just need to find our own answer for them that we can accept."

"Everything I do and everything I am is tainted by her death," Anne replied. "I find myself getting a pap smear, lying on my back and filled with shame, but thinking about Shauna. The feeling as the doctor inserts the speculum is the same as having a spoon or a fork stuck up me," she added, looking at me as if she expected the image to shock me.

"I find myself looking up at the ceiling and then at the doctor, and I feel caged again, this time not by a physical cage, but by my own fear—fear that I won't be able to cover up how ashamed I feel and fear that the doctor will laugh at me or put me down for being afraid of him.

"Most of all, I fear that I will never be able to separate the past from the present. It's been two years since I left the church. I go to school, read books, make my own decisions, and form my own opinions, things Shauna never got to do, but I know I will always have the memory of her with me, reminding me of what she missed and encouraging me to make the most of what I have."

Anne then stopped speaking and just stared at me. What she saw were tears flowing down my cheeks. I had such an intense urge to wipe them away and not make this about me, but I felt the incredible pain and shock that Anne couldn't let me or the world see. I also knew I didn't want to re-create what everyone else had done that day—deny that they had burned to death a little seven-year-old girl.

I was so torn between all the emotion and my brain, which said take back control and be a clinician. However, I think that this was one of those moments in the life of my career that redefined what a clinician might be. I didn't know what to say, and I took a few moments to regain enough composure to speak.

"There's no such thing as letting go of the things we truly grieve, but we can move beyond grief to a calmer place of loss and sadness," I mustered at last. "I don't know that it necessarily gets better than that or has to be better than that."

Anne sat there listening to my words, her calm a vivid contrast to my emotional reaction. Of course, I was doing the feeling for both of us. Part of me wanted her to feel things, but a stronger part of me knew that it was too devastating for her.

"You want to hear something cool?" Anne said suddenly, startling me as if someone had awoken me by shining a flashlight into my eyes. Then I realized this was how she was protecting herself from the painful feelings, one of her defenses that had allowed her to survive all the abuse and torture and incredibly painful memories.

"Sure," I blurted out, not having come close to shifting the focus as Anne had just done.

"Well, you know I have all these stray kitties that kind of live in my yard. Well, a few days ago, I got two more. I kind of think they heard it was a good place to hang out," she said with a smile.

"They're there because you love them, the way you just wanted to be loved. That's one of the characteristics that are common to resilient survivors of severe abuse, especially women. They are often very attached and incredibly caring toward animals."

"What do you mean by 'resilient' survivors?" she asked, looking embarrassed.

"It's a term that means they seem to move beyond survival and thrive again in their adult lives. You have many, if not all, of these characteristics," I said, sitting forward slightly to encourage faith in herself and in her future.

Extremely uncomfortable with any direct praise, Anne said, "In my psychology class the other day I got angry, because people were saying you can't be normal if you've been really abused, and one of the women said that sometimes kids who are abused seem to just naturally attract it. Someone else said it can even be one of those hidden blessings that build character. I wanted to stand up and say something, but I was too angry."

"Why can't you say something if you're really angry?" I asked.

"Because I might say the wrong thing."

"Like what?" I challenged.

"I don't know, just something really hurtful."

"So, tell me something that you think might be too hurtful to say," I pushed, wanting her to begin to trust herself to find her own words, and maybe pulling for the anger that was always missing.

"I don't know. Maybe they have no idea what they're talking about," Anne said.

"Well, my thinking is that if you have something important to say, and it's a truth, then you might be able to find a way to say it."

"Yeah, but then people would think I'm a freak or not talk to me anymore."

"Maybe. Or maybe they would learn something important and realize the impact of their assumptions and their words."

Anne then asked a question I was anticipating. "Do you think they're right?"

"If I promise to talk with you more about this next time, could we wait until then for me to answer? We're past our time," I said.

"Okay," she said, looking forlorn.

But I didn't want her to form one of her self-denigrating conclusions, so I said, "I don't think it has to do with right or wrong. It's about an individual's path, and for most people, it's probably hard to see the kind of damage that's inflicted by child abuse as something you get past. I've seen people never get past it, and I've seen people shine and have wonderful and happy lives. I'm pretty certain you're going to be one of the latter, because you have those characteristics of resilience."

This time Anne smiled, knowing I wasn't going to let up on believing in her.

As I stood to say good-bye, I could see that she was feeling calmer, and I felt that even with the intensity of my emotions, I had handled this session well.

— CHAPTER TWENTY-EIGHT —

Several times during the ensuing week, I had found myself struggling with my sense of human behavior and our capacity to harm our own species at the magnitude Anne had described. In spite of all the atrocities occurring throughout the world on a daily basis, it is much harder to filter out or detach from when it comes alive so personally and vividly. As I reviewed my notes from the previous week for today's session with Anne, I felt my sadness again. When I opened the door to invite Anne in for our next session, her demeanor seemed to match my own.

Without saying a word, she stood up, walked into my office, and sat down on the sofa. She took a moment to hug Madison and, momentarily, her spirits seemed to lift, but then she looked at me and said, "I've had a horrible week."

Folding her arms over her chest and looking at me expectantly, kind of like a school principal might look at a misbehaving student, Anne waited for me to proceed.

I couldn't help but smile a little at her dramatic presentation. "So, are you going to tell me about it?" I asked.

"Why? You can't do anything about it," she said testily.

"That may be true. But maybe I can help *you* to do something about it," I said.

"There isn't anything to be done, and maybe you can't always make it better," she retorted, her tone unchanged.

My intuition told me her anger wasn't really about me, and I chose to look toward the source rather than focus on us in that moment. "Okay," I said. "I at least would like to know what's happening, though, and then we can decide whether I can be of any help. So, what's happened?" I asked, offering encouragement to address what was bothering her.

"For one thing," she started, "I've been looking at some articles on the church on the Internet, and all these new memories are resurfacing."

Before she could continue, I interrupted her to understand an important distinction. "You're saying two different things," I said. "One is that these are new memories, and the other is that they're resurfacing, which says to me you've remembered them before."

"Does it matter?" Anne asked, sounding annoyed with my question.

"Yes, it could be very important. But let's just talk about what you're remembering and feeling, and maybe we'll deal with that later," I said.

"One of them is a memory of being hit by a belt and having to wear the belt and show off the bruises. And one of the articles had a photo of Jonas Smith and some of the other men who hurt me. It took me back in time, and I felt like all the evil was inside me and possessing me again, like an evil spirit. I've found myself disconnecting more lately, doing that dissociating thing. Mickie says it's scary, because I have a glazed look at times."

Anne paused briefly, looking very sad, then continued. "Why me? How could my mom have let this happen to me? How could my father have done these things to me? I was doing a little better, but now I've started hating myself all over again," she added with a pleading tone.

"Mickie likes herself and who she is. I don't even understand how someone could feel that way. Then, someone told me I'm a survivor. Is that what I'll be doing the rest of my life, just trying to survive?"

This was by far the most upset I had seen Anne in a long time, and I found myself much more concerned about the immensity of what she was feeling and the pronounced regression. The dissociative experiences clearly indicated that she felt too overwhelmed.

Knowing that there were likely to be concomitant somatic experiences, I asked, "Is this affecting you physically as well?"

"Yeah, I have earaches in both ears, and I've been throwing up and getting real dizzy."

I was becoming worried that, in spite of how amazingly she had always endured so much, she was nearing a breaking point. So I knew we needed to try to back away from focusing on the past and all the pain for her to stabilize, and I felt pressured to get her there.

With those thoughts in mind, I said, "Well, I'd really like us to focus away from the past for now, and so I'll ask you to not read or focus on any of that stuff for a while. We need to help you feel better physically and back in control emotionally. Okay?"

"Okay," Anne said morosely.

"I want you to also go in for a physical checkup and find out if you have anything happening medically that needs treatment. What's happening at school right now? Can you maybe take a day or two and just do some relaxing and healing things, like anyone does when they feel really lousy, although I don't mean lying in bed—maybe taking some walks and doing some lightweight things with friends?"

"I guess I could," she grumbled, her tone saying, "That's all you can offer?"

"Good. Maybe we could talk more about your question of whether you'll always be in a survival mode. Would that be okay for now?"

Looking a little relieved, probably more because I had opted to take charge and give us a direction than because she presently felt confident in her recovery, Anne replied, "Yeah," sounding somewhat defeated.

"So, tell me what the term 'survivor' means to you."

"Everyone sees me as strong and funny, but I cry every day and feel stupid and very insecure and emotionally out of control. So, how can I be a survivor?"

"I kind of think you're talking about two different things right now. One is about how you come across versus how you feel inside, and the other is about what it means to survive and whether that's enough.

"We all have public and private faces. We usually try to put on a good face in public, even if we're really feeling different inside. I don't know if that's good or honest, but it's what humans do. It's what I do, too, so don't get lost in that one."

Anne looked up at me with an astounded expression. "Do you get depressed or worried about things?" she asked.

Her question caught me off guard. I didn't know if she saw me as someone who never struggled or if she needed me to always be okay. I momentarily questioned whether my own disclosure was appropriate at the moment, but I had already opened that door. And how could I be asking her to express her feelings and quite obviously hide mine?

"Yes, I sometimes get down and sometimes worry and sometimes feel angry, although not with you," I quickly assured her. "And when I'm feeling those things, I do everything I can to not show it, here or anywhere, except when I'm alone or with people who are close to me. So, I'm not really different on that front."

Anne had no response, and I couldn't discern how my sharing had felt to her.

Then she said, "But at least you don't have to just survive." She looked downward.

"Neither will you, eventually, in my judgment. I've told you before that you possess the traits that will allow you to move beyond survival, to whatever one might call that," I said, relieved to see us focus back on her.

"When?" she asked impatiently.

"You know, I'm usually pretty right on about direction, but I'm far less able to know the timing or the pace. I also know that you've taken a lot of steps forward and maybe one backward at the moment, but that's pretty normal.

"I think you may have begun to feel stronger and more confident and felt you could take a further step, like reading about the church and trying to struggle with concepts beyond survival, like why this all happened to you, but you may not be quite ready to go there yet.

"I also think people see a very real part of who you are, a strong, funny, and pretty amazing person, and that doesn't yet fit with how you've always seen yourself, but I know you don't see yourself the way you once did."

I stopped talking, feeling like I was doing a lot of work to make her feel better. Or was it to make her feel less worried so I could feel better? Maybe that was okay, too, I thought, as long as it helped Anne.

"The cages are the worst memories," Anne confessed. "But sometimes what scares me more than the dreams and memories are the ones I haven't remembered yet."

Her statement had been chilling and lacked any discernable boundaries, and I found myself sitting there trying to think of anything I could say to calm that fear—something other than unfounded optimism.

"Also, I'm upset because my father assaulted my mom, and she's in a sanitarium," she blurted out before I could respond.

"You're kidding," I responded, not hiding my shock. "No wonder everything is hitting you, between the memories and the fact that the chaos in your family endures. When you say a sanitarium, are you implying a mental facility?"

"I'm not sure. My brother says she's not seriously injured, so I assume it's because of the mental part. I called my mom, and it was the first time she and I ever talked about all the abuse. She's in denial and acknowledges I was kept in cages, but says it's the best they could do. She says she'll go and stay with my brother after she leaves the place, but I'm afraid she'll go right back to my father. She cried a lot and really needed my support.

"It was really strange. I always saw her as unstable and afraid and jealous of me, because my father was having sex with me instead of her. It was really bizarre being in the middle of their relationship and having them both punish me in different ways. Having her rely on me makes me feel superior to her for the first time. She was even calling me 'darling.' It's like I finally have a mom, but she's more like a child now.

"I even talked to my brother about having sex with me and watching and never protecting me, and he says he's starting therapy to deal with it. That was kind of cool, since I think he's doing that because he sees it's helped me to deal with what our lives were like."

Sadness spread over me as I realized how much Anne remained desperate to have a family, even at the price of her mom's denial and even knowing her mother's situation was probably temporary. Like all of us, she was still a child who just wanted to be loved, especially by her parents.

"You're starting to come to terms with a much larger truth than even the physical pain and emotional trauma," I said. "You're trying to make some sense of the bigger picture, and that's one of those forward leaps. All the sadness and the crying and bad dreams may be saying 'slow down a little, if you can.'"

"I don't feel like I control what my dreams are about or what comes into my head," she replied.

"I know, but I want you to at least see this as maybe positive and not just threatening."

"Could we talk about school now?" Anne said then, with one of her abrupt transitions.

"Sure," I responded, my mind trying to catch up with the sudden transition.

"I feel like I'm going up an escalator the wrong way most of the time and constantly fighting to just stand still. Between school and working at the hospice, I'm putting in sixty hours a week. I probably won't even pass all my classes.

"In my sociology class, we had the D.A. come in and talk about abuse and addressing it criminally and legally. It felt like she completely downplayed the impact on the people who are abused. People don't understand my experience, and the authorities and lawyers think retribution and punishment will be the ultimate healing and consolation."

"Do you think Nathan feels that way?" I asked.

"No, but he's different."

"I think that's my point. Not everyone feels that way, but you're probably right that these people focus on the legal aspects. I guess you have to accept that as part of their discipline and role and find emotional support in other places. It's amazing how many places you run into triggers."

"I told my teacher about Shauna's death, and she was really shocked but really nice. And she reassured me that when anything is uncomfortable for me, I don't have to read about it or stay in the class, and she'll work with me to do something else instead. She also said she really wants me to let her know when things come up."

"I think that was an important step for you, because you took an action to protect yourself and found care and compassion," I said. "And I have a feeling you don't think she views you negatively. She may feel bad for you, but that's okay.

"Well, we need to stop, and we haven't even talked about your trip to Portland next week to testify. How are you doing with that?"

"I'm really nervous, but a police escort is meeting me at the flight and taking me straight to Nathan's house, which feels safe. Nathan said there will be a lot of security at the courthouse and that my case is even in the papers there, but I'll be kept away from any reporters or photographers, and the judge isn't allowing any cameras in the courtroom."

"Well, since I know you'll be with Nathan the whole time, I feel okay, but you know you can call me any time you want to," I offered.

"I know. Thank you," Anne said with a calm smile as she stood up to depart.

— CHAPTER TWENTY-NINE —

Anyone observing the passenger seated in 28F on the United flight from Boston to Portland would have noticed a woman curled in a fetal position, at least as much as anyone could be within the confines of a seat in coach.

Anne Martin had boarded the plane in Boston, taken her seat, and not spoken with anyone during the six-hour flight. She had declined any food or beverage with a barely audible "no, thank you," and scarcely shifted in her seat during the entire flight. The flight attendants took little notice, both because she drew no attention and because they had been flying far too many years to really have anything to do with the passengers.

As the plane touched down on the runway, while the other passengers felt relieved to have landed safely, Anne's fear heightened dramatically. She could feel her heartbeat. Her breathing quickened and grew shallow, and she began to sweat and feel nauseous. Despite numerous reassurances from Nathan, myself, and the police contact who was to meet her flight, Anne had been conditioned to feel frightened in her home state of Oregon.

When the plane pulled up to the Jetway, the passengers jumped into the aisle, jockeying to exit as quickly as possible, but Anne remained in her seat. Portland police had instructed her to exit last, making it easier for them to shield her. They were clearly going the extra mile to reassure her.

After everyone had exited, she retrieved her daypack and headed toward the front of the plane. Turning from the aisle toward the Jetway, she looked ahead to see a policewoman and a policeman waiting for her. One of the flight attendants was also standing there with a surprised look on her face, and Anne momentarily wondered if she thought Anne was being arrested.

"Are you Anne?" the policewoman asked when Anne reached the end of the ramp.

Too frightened to speak, Anne nodded, clutching her backpack in a protective manner.

"I'm Officer Laura Michaels, and this is Officer Tim Burns, Anne. How about if we go and retrieve your bags, and then we'll head to where you'll be staying?" the officer said.

As they headed toward baggage claim, Anne's fear-sensing radar was on heightened alert, searching for familiar faces from the church. If she had been able to give rational consideration to the circumstances, however, she would have realized that even if they were going to show up at the courthouse, they wouldn't have known when nor how she might be arriving.

But Anne's fear precluded any capacity for logical thought. Powerful emotions trump logic, just as powerful intellectualization overcomes the ability to experience emotion.

"You certainly travel light," Officer Michaels commented as she retrieved a small khaki-colored duffle bag from the luggage carousel.

Anne simply smiled, still too overwhelmed with fear to engage in any kind of conversation. She knew that her changes of attire consisted only of a few T-shirts, an extra pair of jeans, and some underwear, because she had long ago learned to diminish her attractiveness, and hence her visibility, as much as possible. It was one of the few ways she felt able to protect herself from male attention.

Anne's anxiety reached its peak as they exited the terminal and stepped outside onto the sidewalk, which was less protected than the airport, so she was relieved to see they were immediately getting into a vehicle parked right in front. Once inside, she relaxed a little and sat quietly, looking out at the rain.

"Now that we have some privacy," she heard the policewoman say, "maybe we can talk about the next couple of days, Anne. As you probably know, we're taking you to Nathan Cohen's home, as per his instructions. There will be police officers stationed at the residence while you're in town and accompanying you to the courthouse. In addition, there will be a detail of other police officers at the courthouse to ensure your safety. Please know that we are very committed to protecting you."

Anne listened closely but derived little, if any, comfort from the officer's assurances. "You don't know these people and how fanatic and committed they are to protecting their world," she thought.

But as they drove through the imposing black iron gates to Nathan's property, Anne felt more at ease. Nathan's home had been a place of refuge for a few days when she had come back to testify previously, and unlike the courthouse where she had been assaulted, the elders wouldn't know this location. Besides, it wasn't just a cool house, it was a really cool mansion. When they pulled under the portico and Nathan and Cliff emerged from the house to greet her, she smiled for the first time all day.

Nathan opened her door and offered a hand to help her out. As much as he wanted to give her a hug, he knew enough to maintain appropriate professional boundaries in the presence of the police detail assigned to Anne. So he simply cupped her hand in both of his. Cliff, on the other hand, made a point of giving her a very warm hug.

Then Nathan and the police officers briefly discussed a few logistics regarding the security procedures for Anne's trip into town to testify, which was to take place two days later. Nathan had arranged to take two days to prepare her to testify, before she had to face what would likely be a very stressful experience.

Nathan and Cliff accompanied Anne into their home, and Cliff excused himself to finish preparing lunch. A casual lunch to Cliff consisted of three or four courses, cloth napkins, and fine wine, and could often last for two hours. He and Nathan were wine connoisseurs, having prominent collections in their homes in Portland and Napa, and loved to cultivate a lavish ambience in the tradition of Parisian or Roman cultures. Cliff adored cooking, and his gourmet kitchen possessed equipment that would parallel that of many fine restaurants.

Lunch also included the police detail that had brought Anne to their home. Nathan viewed them as part of Anne's team, and the Portland police had a vested interest in this assignment, having had two of their colleagues injured on duty protecting Anne previously. In addition, by this time, many law enforcement officials were aware that Deerbrook's elders had managed to elude justice for many years.

As Cliff headed to the kitchen, Nathan accompanied Anne up one of the magnificent winding staircases that ascended from each side of the twenty-foot-high entryway to the second floor of the house. Having four guest rooms allowed them choices in where to house their guests.

"Which room would you like to stay in?" he asked Anne, lifting an arm and sweeping it grandly across the vista of the upstairs hallway.

Anne laughed, never having had the chance to choose anything in her life, let alone choose something so luxurious. During her previous stay at Nathan's home, she had been in a more fragile state, and even a choice like this would have been too overwhelming. This time, however, it was very apparent that her mental health and confidence had improved considerably.

He led Anne to each of the four rooms, watching her eyes widen as she viewed each one, like a kid told to pick out any toy in the store. She looked at each room at least twice, almost as if she didn't know how to choose, before picking the one he'd thought she would. It was the most traditional, with a quilt his grandmother had given him adorning the bed and a rocking chair Cliff had inherited from his parents. He knew that vastly different from his own background, Anne's childhood had denied her almost any traditions she would want to carry forward into her life.

"Why don't you relax before lunch?" he suggested, as Anne sat gingerly on the edge of the bed.

Anne was only too happy to do so. It had been a long trip, and Nathan's bed was luxuriously comfortable. It was only the second time she had slept in a truly comfortable bed in her life, the last time being her first visit to this house.

Later, after a luxurious three-course lunch, Nathan and Anne retired to his study to begin their preparations for her testimony. This was going to be a very different experience testifying, since Anne was both a victim and a witness.

In addition, the accused was a man named Elias Harmon, a father of four and an important elder in The Christian Movement. His credentials as an influential member of the community and as someone who was privy to very powerful information regarding the church ensured that he would be represented by Oregon's best defense attorneys. The defense team would also have greater latitude to confront what it would deem had been Anne's role in the assaults against her. Most especially, the defense team was sure to exploit the jury's possible perception that she had had opportunities to notify authorities, as she had when she'd called the police about Mr. Jenkins. Nathan knew that the team would assert that Anne had chosen not to report Elias Harmon, which could dilute her claims.

Nathan had again lined up several aggressive colleagues to provide mock cross-examinations, reminiscent of their preparations for the Jenkins trial, but committed to being more adversarial and challenging for Anne. They spent twelve hours over the first evening and the following day putting Anne through a very challenging mock trial, followed by wonderful, playful, and luxurious meals served by Cliff.

It was another good cop/bad cop routine, with Nathan draining Anne of her emotional and physical resources and Cliff nurturing her with the comfort and nutrition of great cooking.

The three of them also took walks on the extensive grounds, which surpassed ten acres, and Anne found herself in an incredibly strange mix of great stress and blissful peace and safety, the latter only having existed in her past when she could spend a morning or an afternoon with the animals on the farm. She had virtually never experienced peace and comfort when people were present. But, as she retired that evening, she knew that the ensuing few days would be very stressful and emotionally draining.

Three different defense attorneys joined them throughout the second day, each using a different approach. One of them was very aggressive, and even though Anne fully knew this was a mock experience, she became very angry and hurt during this cross-examination. Another one seemed to be kind and supportive, luring her into a sense of safety and comfort, hoping to seduce her into answering in a certain direction. The third tried to confuse her, making it appear as if she might be uncertain enough about facts and perceptions to nullify her credibility and testimony.

In each case, Nathan allowed the attorneys to proceed for a while to assess their impact on Anne and see how she might respond. Eventually, he would take on the role of a coach, sometimes stopping the process to allow her to calm down and sometimes to give her a way to respond differently. However, he never asked her to respond in a way other than what she actually recalled, although sometimes he advised her not to give as much information as she was inclined to give, and he almost always tried to get her to withhold reacting emotionally, unless the emotions would serve to strengthen her claims.

Along with mock questioning and addressing Anne's responses, the team also focused on how she would come across physically, taking on the role of witness coaches. One of the attorneys helped her use some relaxation techniques and breathing exercises and also addressed the significance of her posture and facial expressions. They assured her it was okay to make mistakes, say the wrong word, or be confused or emotional, since juries strongly identify with human qualities and vulnerability. They also suggested that when she felt overwhelmed thinking about or remembering a traumatic experience, she could try to imagine it happening to someone else.

Albeit overwhelmed by all of the advice and expectations, Anne felt their encouragement, and she knew they truly supported her.

At one point during the afternoon, Cliff walked in to offer a snack, and as he listened to Anne recount some of the abuse she had endured, he began to cry. Everyone present noticed this, and it confirmed to them the power Anne's testimony would have on the jury. Nathan realized that Cliff's attachment to Anne heightened his sensitivity, but he was still a barometer, and this brought added confidence.

Even though Anne had very little understanding of ethics and the legal world, she had a strong sense that Nathan was someone who maintained his ethical responsibilities irrespective of his personal beliefs or concerns. He and Cliff seemed like truly good human beings. She didn't know what she was observing or experiencing yet, but they had a relationship that far better reflected the natural values of marriage than any marriage she had seen in her life. They had very different roles and ways of being, but both contributed strongly to the partnership. Each seemed to embody the best attributes of a strong father and a loving mother.

Anne was far from even imagining ever having any kind of real relationship in her own life, but their world together looked like something that would be nice to have. Nathan remained constantly supportive, even when she lost it or got angry and said she wasn't going to do this anymore. She absolutely loved it when her emotions and her antics got him to actually laugh. She had learned that humor could be a powerful means of disarmament and distraction that provided at least momentary relief or remission.

The following morning, Nathan and Anne met out on the deck on an unusually sunny day for Portland in January. It was chilly, but the sun had the psychological effect of significantly raising the temperature.

Even though it wasn't the first time Anne would be testifying, Nathan was concerned because this time the defense might try to employ what was termed the "nuts and sluts" approach. This was a tactic designed to discredit a victim/ witness by trying to establish emotional instability and elicit any history of sexual behavior that might bring into doubt the notion of involuntary acts.

In Anne's case, there was absolutely no basis for asserting sexual promiscuity. The police investigation, social service reports, and her testimony given at two prior trials substantiated that she had no history of voluntary sexual behavior and had been subjected to sexual abuse since early childhood. Even though her prior testimony wasn't admissible, it was known to all the legal participants who would be involved in this trial. Supposedly, her previous testimony wasn't known to the members of the jury, since that knowledge was one of the elimination criteria demanded by the defense team. So Nathan knew that this aspect of the defense's approach could easily backfire, both on logical grounds and because of the emotional sympathy a jury might have for a victim of abuse.

However, he acknowledged that the defense team had better chances when it came to discrediting Anne's mental faculties. The team was likely to use child abuse experts who would testify as to the psychological and mental damage that was likely to occur with repeated abuse in childhood. They would attempt to substantiate this with evidence that the other abuse victims from the community had incurred such psychological impairment that they weren't even able to testify.

Also, Nathan knew members of the church, including some of the elders, would be in the courtroom, their mere presence, let alone their stares and even subtle behaviors, significantly heightening Anne's fear. They had controlled and tortured Anne for three decades, and she still didn't feel safe from their grasp.

Adding to Nathan's concerns was his experience of Anne's tendencies in the witness box. While her memory was excellent and he could count on her to provide consistent testimony, he knew she had a propensity to become mute when she feared retribution or had to relive traumas. He had also learned from her first experience at testifying in court that she could become highly emotional, ranging from confusion to talking back. Even though all of her emotions were easily justifiable, considering her history, the defense would use this to establish doubt as to her stability and reliability.

Nathan would do anything in his power to support and protect Anne, but his role in court limited him in this. Consequently, preparing her as well as possible for various types of cross-examination was the best way he could protect her.

He also knew that Anne would not be the only witness in this trial. Elias Harmon's middle son would be testifying. That testimony and the fact that Harmon had allegedly inflicted offenses upon his own young child would weigh even more heavily in the minds of the jury, and Nathan felt this gave them a little breathing room. He also hoped that Anne would feel she had company, most importantly from someone within the church, in trying to bring justice to these men who had damaged so many children.

In addition, the son's testimony was crucial to Anne's case, since it would corroborate her charges that Harmon had, several times, assaulted her while she was still a minor.

So, all in all, Nathan was optimistic. The combined sentences for all the charges could conceivably put Harmon away for the rest of his life, a conclusion that would prevent him from doing further damage and reassure Anne that there was no possibility he would ever be free to seek revenge. He knew well, having worked with many victims of abuse, that behind any sense of justice, lurked the fear that someday this person, whom you helped put in prison, would come looking for you.

— CHAPTER THIRTY —

On the morning of the third day, Nathan woke Anne at 7:00 a.m. and told her they needed to be on the road in an hour, as he knew she would be the first witness for the prosecution.

The prosecutor had chosen to present the evidence regarding the assaults against Anne first, since the charges against Harmon for having sexually abused his son would seem even more egregious and leave a powerful last impression on the jury as it contemplated a verdict. And, if the prosecutor managed to prove both sets of charges, the jury would perceive the accused as being a serial rapist and, consequently, a danger not just to children but to society overall. When Nathan had explained this strategy to Anne, she better understood the importance of her role in keeping Elias Harmon imprisoned for a long time, leading her to feel both more comforted and more pressured by her role.

In spite of the early hour, Cliff had a sumptuous breakfast laid out when Anne came downstairs. But, compared to her jovial and boisterous mood the prior evening, she was withdrawn and motionless. She provided only one-word responses to Cliff's attempts to make conversation and picked at her meal so as not to insult him, but had no appetite.

Following their subdued breakfast, Nathan and Anne departed for downtown Portland with the police officers. Like the last time Anne had testified, a detail of four more officers met them as they pulled into the courthouse's underground garage.

The case against Elias Harmon stemmed from an investigation that had begun within a few days of Anne's 911 call. When police had initially questioned her, Anne had been too frightened to provide details, but she had later confirmed that there had been other children, all girls to her knowledge, who had been abused in the church community. Anne hadn't provided any names, but she had indicated the church elders had been instrumental in the abuse.

The police had fanned out to the elders' homes, one of which was Elias Harmon's, where they found four children. The third oldest was a boy named Nick, a thin, red-headed, nine-year-old, who had been withdrawn and nervous during the subsequent interview.

Nick had revealed a long history of having been molested by his father and having been forced to do things to his younger sister. In addition, Nick made references to Anne having been a live-in babysitter for the family and indicated that his father was often very mean to her, sometimes to the point of hurting her physically.

When the investigators had interviewed Anne a few days later, she acknowledged a history of physical, emotional, and sexual abuse perpetrated against her by Mr. Harmon. This information had provided the first confirmation that Anne was not only a witness, but a victim as well.

At the age of sixteen, Anne had become a live-in babysitter and nanny for the Harmon family, during which time Mrs. Harmon had given birth to the two youngest children, born a year apart. This meant that Anne had been a minor at the time, since the age of consent was eighteen in the state of Oregon.

Anne had left the home when Nick had been only two years old, so she'd had no knowledge of the abuse toward him.

Over the ensuing years when she had run into Nick on the farm or in Deerbrook, she had noticed his somber demeanor and nervousness, but never connected the similarities in his behavior to her own, because she had never known any of the boys in the church to have been abused.

To Nathan's relief, the police, as they had done when Anne testified against James Jenkins, escorted them past the press and public to the courtroom. Nathan didn't want Anne to be subjected to any exposure to the public or to any church members, as this could easily unnerve her and compromise her ability to testify.

After taking their seats, Nathan tried to find trivia to distract Anne, but had little success in dissipating her anxiety. Nor did the female judge's entrance provide any relief, as Nathan had hoped. While understanding that a judge's role is to be impartial, nevertheless he felt she might have greater empathy for what men had done to Anne.

The attorneys' courtroom theatrics during opening remarks, which lasted more than two hours, further increased her anxiety, making her feel trapped in the courtroom. It was, therefore, somewhat of an unexpected relief when the judge asked the prosecution to call its first witness, and Anne had to step forward to be sworn in.

Nathan stood up as Anne moved toward the witness box, wanting to assure her he was with her every step of the way. He then stepped forward and began his examination.

"Ms. Martin, would you please tell the court what your relationship was to the Harmon family?"

"I was their babysitter and nanny for three years."

"What were the circumstances of your role as a babysitter?"

"It was part of my service in the church."

"Was this a paid position?"

"No, it was a service I did for the church."

"In other words, you were doing this as a requirement or assignment from the church and did not enter into a separate contract or agreement as an employee?"

"That's correct. Everyone had to do services like this for the church. I often babysat for different families." Anne's tone and words were clear and precise, helping to make Nathan's points to the jury.

"Did you have a choice as to whether you performed a service like this for the church?"

"Not really. I couldn't have really refused."

At this point, the opposing lead attorney, Ms. Jones, stood up.

"Your honor, I don't see how this line of questioning relates to anything," she said dismissively.

"Mr. Cohen, do these questions relate to the nature of the charges or purpose of this trial?" the judge asked, obliging Ms. Jones.

"Your honor, I am trying to establish whether the church itself may be held responsible for the damages experienced by Ms. Martin while under its jurisdiction," Nathan replied, "especially in light of the fact that she was a legal minor under its direction, and that she was fulfilling a duty for the church and was injured in such service, not unlike any employee or volunteer for an organization."

Nathan knew that opposing counsel was astute enough to realize he was seeking to establish grounds for at least civil liability on the part of the church.

"Okay, I'll allow it," the judge agreed. "But I think you have adequately established your point, Mr. Cohen."

Nathan stifled a satisfied smirk. Paradoxically, the prosecution's objection had backfired, because it had enabled Nathan to assert his point directly, without needing to use his witness to circuitously do so.

"Ms. Martin, can you tell us why you were assigned to babysit for the Harmons?" he continued.

"Well, Mrs. Harmon gave birth to the two youngest children, Nick and Amy, about a year apart. I was there to help take care of the two older children and eventually help out with Nick when she got closer to giving birth to Amy. I lived in the home for that time."

"What was your relationship like with the children?"

"I really loved being with the children, and it was really cool to take care of a newborn. The children and I would have lots of fun together when it was just us and Mrs. Harmon." Anne's smile confirmed her affection for them.

"What was your relationship like with Mrs. Harmon?"

"I liked her a lot. She was very nice to me, but she was very different when Mr. Harmon was home. When he wasn't there, she would sometimes play with us and was more relaxed. We got along really well, and she kind of felt like a friend."

"Can you tell us what your relationship with Mr. Harmon was like?"

"He wasn't around that much, and he was really stern and not friendly. So I didn't feel comfortable around him. And when he was home, the kids were really different and Mrs. Harmon was too. It was like no one smiled or laughed, and we would stop playing when he walked in," Anne said, her downward gaze reflecting the sadness this evoked.

"During the time you served as the nanny and babysitter for the Harmons, did Mr. Harmon ever do anything to hurt you, either emotionally, physically, or sexually?"

Looking directly at Nathan, Anne responded, "Well, he'd sometimes push me against a wall and hit me on the backside or make me bend over in front of the kids and whack me. Or he'd say I was stupid and useless and make me repeat it to the children."

"How would that make you feel?"

"I'd feel really humiliated and embarrassed," Anne said softly.

"Did he do other things that caused you pain or discomfort?"

Anne looked down. Recognizing her hallmark of discomfort and fear, Nathan quickly added, "Anne, it's very important that you speak up, so that the members of the jury are able to hear what you are saying."

Feeling somewhat chastised, Anne spoke up. Her words, in fact, came out a little too loudly, and so were all the more arresting. "One time he cut our arms to join us in blood kinship."

There was a stir in the courtroom audience, and someone in the jury box gasped.

"Quiet in the court," the judge said. "Mr. Cohen, please proceed."

"Did you go along with him doing this to you?" Nathan continued.

"I didn't really have a choice. He said this was part of getting rid of the sin and evil inside of me, and if I had tried to stop him, he would have hurt me worse."

"Now, I know this is very difficult to talk about in front of all these people," Nathan continued, "but I need you to tell us whether Mr. Harmon tried to do anything sexual with you, and it's very important that you continue to speak up so that we can all hear what you are saying."

Anne again began very quietly, but when Nathan raised his hand as a signal to speak louder, she raised her voice.

"He would make me have sex with him when he came into my room, usually during the night. I'd wake up, and he'd be on top of me," she said.

"What would he be doing on top of you?"

"Sometimes he'd be masturbating, and sometimes he'd make me have oral sex or intercourse."

"How often did this occur, Anne?"

"A couple of times a week sometimes."

"Did he ever say anything to you when this was happening?"

"Well, a couple of times he told me that he'd told the church elders bad or sinful things I had done so they would agree that I should be punished. I think they sort of authorized him to get the evil out of me as a form of absolution. This was really unfair."

"Did you ever try to stop him from doing any of these things?"

"Not really," she said, looking hurt. In spite of all the anticipation and preparation around this question, Anne seemed to have taken his question as a criticism.

Nathan had expected Anne to explain why she'd stayed silent, as they had discussed. So he tried to prompt her, worrying that she might not answer this crucial question. "Why didn't you try to stop him, Anne?"

"Because it would have only made things worse," she promptly said, as if a switch had been turned on again. "And I might have also been hurt more, and this is what God said I deserved. I'd learned long before that my survival depended on not fighting. Some of the people who fought disappeared or had been found mysteriously dead from different kinds of strange accidents."

At this, Ms. Jones shot out of her seat.

"Your honor, this is hearsay," she said loudly, as if trying to drown out Anne's words.

But before the judge could even respond, Anne interjected. "I'm trying to explain what I've heard that's frightened me away from fighting," she said vehemently. "And as for my testimony being 'hearsay,' some of these strange deaths were in the newspaper. So, does that make it seesay?" Anne asked with a sarcastic tone.

Nathan was stunned by both the tenacity and the power of Anne's words. She had issued a preemptive strike before cross-examination even began, and, no matter what the judge instructed the jury regarding her outburst, they had clearly heard and absorbed Anne's words.

All eyes had shifted to the judge, who took a moment before addressing the courtroom. "I will allow Ms. Martin's statement, as it substantiates the basis for her not fighting.

"As for hearsay or seesay, Ms. Martin has stated that these were things she had learned that had frightened her. I myself have read some of the articles and police reports concerning these mysterious deaths, so this is public information, whether it be rumor or fact.

"The jury, however, is not to construe Ms. Martin's statements as anything more than rumor. To my knowledge, all of these deaths were ruled accidental or self-inflicted."

The court was silent for a few moments, and then Nathan said, "I know this hasn't been easy to talk about, Anne, and I'm going to ask you to do one more thing for the court. Is the man who molested you repeatedly, the man who hit and emotionally abused you when you were a minor, is that man in this courtroom?"

"Yes," Anne responded, quite emphatically. As terrified as she was in the courtroom, she had been waiting for this moment for a long time—to literally point a finger at Elias Harmon.

"Would you point him out at this time, Anne?"

Without saying a word, Anne looked up enough to know she was aiming in the right direction and pointed at the defendant.

"Let the record show that the witness is pointing at the defendant, Mr. Elias Harmon. I have no further questions for the witness at this time, your honor."

— CHAPTER THIRTY-ONE —

Anne's heart began racing and her breathing became very shallow when she heard Nathan state that he had no further questions. She knew it was now Ms. Jones's turn to interrogate her.

As the defense attorney moved toward the witness box, Anne avoided looking at her face, only seeing the hem of her smart, navy blue, pin-striped skirt and black patent leather high heels as Ms. Jones approached her. Fitting with Anne's sense of the theatrics that defined so much in the legal process, Ms. Jones looked like she had just entered the stage from the wardrobe department. It was often difficult for her to understand to what degree the legal process was about right and wrong as opposed to mere perception. When she'd questioned Nathan about this, his response had been that perception was, essentially, the truth that defined people's lives and decisions.

Nathan had again explained to Anne that the prosecution's choice of a female defense attorney was in itself a part of its strategy, hoping to influence the jury by presenting a woman who strongly believed in the credibility of the male accused, Elias Harmon.

"Think about the way you once believed that you deserved the elders' abuse," he'd said, "and remember how you believed it was justified by God."

But Anne still had not understood. That hadn't been about perception, she'd thought. It had been about what the Bible said, which was the truth, not perception. Her reverie was interrupted.

"Good morning, Anne. How are you doing?" Ms. Jones began, interrupting Anne's momentary escape.

So, Anne surmised, this is going to be the "nice version" approach they had rehearsed. Thanks to Nathan's coaching, she recognized Ms. Jones's tactic of using her first name as an inducement to diminish her guard. Despite all her thoughts, however, Anne responded to the opening question with a quiet "Okay."

"You told us earlier that you had been involved sexually with Mr. Harmon on numerous occasions," Ms. Jones proceeded. "Was Mrs. Harmon in the house during most of these occasions?"

"Yes, but she was in her bedroom and usually asleep."

"And were the four children also in the home?"

"Yes, they would also be in their rooms and asleep."

"How large is the Harmon's' house, Anne?"

"I don't know. It's the same size as most of the houses on the farm."

"Approximately how many square feet are these houses?"

"I don't know, maybe a thousand square feet."

"Actually, Ms. Martin, the house *is* about one thousand square feet, a relatively small space for seven people, and especially for none of them to ever hear anything happening on the numerous occasions while you were having a sexual relationship with Mr. Harmon."

At this, Nathan literally jumped out of his seat. "Your honor, I strongly object to counsel's reference to the sexual, physical, and emotional abuse of a minor as a 'sexual relationship.' That term implies consent, and this is far from any such kind of relationship. Nor is consent even in the realm of possibility, either legally or morally. Ms. Jones is also providing a conclusion rather than questioning the witness."

"Objection sustained," the judge concurred, as Ms. Jones began to defend her wording. "Please refrain from implying this was a 'relationship,' Ms. Jones," he said, shifting his glance from Ms. Jones to the jury. "The jury will strike that phrase from their record of this proceeding. In addition, Ms. Jones, please direct your efforts toward questioning the witness, rather than providing us with your perspective."

"Ms. Martin, could you hear the children from your room when they were playing?" Ms. Jones asked, regaining her composure following the reprimand.

"Yes, if they were laughing or playing a game where they would be talking."

"Could you hear Mr. and Mrs. Harmon from your bedroom, if they were talking in their bedroom?"

"I don't know."

"Let me phrase that differently. Did you ever hear them when they were talking in their bedroom from either your room or from the living room or the kitchen?"

"Are those three separate questions?" Anne asked, her tone slightly smug.

"You are welcome to answer them separately, if you'd like."

"Yeah, I sometimes could hear them from the living room or the kitchen, but not usually from my bedroom unless they were fighting."

"Did you ever make any sounds when Mr. Harmon was allegedly having sexual or inappropriate contact with you?"

"Only a few times when it would really hurt."

"You mean you never said anything else to him?"

"Not really."

"So, you never even asked him to stop?"

"It wouldn't have mattered."

"Please, just answer my question, Anne. Did you ever ask him to stop?"

"Not really," Anne said, more softly, sensing the trap.

"Did Mr. Harmon ever say anything to you or make any sounds when he was in your room with you?"

"Yeah, sometimes he would say things or make grunting sounds or strange sounds with his tongue." Anne briefly glanced toward Nathan to see if she might have offered too much information. She felt comforted by his smile and nod.

"So, if we are to believe you, Ms. Martin, you are telling us that you could hear the Martins talking in their room and the children playing in their rooms from your room, but you would have us believe that they could never hear you."

"It isn't a belief. It's the truth." Anne then just looked at Ms. Jones, not sure if she was supposed to answer, since the attorney hadn't really posed a question.

"Would you agree that it is somewhat strange that you could hear everyone else, but they could never hear you?"

"I never said they never could hear me," Anne responded, her tone more defiant.

Nathan felt a twinge of discomfort hearing Anne digress from her role of only answering questions to adding her own comments.

"Well, Anne," Ms. Jones continued, "when we interviewed the two older children and Mrs. Martin, they all denied ever having heard any sounds coming from your room at night. Doesn't that strike you as interesting, in light of you being the only person in this small house to allege that Mr. Harmon would come to your room at night, let alone initiate sexual events and make any sounds?"

Nathan was keenly aware that Ms. Jones was treading on thin ice, bringing up statements from a wife who was exempt from providing testimony by claiming spousal privilege.

"I don't know that I find it particularly interesting actually," replied Anne. This brought a few snickers from a couple of the jurors and members of the audience.

"How many bathrooms are in the Harmon's' house, Ms. Martin?"

"One."

"Where is that bathroom located in relation to your room?"

"It's next to my room."

"So, if anyone needed to go to the bathroom during the night, they would have to use that bathroom?"

"Yes."

"So, are you to have us believe that on the numerous occasions on which you allege these events to have occurred, that no one ever would have come across Mr. Harmon either entering or leaving your room?"

"I don't know if that would have ever happened."

"Do you usually have to go to the bathroom during the night?"

"Sometimes," she responded, feeling embarrassed by the question.

"Would you say you get up at some point at least half the nights to use the bathroom?"

"Yeah, I guess so," Anne replied, obviously annoyed and turning toward Nathan with a pleading look. He knew where this line of questioning was heading and saw nothing to which he could object, so he smiled to offer some encouragement.

"So, knowing how easily sounds can be heard between the rooms in this small house and the likelihood that, at least a few times each night, someone in the family would be going into or exiting the bathroom that was right next to your room, doesn't it sound incredible and hard to imagine that no one ever ran into Mr. Harmon entering or exiting your room, nor ever heard any sound coming from there?"

"I don't know," Anne responded cautiously, aware that Ms. Jones had made her point.

"Would you agree that it might seem likely that someone would have run into him or heard something?" Ms. Jones asked, looking pleased with herself.

"I guess so."

"With such an amazing coincidence of Mr. Harmon never having been seen or heard, would you still have us believe that he was coming into your room at night and having sex with you?"

"All I know is, it happened many times, as I have said."

"Isn't it true, Anne, that you are exaggerating what happened?"

Anne began to shake. She looked at Ms. Jones directly. "I'm not exaggerating anything. It all happened just as I said," she said, her lip quivering.

"Isn't it true that you had come to resent Mr. Harmon and were resentful of how serious and stern he was with the kids? And isn't it true that you would like to hurt him by making up such a story?"

"I didn't make up anything," Anne raised her voice.

"Aren't you just trying to get attention and get back at him for his emotionally inappropriate behavior in embarrassing you in front of the children? Didn't you make up the sexual abuse to really get him back?"

Anne began to curl into a ball on the witness stand, bringing her knees up and holding onto her shins. Then she began to cry.

As Ms. Jones was about to continue, the judge interrupted, turning to Anne.

"Ms. Martin, would you like a few minutes before we continue?" she asked.

Anne didn't reply and appeared to not even have heard the judge.

She then asked, "Ms. Martin, are you okay?"

Seeing no response, Nathan stood. "Your honor, would it be okay for me to approach Ms. Martin and see if I can help calm her down, and could we maybe take a recess?" he asked.

"That would be good, Mr. Cohen, and the court will take a thirty-minute recess," the judge said, relieved.

But, as Nathan began to step forward, Ms. Jones objected. "Your honor, this is a crucial point in my cross-examination, and it would be highly irregular and unfair to my client for the prosecution to be able to intervene and coach the witness at this time."

"Your point is well taken, Ms. Jones, but I am not going to allow this woman to be pushed further at this time," the judge determined. "I am instructing Mr. Cohen to refrain from any discussion of this testimony during the recess and not to provide any guidance regarding her prior or future testimony."

"Your honor, it would be very difficult for me to believe Mr. Cohen would not use this opportunity under the guise of helping her to feel calmer."

"Well, Ms. Jones, I'm going to allow him an opportunity to prevent the witness from emotionally breaking down and being harmed as a result of testifying," the judge said sternly.

Turning to Nathan, she said, "Mr. Cohen, I will ask the witness, who will remain under oath, if any such coaching or comments occurred when we return, and I will hold you personally responsible, under the penalty of contempt of court, if you abuse this opportunity."

Still unsatisfied, Ms. Jones again began to speak, but the judge, in a louder voice, reiterated, "That is my decision, Ms. Jones. Let the court notes reflect that you object, but I'm not going to further this discussion until the witness has had a chance to calm down."

Nathan was fully aware that Ms. Jones was trading the unlikely opportunity to have grounds for requesting a mistrial or setting up an appeal, for a significant loss of respect or alliance with the jury. She was, in essence, arguing with a judge who was trying to be merciful toward a highly distraught victim of child abuse.

He approached the witness box and opened the door, holding a hand out toward Anne, a gesture that did not go unnoticed by the jury members as they filed out. In spite of all the instructions, all the rehearsals, and the judge stressing the importance of evidence outweighing all other factors, such moments had the potential to powerfully affect a jury's deliberations and eventual verdict. But, at this particular moment, Nathan wasn't aware he was being observed. His entire focus was on Anne. She was, he realized, very close to that breaking point that both of them had feared.

Nathan directed Anne toward a door in the front of the courtroom.

As they passed through, the bailiff, a large black man whose massive physique contrasted with the gentle smile he gave to Anne, held it open, and they entered the waiting room.

Nathan directed Anne to a sofa. "Lie back, Anne. Just relax for a minute," he said gently. He then took a chair, and they sat silently for the next few minutes.

Nathan felt it best to allow Anne time to regain her composure before trying to talk with her. He also needed a few minutes to organize his thoughts so that he could address her approach to Ms. Jones's cross-examination without touching upon any of the content that related to her testimony.

When Anne's breathing appeared to have returned to normal and she was no longer visibly shaking, Nathan asked, "So, how are you doing?"

"I'm okay, I guess," Anne said.

"You obviously became very upset on the stand. What was going on for you?"

"She pissed me off, telling me I was making things up. I've never made up anything."

"I know that, Anne, and I'll tell you a secret. I'm sure the defense attorneys know you're someone who tells the truth, but sometimes their job is to try to make it look otherwise. She may seem really mean and probably isn't someone you or I would want to hang out with, but she's doing her job. You need to keep that in mind and not take it personally or even think it's what she believes. We've talked a lot about this before, how important it is. Even if it's really hard to do, you can't take her tactics personally, even if she says you're not being honest."

"Yeah, she may believe I'm telling the truth, but lots of other people may think I'm lying if she says it."

"You may be right, but I'm pretty sure everyone on that jury and most of the people in the courtroom see you as an honest person."

"Why does she keep asking me about what other people might have seen or heard in the house? Why doesn't she just say what she wants to hear?"

Nathan knew they had talked about this numerous times, but he also realized that the lay public and witnesses often struggled to comprehend that testimony was the only means of revealing evidence, beliefs, or circumstances in a courtroom, with the exception of opening and closing summations.

"Do you recall us talking about this before?" he asked calmly.

"Yeah, but I still don't get it," Anne responded, her tone sounding more annoyed than confused.

"I have a feeling you're saying you think it's a pretty ridiculous system, aren't you?" Nathan asked, nodding his head.

"Yeah, I think it's pretty stupid. If you want to tell people something, then you should tell them—not get someone else to do it."

"In almost every other situation in life, you'd be right, but in a courtroom it's done in this strange and ridiculous way. And I'm fine for you to feel it's ridiculous, but we still need you to cooperate and go along with this system if you want us to be able to convict Mr. Harmon for hurting you and Nick, and maybe stop him from hurting others. So, can you just tell yourself this is a dumb system, but go along with it for me for today?"

"Yeah, I guess so, but not if she's going to call me a liar again," she said with a defiant tone.

"I'll make you a deal. If she calls you a liar, you can say this in response. 'Sticks and stones may break my bones, but names will never hurt me,'" Nathan offered.

"Can I really say that?" Anne asked with a mischievous smile.

"Well, you probably better not say I told you to, but by the time anyone stops you, the jury will be laughing and Ms. Jones may find herself in an awkward place."

"Okay, that's cool," Anne said, her body relaxing.

"So, do we have a deal? You're not going to let her questions or comments get to you, and you're going to tell yourself she's just doing her job. And if she accuses you of something or calls you something like a liar, you can use the little poem."

"Yeah, it's a deal," Anne agreed.

With that said, Nathan suggested they go back into the courtroom and led Anne back through the door and to the witness box.

"This courtroom is back in session," the judge pronounced after Anne was settled.

Nathan gave Anne a final quick smile. "Do you feel you're okay to continue now?" the judge asked.

"Yeah, I think so, but could you ask that woman not to be so mean?" Anne said softly, but her words carried across the courtroom and brought outright laughter from the jury and from others in the courtroom. Even the judge suppressed a smile.

"You may continue with the witness, Ms. Jones, and she would like you to not be so mean," she allowed herself, and Ms. Jones had enough of a sense of humor or at least the wherewithal to appear amused, the feigned effort still obvious.

"Thank you, your honor. I worked on smiling more during the recess," she quipped before approaching the witness box once more.

"Anne," she resumed, "Did Mr. Cohen and you talk about your testimony during the recess?"

Nathan jumped up. "Your honor, this constitutes a harassment of the witness. Ms. Martin was not charged with the responsibility to adhere to your order. I was, and it seems highly inappropriate for her to be interrogated by Ms. Jones regarding this.

"This certainly isn't Ms. Jones's courtroom, although she'd like to have that power, obviously. There has to be a limit to her right to harm a witness, and I'm asking you to help me protect my client from this kind of aggression."

With this, Nathan realized, he had risked stepping on the judge's toes. He had aimed directly at Ms. Jones without even firing a warning shot.

"Mr. Cohen, I am quite able to determine how my courtroom will be run, and I expect you to maintain decorum in my courtroom," the judge retorted, cutting off Ms. Jones, who had started to respond. "You are free to object, but I am not going to allow the opposing attorneys to start attacking each other and distorting why we're here."

She then turned to Ms. Jones. "Ms. Jones, you will stick to testimony regarding the events in question and the charges related to the accused and any testimony the witness might provide regarding these matters," she admonished.

"If you have concerns regarding the behavior of opposing counsel, then you will address them with me. Do not ever use a witness as a pawn on a chessboard in my courtroom."

Ms. Jones knew she needed to act contrite at this moment, and it was a real stretch for her. "I apologize, your honor, and I apologize to Ms. Martin if I placed you in an unfair role just now," she said, turning from the judge toward Anne.

The judge then also turned to Anne. "Ms. Martin, you are still under oath, and I want to ask you a question regarding the recess. Did you and Mr. Cohen discuss any of the testimony, the questions or your responses, that occurred prior to the recess?"

Anne was visibly shaking again, wondering if she was in some kind of trouble. "We only talked about my being upset and not to take things so personally and what I could do if she called me a liar again," she managed.

"Did you talk about any of the content of your testimony or the questions posed by Ms. Jones?"

"No, but we did talk about Ms. Jones," Anne admitted.

This elicited more laughter in the courtroom. Anne's humor had an endearing quality, in part due to how much it reflected her striking honesty and literal thinking.

"All right, thank you, Ms. Martin. I feel satisfied that Mr. Cohen and you adhered to my request. Please continue with your witness, Ms. Jones."

Ms. Jones had unbuttoned her suit jacket, as if to seem less intimidating. "Ms. Martin," she began. "Do you understand what it means to be under oath?"

"It means I have sworn to God that I will tell the truth," she said.

"Have you ever lied about anything, Ms. Martin?" Ms. Jones asked.

"No. It's a sin to tell a lie, and God would punish me."

"So, you are under oath, Ms. Martin, and are telling the jury that at no point in your thirty-year history have you ever told any kind of lie?"

"That's right. I don't lie."

"Ms. Martin, when you were twelve years old and the police and social services removed you from your home and asked you if you had ever been abused, did you answer their questions truthfully?"

"Objection! Your honor, this witness's history of abuse is completely inadmissible according to both legal precedent and agreements reached between yourself and both parties prior to the commencement of this trial," Nathan interjected.

But Ms. Jones had a ready rebuttal. "Your honor, I am not bringing in any of the events of such history nor asking for any details about her history. I am merely trying to establish or, in this case, question her credibility, since it has tremendous bearing on this case and the life of my client."

"I will only allow the question you have put forth regarding her prior history," the judge said. "The witness is instructed to answer."

"I didn't respond to their questions," Anne said.

"Is that being honest, Ms. Martin?"

"It isn't lying."

"Is it being honest?"

"It's not saying anything, which isn't lying."

"Do you believe that not providing information to the police when they are investigating a crime is right, Ms. Martin?"

"It isn't the same as lying."

"That wasn't my question, Ms. Martin," Ms. Jones stated more sternly. "Please answer the question. Do you believe that when a policeman asks a question and you refuse to answer that this is right?"

Anne seemed flustered again, but she responded, "No, it isn't right, but it's different from lying."

"Thank you for at least being honest that you agree that this isn't right. I assume you agree that your withholding of information previously wasn't right," Ms. Jones concluded.

"Your honor, the prosecution is putting words in the witness's mouth," Nathan objected. "That was not what she said."

"I'll rephrase the question, your honor," Ms. Jones offered.

But the judge declined. Turning to Nathan, she said, "Mr. Cohen, your objection is denied. Both the jury and I are smart enough to understand that Ms. Martin didn't necessarily make this exact statement. Can we move on, Ms. Jones? Unless you feel it necessary to further belabor this point, which is, essentially, philosophical, since the witness has denied giving a false answer during her lifetime. Whether this be true or false, the jury will reach its opinion based upon this response."

Ms. Jones took a different course. "Ms. Martin, would you tell the courtroom where you grew up," she resumed.

"In Deerbrook," Anne replied.

"Are you saying you actually grew up in the town of Deerbrook?"

"Well, the farm was next to Deerbrook, and we considered ourselves to be living in Deerbrook."

"So, you actually grew up on a farm and not in a town or a city or even any suburbs, isn't that correct?"

"Yes, unless the farm might be considered to be in the suburbs of Deerbrook."

"Well, we don't really think of a town of maybe a thousand people as having suburbs," Ms. Jones said. "Did you consider yourself to have a normal upbringing, Ms. Martin?"

Again Nathan felt behooved to object. "Your honor, it is my understanding that the witness's past remains off-limits, and this is clearly an attempt to inquire about her past."

Ms. Jones quickly interjected, "Mr. Cohen is clearly using a very broad stroke to paint his canvas here. We have an agreement that any history of abuse or inappropriate sexual conduct is off-limits, but not her entire past. Anyone's upbringing, cultural environment, or childhood could have an important impact on perceptions or beliefs, which could be important in the jury's interpretation of Anne's credibility or ability to accurately understand later events."

"I'll allow generic questions related to her upbringing or early history, but don't tread on the grounds we have agreed upon as sacred, Ms. Jones. The witness will answer the question," the judge deemed.

But Anne just sat there, uncertain if she was to respond, until Ms. Jones repeated the question.

"Yeah, I guess I had a normal upbringing, as far as I knew at least," she said.

"Did you attend school while growing up, Ms. Martin?" Ms. Jones continued.

"We attended church classes on Sundays."

"Did you have any formal schooling besides that?"

"My father taught me to read from the Bible."

"So, other than when your father taught you from the Bible, and other than attending church classes on Sunday, you attended no school or classes growing up, is that correct?"

"Yes, that is correct."

"When you were interviewed by the district attorney, you indicated that you were placed in cages, along with other girls on the farm, and at times left in those cages for many hours. Is that correct?"

"Yes, that is correct," Anne said, and Nathan detected, with an uneasy feeling, a sarcastic tone in her voice, as if she were attempting to mimic the attorney.

"You also talked about many incidences of physical, sexual, and emotional abuse during your childhood. Is that correct?"

"Your honor, this is in violation of the agreement not to delve into the witness's past," Nathan objected wearily, before Anne could respond. He could barely believe Ms. Jones was again trying to circumvent this term.

Ms. Jones cut in, "Your honor, I am not intending to ask the witness to discuss any details of her history beyond acknowledging in general what the conditions of her world were like. I am trying to establish whether Ms. Martin grew up in a normal or highly unusual environment, and my questioning relates directly to the question of her perception and credibility."

"Objection overruled. I will allow it only as far as you've gone, Ms. Jones, but you are treading on very thin ice here. The witness will answer the question."

With the judge looking at her, Anne very quietly responded, "Yes."

"So, Ms. Martin, you would have the court believe that, in spite of never having been to school, in spite of having been kept in cages during part of your childhood, and having often been abused, emotionally, physically, and sexually, you had a normal childhood. Is that correct?"

"It was normal for me and the only childhood I knew."

"Thank you. That is my point exactly, Ms. Martin."

Anne looked fearfully at Nathan, feeling she must have walked into some kind of trap and failed. But Nathan smiled back and gave her a thumbs-up. He knew she'd had no way of avoiding Ms. Jones's snare.

"Ms. Martin," Ms. Jones continued, "you have told us that Mr. Harmon repeatedly tried to have sex with you against your will. Did you ever tell anyone about any of these experiences?"

"No."

"Why didn't you ever report any of these experiences, if you didn't like having them happen?"

"Because he said it was God's will," Anne replied, her voice shaking.

"And you therefore simply complied and went along with all these experiences?"

"It was God's will," Anne repeated, visibly more upset.

"Did you ever try to fight or resist or even ask him to stop?"

"It wouldn't have done any good anyway," she pleaded.

"Isn't it true, Ms. Martin, that you went along with it because part of you enjoyed the attention and affection?"

Anne curled back into a ball and began sobbing, uttering in muffled tones, "It was God's will. It was God's will. It was God's will …" She then began wailing almost uncontrollably and shaking. Nathan reacted by jumping up and moving toward her. It appeared to him that she had gone into some kind of a dissociative state. As Nathan came within a couple of feet of the witness box, Anne began swinging her arms, not even looking up, but seemingly trying to protect herself from an assault.

"It was God's will. It was God's will," she repeated, and she did not respond to Nathan's voice.

"Call the paramedics," the judge instructed the bailiff. "The court will recess for the day. Please vacate the court."

Nathan wasn't sure if the judge was trying more to protect Anne or to preserve the trial from being declared a mistrial.

Within moments, a paramedic team arrived with a stretcher. Nathan stood out of the way, but quietly repeated, "Anne, it's me, Nathan. I'm here, and you're safe."

Perhaps responding to his voice as well as to the calm voice of one of the female paramedics, Anne had started to come around.

"Anne, my name is also Anne," the paramedic soothed. "I'm a paramedic, and my partner and I are here now and will keep you safe. We're going to help you step down from where you are, so you can lie down on the stretcher. We'll give you something to help you relax. Is that okay, Anne?"

Anne didn't speak, but her shoulders slumped a little and her sobs became gasps for breath. Her eyes remained closed, and she grabbed her body with her arms, reverting into a fetal position, as much as one could in a chair.

Having no real indication whether Anne was hearing her, the paramedic continued. "Anne, I'm going to take one of your arms, and my partner is going to take the other, and we're going to help you step down and onto the stretcher."

The paramedics stepped forward simultaneously, taking Anne's arms and guiding her gently down the single step from the witness box. Then they slowly helped her to lie down on the stretcher.

They could see, now that Anne was cooperating with them, that she was again capable of listening and responding to direction.

Anne rolled onto her right side, back into a fetal position. While the female paramedic kept a hand on Anne's shoulder, her partner prepared an injection.

"Anne, we're going to give you something that will help you feel much better in a couple of minutes. I'm going to raise your sleeve, so we can give you an injection," the paramedic said soothingly.

Anne didn't respond or flinch when they inserted the needle, and within a minute, her body began to relax, so the paramedics gently rolled her onto her back.

"Anne, we have to put some straps on you to protect you from falling off the stretcher," the female paramedic said. But Anne showed no response. She seemed, in fact, to have dissociated again, since her complete lack of any response was beyond the likely effects of the sedative.

Standing a few feet away from the paramedics, Nathan wondered if he had done all he could to protect Anne during the cross-examination. Standing next to him, Cliff was wiping tears away from his eyes. All he could think was, "Dear God, hasn't she suffered enough in her life?"

CHAPTER THIRTY-TWO

Several hours later, Anne awoke in Nathan and Cliff's home. As her eyes adjusted to the darkened room, she saw Cliff sitting on the credenza beneath a semicircular window.

"Hello there, honey," Cliff cooed, seeing her eyes open. "We've missed you the past few hours."

"What happened? I don't remember coming back here," Anne asked, obviously disoriented.

Cliff rose from the windowsill and, crossing the room, took her hand.

"Well, you don't remember, because you were given a pretty strong sedative. Do you recall collapsing in the courtroom?"

Anne thought for a minute. "Yeah, I got really angry when that horrible woman started making up lies."

Her face flushed a little, and, seeing she was quickly becoming riled again, Cliff hurriedly interrupted her. "Hey, Anne, calm down. You and Nathan will have time to talk about all that. But I need you to stay calm for now, at least until he gets home."

Anne looked instantly contrite. Clearly not wanting to upset Cliff and reminding herself to behave in their home, she relaxed. "Where *is* Nathan?" she asked quietly.

"He's down at the courthouse, meeting with the judge. He'll be home by dinner, and then you can talk to him about everything," Cliff consoled her.

"I don't want to testify anymore. It's too upsetting to have to think about everything, let alone be attacked and told I wanted Mr. Harmon to have sex with me," Anne griped.

Cliff had always maintained a solid boundary between Nathan's legal work and their family life, so he didn't want to talk about the events in the courtroom, although having witnessed the experience made resisting difficult since he wasn't without his own anger toward the defense attorney. But he calculated an appropriate response.

"You know that I've always been on your side, Anne, and I'm totally there right now. But you and I have worked to keep our relationship free of legal stuff, and I'm really trying to do that now, as hard as it is. I just want to help you feel safe and comfortable, and you and Nathan can talk about everything as soon as he's home, okay?"

Instantly feeling guilty for pressuring Cliff, Anne looked forlorn. "Yeah, I'm sorry for doing that to you," she said, looking down at the bedcovers. "I know you really don't want to get into all of this. You've been so good to me, and I feel really bad for doing that."

"Hey, don't you ever feel sorry for that," Cliff said, his heart aching for having made her feel bad. "You're hurting, and you've had a really rough day. Wanting to talk about it is both normal and good, and I love talking with you. I never feel pressured when you just want to talk about your life or your concerns, but I try to stay away from the legal stuff. That's all. How about if I get us some tea, and we can at least dish the bitch?"

With that Anne laughed. "Yeah, that would be cool," she agreed.

They were still laughing when Nathan arrived a couple of hours later, and he had little doubt that his opposing counsel was the topic of their shared humor. He also knew that their reverie would quickly dissipate when he informed Anne that she would have to continue her testimony the following morning.

But before he could even think of bringing this up, Cliff gave him a look that clearly said, "Tread carefully," not unlike any mother protecting her child. Rising to clear the cups from the table, Cliff continued in a sing-song voice, "Dinner will be ready in thirty minutes, and this time 'Miss Anne' here is going to eat. Right, Anne?"

Nathan felt a rush of appreciation for Cliff's good judgment. Eating dinner before bringing up the case was, of course, the best approach. And, after all, with mealtime approaching, he had entered Cliff's domain, he thought, anticipating with pleasure the delicious aromas he knew would soon be emanating from the kitchen.

Nathan's expectations were not disappointed. The three of them enjoyed an elaborate five-course meal with a velvety bottle of pinot noir accompanying a rack of lamb, and they managed to have fun and laugh some more without touching upon the day's proceedings.

After dinner, Cliff excused himself from the conversation as he headed into the kitchen to start cleaning up, and Nathan invited Anne into the library, where she reluctantly followed him, knowing what he was going to address.

"Look, I know that you've had a horrible day and that Ms. Jones took some very cheap shots …," Nathan began, once they were settled.

But before he could finish, Anne interjected, "She's a lying bitch. And Cliff agrees with me."

Nathan allowed himself the smile he felt. Her response reminded him that, in many ways, Anne was still emotionally a child, so he needed to cajole as much as to reason with her. "I have little doubt that Cliff agrees with you, and, off the record, so do I, but we're still at trial and need to deal with the legal process," he coaxed.

But Anne was not persuaded. "I'm not answering any more questions from that liar, and I'm not going to testify any further. I've told them everything I know," she said vehemently.

Nathan looked into Anne's eyes, which he knew inclined her to look downward.

"You know I'll do whatever it takes to protect you physically and legally, but I can't completely insulate you emotionally from all of this. At the very least, you can be legally required to testify or face contempt-of-court charges, but I'm doing everything I can to make it safer and better."

His approach was working. Anne seemed less agitated, and softened with the recognition that further argument was futile and could result in some kind of punishment, a circumstance she had faced many times in her life. She had no clue, however, what contempt-of-court charges implied.

"And you know we *both* want Mr. Harmon to go to prison," he appealed. "If you don't cooperate, that might not happen."

"Yeah, but that woman made up lies and said them to the whole courtroom, and she's a bitch and a liar," Anne resumed, although this time her voice had a whiny tone.

Feeling he was gaining ground, Nathan spoke quickly. "Okay, hear me out, because I've been in a meeting for the past three hours with Ms. Jones and the judge, and we worked out an agreement that won't allow her to repeat any of her behavior."

"What kind of agreement?" Anne asked suspiciously. "Can't you or the judge ask the questions for her and just leave out the lies?"

"Please relax and listen, Anne. The judge clearly feels Ms. Jones went overboard, and she came down very hard on her. The judge knows you've been through so much, and she wants to do whatever she can to take this trial forward and protect you from further pain. So, she's stipulated that Ms. Jones has to submit any questions to her before we convene again tomorrow morning, and that she will not allow any tactics like she used today.

"The judge must allow the defense to finish with any further reasonable and fair questions, or there's likely to be a mistrial, and Mr. Harmon could get a significantly reduced sentence or even an acquittal if your testimony isn't allowed. I think this is a fair offer, and I fully trust the judge to be caring and responsible here.

"Ms. Jones reluctantly agreed to this option, and, as far as we can discern, it remains a legal option, since the defense will still pose her questions, and because it's similar to how a judge might protect a child having to testify."

Nathan paused for a moment, watching Anne's face. She didn't seem convinced, but neither did she offer further protest, so he made his final plea. "Anne, we need you to go forward. In truth, I think Ms. Jones was about done with her questions anyway and hadn't succeeded in damaging your testimony or credibility, so she took a really cheap shot. And she did so because you did an incredible job today. You beat her at her own game," Nathan said with the smile of a proud parent.

Anne sat there silently for a moment and then asked, "You really think so, even though I lost it and had to go to the hospital?"

"I don't just think so, my dear. I know so," Nathan said, taking her hand in his hands and looking deeply into her eyes. Anne relaxed even further in response. She trusted Nathan, and he believed in her.

Any relief Nathan might have felt at having achieved his objective, however, was supplanted by how lousy he felt knowing Anne had been bullied her entire life. His one consolation for having had to coerce her was that, unlike others with whom she had of necessity complied, he truly cared about her. He also held onto the awareness that he was doing this to win justice for her, too. "So, can we agree you'll go forward under these agreed-upon terms?" he asked gently.

Anne did not at first reply. But, after a second, she looked up. "Okay, but she's still a bitch and a liar," she said.

"Objection sustained," Nathan agreed, and Anne gave a slight smile.

Ironically, the testimony the following morning took less time than Anne and Nathan's ten-minute conversation in the library the night before.

The defense limited its questions to simple factual issues, including time frames and settings of alleged assaults. It was clear the defense was hoping Anne's memory would be inconsistent or vague enough to minimize certainty beyond a shadow of a doubt. But Anne displayed tremendous recall and consistency, enough so that Ms. Jones obviously halted her questioning prematurely.

— CHAPTER THIRTY-THREE —

Having learned that one of the girls she'd grown up with, whose family had left the farm, was in hospice with terminal ovarian cancer, Anne had planned, prior to heading home to Boston, to visit her after completing her testimony. She had arranged through her friend Kate's mother to come the following day.

Anne expected the visit to be a very difficult experience, in part because Anne knew that, while Kate's life had been incredibly painful like her own, Kate, in her thirties like Anne, did not have the chance to create a better life, as Anne was hoping to do.

So, after visiting a couple of hours, it was with a heavy heart that Anne said good-bye. Kate's mother offered to accompany Anne outside to her taxi, and as they started down the long, sterile hospital hallway toward the exit, Anne, her head hanging down, knew it would probably be the last time she ever saw her childhood friend.

She'd been so deep in thought as they pushed open the glass hospital doors and stepped out into an unremitting sunlight that felt incongruous to her mood, that she hadn't seen the two unmarked vans parked in front of them.

Suddenly, before the door had even closed behind them, a dozen members of the church threw open the van doors, jumped out, and rushed toward the two women.

It took Anne a few seconds to actually comprehend what was happening, and then she was inundated with pain, especially in her stomach. Almost as instantly, her awareness disappeared and, while she continued to register physical distress, her emotions and any understanding of her circumstances were eclipsed by the process of dissociation that took over whenever she was severely threatened.

Had Anne been able to register the facts of the situation, however, she would have observed five of the attackers punching her and tearing off her clothes in a fumbled attempt to rape her, an assault that was interrupted within two or three minutes by the wailing of sirens.

Somewhat ironically, just as members of her church had anticipated that Anne might visit her friend in hospice, local police had been tipped off to be alert for any members of the church showing up to either assault or harass Kate and her family. However, being a small-town, local force, it lacked the experience or sophistication to anticipate The Christian Movement's cunning and determination. They were, therefore, a little more prepared to possibly have saved Anne's life, but not enough to prevent the assault. Within minutes they had countered the attack and placed the assailants in handcuffs.

As ambulances arrived, Anne was becoming more aware of her surroundings, and she began to understand some of what had happened. A hospice nurse had covered her in a blanket, but as she probed beneath it toward her abdomen, from which sharp pains shot down her legs and into her chest, she realized her pants and underpants had been torn away.

Intense fear that she had been sexually assaulted gripped Anne, but she couldn't really comprehend what had transpired. She observed several policemen and then saw Kate's mother lying on the ground bleeding. She was moving, though, and Anne took this as a hopeful sign. She wanted to ask about the mother's condition, but words wouldn't seem to come out.

"Please don't move, Miss," a policeman, who'd kneeled down beside Anne, said. "We have emergency people arriving now, and we'd like them to assess you before you move, okay?"

Without making a sound or moving at all, Anne very slightly nodded. Her eyes were wide and darting around, which told the policeman that she was frightened of further assault. Somewhere in her mind she knew she was reliving a similar moment in her history.

"We've apprehended these men. They're in handcuffs now," he assured her. "You're safe. I promise you."

Even though she'd heard similar empty promises before, she somehow believed him, but she was terrified of medical help from strangers and of losing control. Then one of the emergency medical team nurses crouched down beside her. "What's your name, Miss?" he asked gently.

"Anne," she whispered.

The next couple of hours involved an on-the-spot assessment and then transport to a nearby emergency room.

Sometime during the several hours she was there, Nathan and Cliff arrived. When Anne first saw them, she realized they were extremely shaken, and this felt comforting, knowing that their concern represented truly being loved and cared for.

With their arrival, she began to cry for the first time. It was also the first time either of them had ever seen her cry. They were devastated, knowing her incredible threshold for physical and emotional pain had finally been overwhelmed. It wasn't surprising, considering that forty-eight hours earlier, she had been on a stretcher after collapsing in a courtroom and had just spent several hours saying good-bye to one of her closest childhood friends, who was dying. Nathan sat down on the edge of the bed and said, "We're here now and not leaving your side. I am so sorry we let you go."

Seeing Nathan's pain, Anne stopped crying. "I chose to go," she offered, hoping to ease his guilt. "I want to get out of here. Can we go?" she then asked.

"From what we've learned so far, you don't have any internal injuries nor any broken bones, just some bruises. But they're concerned you may have been sexually assaulted and want your permission to do some tests."

"No, I don't want them doing anything. I'll see Dr. Pearl when I get home. He's the only one I trust to do that."

"I understand, but you have to realize that if we want to obtain anything that could be used as evidence, then we have to take those samples now."

"I don't care about evidence. I'm done testifying," Anne said.

"Okay, okay. The good news in all this is that the police arrived while the assault was taking place, and they are solid witnesses. So you're not likely to be needed to confirm anything. There are also numerous other witnesses," Nathan said, thinking aloud.

"Can we just go to your house?" Anne pleaded, tired of all the legal talk.

"I can tell you that's very much Cliff's and my plan, so let me check with the doctors and see if they can release you now. I also need to confirm that they've set up police escort. This is a very big deal. It appears that almost all of the rest of the leadership of the church has been arrested and this may bring an end to The Christian Movement, but we need to have you under police escort while you're still in Oregon."

"Okay, but how many?" Anne asked, her smile more serious than playful.

"How many would you like?" Nathan asked, smiling.

"Maybe twenty," Anne grinned, wincing when it cost her a sharp pain in her jaw.

Nathan left and arranged for Anne to be released.

The trip back to Nathan's house was painful for her, but uneventful, and after getting settled back in her room, she asked Nathan if she could call her mom. He brought her a phone, and she dialed the house. When her mother answered, she shared what had happened, omitting the possibility of a sexual assault. Her mom's response was neutral. She had little to say except to ask if she was okay. Not wanting to alarm her, Anne feigned that she was.

Then her father got on the phone, and she briefly related to him what she had been through.

"Nobody should abuse my daughter without my permission," he interrupted angrily. This was his only comment and, as Anne hung up the phone, she told Nathan, who was standing beside the bed, what he'd said.

They stared at each other, stunned and perplexed by the intent of the strange statement, and wondering if this was her father's bizarre way of saying he in some way wanted to protect her, or an acknowledgement that it was okay to abuse her, if it was cleared with him. It was an answer that might never really be known.

Anne remained a few days with Nathan and Cliff, not venturing out of the house at all. She remained under police escort to the airport, where it had been arranged for her parents to see her inside the terminal. She had a brief visit with them, but her mother was the only one to speak. As Anne headed toward security and her gate, her father got up and followed her, speaking in tongues the whole time. She had no idea what he was saying, but just hearing him speak in tongues triggered powerful images of all the abuse. She was also very embarrassed and was immensely relieved to reach the security checkpoint, where security personnel stopped him. Except for knowing she would miss Nathan and Cliff, she was enormously relieved to be heading home to her life in Boston.

— CHAPTER THIRTY-FOUR —

It was Christmas week in Boston, a time when our disdain for freezing temperatures and traffic-crippling snowfall is eclipsed by the desire for the proverbial white Christmas.

I was always pulled in two directions regarding taking off the holiday period, one being the absence of at least half my clients and the other being the increased depression that many people experienced during the holidays. I had long ago learned that holidays serve to magnify the point at which one finds oneself in life. If life felt good, fulfilled, and connected, then the holidays usually increased that joy. If life felt isolated, struggling, or unhappy, then the holidays magnified the emptiness and depression. So, I had come to a compromise over the years, and I usually worked one or two days during the designated Christmas week, affording my clients who were struggling, a place of refuge and support.

Consequently, as Anne had returned from her disastrous trip to Portland the beginning of the Christmas week, we had committed to a couple of hours of what I thought of as a debriefing. I had received a call from Nathan following the assault at the hospice and had spoken with Anne briefly that evening. I was also aware that she had declined to be evaluated for a possible rape, and it needed to be addressed.

Opening the door to my waiting room, I observed Anne as being considerably more demure and subdued than when I'd last seen her. She looked up slowly, revealing several bruises on her face that looked very tender. As she walked into my office, I could tell she was in pain. Once we were seated, I said, "I know we've talked some, but how about letting me know how you're doing now."

"I'm kind of okay, I guess. I'm more shaken up than hurt," she said without visible emotion.

"That's what I understood. Are you in physical pain now?"

"My ribs hurt where they punched me, but they're not broken or anything. I guess I'm okay otherwise," Anne responded, her affect remaining flat.

"How about emotionally?" I asked, looking at her more intently.

"I've been crying a lot more again and waking up really frightened. I have been dreaming about what happened, and it's harder to get back to sleep. But it's not as bad as a couple of days ago. I feel better just being back here."

"That's good, and you'll heal from this, like so many other things you've had to find your way through."

"Yeah, I figured you'd say that," Anne commented, her tone flat.

"Well, more than me saying that, do you believe it?" I asked, wondering if I had been patronizing.

"Yeah, for the most part, but I don't think I'll forget it."

"I think we both know that isn't a realistic goal, but in time it will be less of a focus, and you'll feel physically and emotionally stronger again. I do want to ask a question, though, because I need to help you make some choices. I know you decided not to have any gynecological exam done in Portland, and I can understand why. But I also understand you may have been raped during the assault. What do you remember or think happened?"

"I don't know. I don't remember anything like that happening, but I don't remember most of what happened after the first moments."

"Okay, so what do you believe at this point? Is your best guess that you were sexually assaulted?"

"I'm really not sure."

"Well, since you're not sure, what do you feel you should do at this point?"

"Do you mean should I see Dr. Pearl?" she asked.

"That's one of my concerns. The other is that whatever happened may still surface, and we want to talk about ways and resources to deal with those images or memories if they arise."

"Are you worried I could be pregnant?" she asked, her tone more challenging than fearful.

"That's certainly one of my two concerns. The other is that you're at risk for sexually transmitted diseases, and if they're caught right away, you can almost always be treated and be fine."

"Yeah, I thought of that, too," she said quietly.

"So, would you be willing to agree to call him after our meeting today?"

"Could you call him for me and tell him what happened?" she asked somewhat plaintively.

"Absolutely. How about if I call him right after our session and ask him to call you to make an appointment?" I responded, knowing this wasn't one of those times when having her take a step was as important as the step itself.

"Thanks," she said quietly. Then, shifting our focus abruptly, she added, "I wrote a poem about Shauna, but I think I'll just keep it. Is it okay if I don't show it to you?"

"Of course, it's okay. Would you prefer to just keep it something between you and her?" I asked, wondering if I was disappointed.

"I guess so. Is that strange?" Anne asked carefully.

"Do you think it's strange?" I parroted back.

"I guess not. Some things can be private between real sisters, I guess."

"Absolutely, and maybe you're finding that relationship now."

We hadn't talked about Shauna since the session when Anne had shared her horrendous first childhood memory. It had, I thought, been a cathartic moment for her, providing some release of the intense pain she had harbored inside for so long. For me, however, it had been the opposite. I had absorbed something incredibly heinous and depressing that I had held inside without any outlet to express what I had felt. But now, Anne's poem to her sister appeared to portray a sense of peace with this almost unimaginable tragedy, and that was inspiring and helped me to feel calmer.

"What inspired you to write this now?" I asked.

"I don't know. Maybe because I was back home near where it all happened. I also wrote a story giving Shauna a childhood and mailed it to my father. He became irate and admitted he knew about or had something to do with the murder of the two girls they found a few months ago. So, I brought up the will and my inheritance on purpose, like we talked about a while back, and he didn't say anything in response.

"You have more than equaled the playing field," I commented, smiling and feeling proud of Anne.

"What do you mean?" she asked, looking puzzled.

"I clearly see you using your leverage and your inner strength to confront him and challenge what you feel is wrong. This is such growth and evolution from where you were two years ago. I'm sure you can see that."

"Yeah, I can," she said, her tone somewhat ambivalent, however. "I'm still really shaky talking to him, but I'm not afraid of his anger anymore."

"You know, I think it's fine to be shaky, and it's really great that you aren't afraid of his anger. What do you think the shakiness is about if it isn't about a fear of him?"

"I don't know. Maybe it's a fear of my own anger coming up."

I just smiled and slowly nodded. More and more, Anne was reaching her own insights without having to rely on me. I didn't want to say anything. I just wanted her own words to resonate with her—with us.

"Did I tell you I saw my parents at the airport briefly, and my father followed me all the way through to security speaking in tongues? It was really bizarre, and they stopped him from following me through security."

"I didn't know you were planning to see them," I said.

"Yeah, I decided to. The police were still concerned that it might put me in danger, but they agreed it would be okay at the airport, since they had so much security there anyways. I wanted to see my mom, and I didn't know if my father would even be there."

"I do have a question now that we're talking about Shauna," I said after a brief silence. "I don't know if you've thought about it. Since the elders also saw you as being this evil being who needed to be absolved of sin, why do you think they killed Shauna, but not you?"

"Because she didn't exist legally, and no one would have ever wondered about her being gone," she answered without hesitation. "I was adopted, and there were records of my existence. Shauna was born within the church and probably never recorded anywhere, and since she was probably the child of Father Jonas and a young girl who lived on the farm, no one would dare challenge him. I've actually been wondering if this was also the case with the other girls whose bodies were found. They were all probably children who didn't legally exist, and that's why the police can't figure out who they are."

What Anne was saying made sense, but the whole tragedy felt even more eerie at that moment as I contemplated an even more macabre world in which children could be discarded.

"So, how are you doing with your feelings about Shauna after having shared her history with me?" I asked, maybe being the one who needed to change topics this time.

"Well, I'm glad you know about it, but I can still see images of her face and her screaming, and it seems like that will always be there."

"Yeah, I can understand. I think there are some things in life that are too hard to ever really resolve. We're just calmer in coping with them. She will always be your sister, and she will always be a little girl who should have been loved and protected. So this may always be about loss and wrong," I offered, hoping my words conveyed what Anne was needing in that moment.

"One of my teachers said I should write a book about my life, but I told her it would be too overwhelming to have to spend all that time focusing on all the details again. But, I was thinking maybe I could write it as if it's about someone else."

"In truth, you don't know if it would be more upsetting or more cathartic, and it would likely be both. I'm not sure I believe that writing it about a supposed someone else would really alter the impact. You'd know it was about you. Maybe the readers would be fooled, but you wouldn't. Is it something you want to think more about?"

"Not really. It was just a thought. I'm really pretty certain I want to go to law school, and I'm even getting information about programs in the area. Besides, I've just begun to really read okay. And between law school and work, I'll have more than enough on my plate. And maybe I'll even try dating this woman I met," she said, a big grin on her face.

"I think you're right. So, wow, law school. What area of law are you thinking you'd like to pursue?" I asked, deciding to let her tell me about this new woman when she felt ready.

"Oh, I know I want to work with abused children or maybe kids in foster homes and adoption," Anne responded, sounding resolved with this decision.

"The circle of life," I mused.

"Why do you say that?" she asked with a confused look.

"Oh, I guess I believe that a lot of life goes in circles, and you've come around the circle, from all the abuse you've endured to deciding to work to help other children who've also suffered and struggled," I reflected, nodding.

"Yeah, I want to try to help them not go through all that I went through."

"You know, they could hurt your body and terrify you, but they couldn't break your spirit."

Anne pursed her lips, her way of saying thank you. We more and more shared not only a language of words, but also a growing language of expressions and behaviors that conveyed so much.

"Well, we need to stop, so I'll call Dr. Pearl and let him know you need to see him right away and why, okay?"

"Do you think he'll be mad at me for not having let them examine me in Portland when this happened?"

"I can guarantee that he won't be mad, but he may be upset this happened to you, since he cares about you. So, don't confuse upset with mad. Remember to look for evidence before you assume someone feels something negative about you. Okay?"

"I met this woman at church. Her name is Nicole, and we've kind of had a second date. It was really comfortable, and there wasn't any sense of pressure. She's also from Oregon, so that's really cool. But I haven't told her anything about my history," Anne said, her smile reflecting the comfort of switching topics.

"I can understand that, and it seems fine. If things go forward, you'll find the time and place to share things with her. Where did you go on your two dates?"

"Well, the first one was going to lunch after church a couple of weeks ago. But we went with some mutual friends, so it wasn't like a real date. But then we went to dinner alone for the second date, and that seemed like a real date."

"Very cool," I remarked, using one of her expressions to emphasize my support.

"Yeah," she agreed, grinning again. "Do we have one more minute so I can show you a quilt I made about Dr. Howard?"

I wondered if Anne knew how seductive an offer that always was, since I was so enamored of the quilts and their power in her healing. I also wondered what kind of images could depict a psychiatrist.

"Sure. For a quilt, I'll even take two minutes," I said, smiling in return.

She unraveled a quilt sewn in gold, burnt orange, forest green, and tan.

"I used autumn colors as a reflection of him being older and, therefore, later in life since autumn is later in the year. I also decided to use ugly fabric to show how I think he sees me, that he sees me as maybe psychotic at times. You see the tumbling blocks?" she asked, pointing. Looking up at me, she said, "They are me, and the thread around the blocks is holding all the parts together. I used the last piece of the one childhood dress I had. Dr. Howard is red, since he felt dangerous at first. Also, because his tie seems so official and stern, he seems scarier."

"I really love this one," I said. "The colors are incredible, and I think the meaning is fascinating."

With a look that had grown more appreciative than perplexed, Anne asked, "You really mean you like it?"

"Yeah, a lot."

After Anne departed, I spoke with Dr. Pearl and filled him in on what Anne had told me, including her fear he would be mad. His initial reaction was "How could she think that?"

— CHAPTER THIRTY-FIVE —

It was one of those perfect spring days in April, with a spectacle of white magnolia blossoms lining the streets of Boston's Back Bay and parts of the South End. The flowers were one of the truest rites (which after the long winter I considered "rights") of spring, and I enjoyed them all the more because, on this particular day, it was my fiftieth birthday.

The milestone of turning fifty wasn't as difficult, because too many friends had died too young from AIDS. I had learned to simply be grateful for the chance to have these years, and this eclipsed the more difficult challenges of aging most of the time. I could identify with one of the birthday cards I had received, however: The card had quipped, "You know you're 50 when you bend down to tie your shoelaces and wonder, 'What else could I get done while I'm down here?'"

Since it was my birthday, I'd scheduled only two clients, and Anne was the first. She seemed happy as she entered my office. She sat down, giving me a generous smile but said nothing. I waited a few moments and then said, "So, you're smiling this morning."

She looked right at me. "Happy birthday," she said, handing me a card, then directing her gaze shyly downward again, uncomfortable with the personal interaction.

Moved by her thoughtfulness and her bravery, I smiled. "Thank you. How did you know it was my birthday?" I asked.

"I asked Dr. Pearl if he could find out when it was, and he did," she grinned.

"You are resourceful. Should I open this now?"

"If you want, or you could just open it later," she said a little awkwardly.

"Hmm. I think you just told me you'd rather I open it later," I said, honoring her discomfort.

She smiled slightly, confirming my hunch that she felt a mix of desire and awkwardness with the personal side of our relationship.

So I just said, "I'll do that," and smiled back.

"So, what are you going to do for your birthday?" she asked. "How old are you, by the way?"

Since this was clearly one of those infrequent opportunities for her to learn more about my personal life and a way of building a sense of comfort and natural equality in the relationship, I answered, "I'm fifty," without needing to overly analyze anything.

"That's cool. What will you do to celebrate?"

"A group of my friends are having a dinner party tonight to celebrate with me."

"That's cool. I've never had a birthday party."

I realized this was important to talk about, but I was trying to discern if that was what she needed at the moment or if she needed to talk a little about my life—another fork in the path. So, after pondering a moment, I asked, "What does it feel like to talk about my birthday party?"

"My father wouldn't allow any celebration of my birthday," she said quietly, her eyes still lowered. "My mom would kind of secretly do something like make a little cake that was just for the two of us when he wasn't around, but no one sang *Happy Birthday*, and there were never any presents or anything. It was different for my brother, though. The family would celebrate it with a party, and he'd get presents."

The tone of our conversation had dramatically shifted for both of us. I felt so sad for her, and she seemed to feel awkward that our focus had changed from my birthday party to her lack of them. Her questions seemed to have ended, and we sat for a few moments while I studied her and she studied the floor.

"So, how is it to hear about the celebration of my birthday?" I resumed after a minute.

"Oh, I think it's really cool, and maybe someday I'll get to have a party."

This sounded so much like the wish a child might have. It was another part of what had been taken from her, and I shared the first idea that came to my mind. "Well, maybe you should have a party when you graduate next year," I suggested.

"Yeah, that would be really cool," she said wistfully.

I so hoped someone would choose to do that for her. I knew her friends would want to celebrate with her, but also suspected they wouldn't know that she had never been celebrated in her life. But that was something that I couldn't change, and I doubted she was ready to address it in more depth, so, after a few moments, I asked, "So, how are things otherwise this week?"

"Okay. Can I show you a quilt I made for Dr. Pearl?" she asked, brightening.

"Sure," I replied, wondering if her more recently prolific creativity was a reflection of more difficult memories and emotions surfacing.

Anne opened up another incredible piece of art and explained what was in front of us. "It has a lot of green in it. That represents being trustworthy to me. It goes from orderly to disorderly patterns, since he'd say things and sometimes they would make sense and sometimes they became jumbled in my mind. Even the stitching is erratic and represents my confusion. The larger stitching represents things that have felt intimidating and overwhelming. It becomes smaller, like I would when I'd disappear. But the smaller stitches are orderly and calm again. The other main color is blue, which is also calming. He always talked calmly when he stuck his hand inside me."

Her last sentence interrupted the poetic mood with the harsh truth of her experience. I had no concept, as a man and as someone who had never been sexually abused, what that might be like, and I didn't know what to say.

"Will you give it to him?" Anne asked, since I hadn't said anything.

"Why wouldn't you give it to him?" I asked, relieved she'd spoken first.

"Because I'm embarrassed. He might think it's silly or stupid."

"He'll be very moved by it. I can assure you of that. But if you really feel too uncomfortable, I can get it to him. But," I added, "the operative word here is 'get,' which is different than what it means for you to 'give' it to him."

For a moment I wondered why I hadn't challenged her to take this interpersonal step, but I decided that she was taking lots of incredible steps and, once in a while, it was okay to just make it easier and help her out.

"Yeah, yeah, yeah," Anne's expression seemed to say. But all she actually said was, "I'd rather you give it to him."

We folded up the quilt together, and I put it on my desk. We sat there in silence for a minute or two, and then Anne smiled slightly.

"So, I guess you want to talk about Nathan's letter," she said.

"I think we need to talk about Nathan's letter, don't you?" I answered, noting that she had initiated doing so.

"Yeah, I guess so."

I had, earlier that week, received a copy of an e-mail Nathan had sent to Anne. It read:

Dear Anne,

I thought it would be beneficial for me to put down exactly what is happening at the moment, so that you have a chance to consider what our response should be. I think it would be most beneficial for you to talk to Dr. Hirsch (and, of course, to the glorious Madison) before you respond, but please respond directly to me this time.

The authorities were given a collection of journals by Anna Smith, Jonas's wife, which appear to have been written by Jonas, several other elders, and your father. They chronicle the abuse carried out by them between 1977 and 1992. There are several volumes that relate specifically to you beginning in 1977, and these are, according to the police, the most disturbing. Maybe of the greatest significance is information related to one particular couple, the Reillys, who are clearly implicated as perpetrators of your abuse. They are certainly likely to face prosecution, based upon this preliminary evidence.

Much of the evidence contained in the journals has already been prosecuted, but there is a sizable amount of new information. It is not realistic for us to expect the police to ignore this, and I am certain they are going to request a response from you regarding certain items. They are currently looking at what constitutes new evidence and state they will have a plan of action in the next month or so.

Everyone is sympathetic to the fact that you do not wish to rehash these issues, and your opinion will hold weight in their decision-making, but it is sensible for us to cooperate with the investigation at some level. To this end, please do not send any more unsolicited e-mails to the detectives handling this investigation, particularly ones that contain suggestions as to what they may want to do with their evidence. Thank you.

Initially, what I need to know is how much (if any) involvement you are prepared to have with any potential investigation. I am copying this e-mail to Dr. Hirsch, as well as a separate e-mail asking him to discuss some pertinent issues with you. In the interim, good luck with your midterms. I know you'll do splendidly.

Nathan

I walked over to my desk and retrieved a copy of my response, which I handed to Anne. "Here's my reply," I said.

Hello, Nathan.

Thanks for the heads-up regarding your communication with Anne about the journals. I have little doubt she will be upset having to return to provide testimony again, as she simply wants all of this to end and to be able to move forward in her life now, without having to continue to be trapped by the past. I know she and you have previously discussed the idea of reaching some kind of agreement regarding an eventual time frame for termination of her 'responsibility' as a witness. I feel it is imperative, because it not only retraumatizes her, it also prevents her from really moving on in her life. I will see her this afternoon and discuss her concerns and readiness to deal with questions and again provide information, especially since this could include material and issues she hasn't even known about. One point of clarification that might help is the duration of the agreement in terms of how much longer she might be asked to provide testimony regarding the journals and any other potential cases derived from future findings.

Lastly, I have little doubt she has more information (which I can't necessarily disclose) regarding other significant events. I have spoken with Anne over the years regarding informing on her father. I have little doubt regarding his capabilities and culpability. Not atypical for a victim of abuse perpetrated by a family member, she remains protective regarding him and the fallout it would portend for her mother. As he is eighty-five and clearly no longer a risk to minors, I understand the value of further prosecution and incarceration is more of a cost than a benefit. You can be sure I am personally conflicted supporting anything other than fairness and justice for Anne, but I have to manage those feelings and support what Anne wants and needs. She has also alluded to the alleged disappearance of a boy who was about five, somewhere around five years ago. His family apparently eventually left the church after his disappearance, and she wonders if something had been done to him. I want to strongly support her here so she doesn't carry further regret as she has regarding not having told authorities about everything when she was taken by social services as a child.

 Bob

After Anne put down the letter, I said, "I received a brief communication from Nathan indicating that he wanted a few days to feel out the possibility of negotiating a real and binding agreement that might include a permanent end to having to provide any future information or testimony, but reiterating the need for me to help you accept the idea of some kind of agreement or compromise here."

"I won't testify in court," Anne said angrily. "Either you or Nathan can ask me questions, but I want to do it by phone or e-mail."

"Okay, I understand you're very done with it, but there's also a chance for the first time to get a commitment to end your role."

"Why can't I do it by phone?" she pleaded.

"You know, I can't really answer that, but it's a fair question for Nathan. My guess is that there are legal issues here like allowing for a defense attorney to be present during any deposition."

"Yeah, but will the Reillys be there? And what if other members of the church show up again?" she asked with a whiny tone.

"Well, we're not talking about a trial right now, and I know that Nathan and the authorities will be very protective here. I'm sure we can work out those details with Nathan," I said, observing Anne's anxiety escalating, and searching for words of comfort.

"You're just taking Nathan's side," she said sullenly.

"Well, in a way, that's true, but he's actually on your side, so I'm still on your side. It does seem like you view me as being against you at the moment, though."

"Because you're trying to get me to do what he wants," Anne responded argumentatively.

"You need to talk with him about how you view his role and how you feel toward him as well. What do you think I should be doing or saying right now, as your therapist?" I asked, wanting to get out from between her and Nathan.

"That I'm right, and they should all leave me alone," Anne pouted.

"It sounds like you want me to be saying what the burned-out and frightened part of you wants, and that's valid, but it isn't really what I should be saying."

"Yeah, yeah, yeah! Well, you and Nathan go figure it out in some little chat room and let me know what I should do," she said with increasing anger in her voice.

"In a little chat room? Hmm!" Boy, had my birthday wishes disappeared from the room. Anne and I had experienced many tense and uncomfortable moments, but we had never had an argument.

This made me fairly anxious, since I didn't really know where it would go or whether she had the security and the tools to get through it without becoming threatened. In the back of my mind was the fear I always carried that a client could just walk out and never come back, something that had happened a couple of times following a perceived confrontation.

We sat for several minutes, and I was hoping Anne would break the ice in the room, maybe to assure me she still wanted to engage. But she held on tightly to her silence.

"Since this is really between you and Nathan and the police and the district attorney in Portland, would you prefer I stayed out of it or tried to help you find your way?" I asked.

Anne remained silent, but seemed to relax slightly and finally said, "I know you're trying to help me, and I want your help. But I'm so done with all of this, and if I don't go, I know that the terms of my witness protection could be changed or ended."

I was very surprised to hear this, considering it could put her life in jeopardy. "What makes you say that?" I asked.

"Because it came up before when I didn't want to testify against Elias Harmon, and Nathan told me that."

"Okay, then you must feel like you're damned if you do and damned if you don't, don't you?"

"Yeah, it's a catch-22," Anne said, her smile reflecting a light sarcasm and a calming of the tension in the room.

Even Madison had begun to sit up, something that didn't go unnoticed by either of us.

"So, how about if we talk about the Reillys?" I said, taking advantage of the shift in mood to change the subject.

"Yeah, I guess so."

"So, what happened at the Reillys'?"

"I lived with them for two years, after I returned from my mission work. I was there to help take care of their six children, but was like an unpaid slave. He was really mean to me, vicious at times, and would beat me with a belt until I bled, for things like making the eggs too runny. He would also come into my room at night and force me to have sex with him. I was terrified to try to stop him, and he threatened to hurt me like I hadn't seen yet if I told anyone. He also beat the children, and sometimes I was beaten for trying to protect them. But that was okay."

Feeling back in that despondent place I often went to when learning about further pain in her life, I responded, "Well, it was far from okay, but I get what you mean, that you felt it was okay to protect them, even at a cost to yourself. And these people do all this under the banner of God," I added, not able to completely contain my anger in that moment.

She nodded, but her silence reflected the turmoil and confusion she felt regarding her spirituality.

"And why is Mrs. Reilly being implicated here as well? Was she involved?"

"She wasn't involved in any of the sexual stuff, but I'm sure she knew about it, and she also didn't stop him from abusing the children. I gather the journals may say something about that. She was also physically abusive toward me and the kids."

For the remainder of the session, we managed to work toward a preliminary agreement for Anne to return to Portland under specific conditions that included the Reillys not being present and concrete assurances of physical and emotional protection from church members and their attorneys.

As we wound up for the day, I'm sure we both realized we had endured our first argument, and we had been able to listen to each other and find our way together. In the end, that felt somewhat comforting for me, as I hoped it did for Anne.

A few days later, Nathan and I corresponded again. Nathan wrote:

Dear Bob,

My feeling regarding the prosecution of the Reillys (and I feel I can be fairly certain) is that there are ultimately other factors that affect time (i.e., the cost of prosecution and statutes of limitations), and so the police will be looking to have the Reillys put in prison for the rest of their lives and will prosecute until they achieve this. From the journals, they can be successfully prosecuted and put away in the short term without too much input from Anne, except for maybe a little clarification and explanations of some terms from her. Then, once that has happened, they can be arrested, on what is believed to be their anniversary, if all goes according to plan. There is a certain intended poetic justice in that particular timing, since family values were one of the cloaks they hid behind.

Then, the main investigation will commence. This is where Anne will become important, and her evidence will be key. The police will go slowly and steadily, as the Reillys will be in jail by then.

I estimate this whole prosecution and sentencing could take up to three years, but is more likely to be done in eighteen to twenty-four months. This does not take into account appeal processes, which wouldn't likely need to involve Anne.

If Anne knows information that you and she feel is important, she should tell the police. The only way she can totally cover herself and assure they uphold the agreement with her is by telling them everything (whether that involves the Reillys or others). I am sure that there are many things that we will never know, but I have consistently encouraged her to tell us everything, as this is the best way forward. Technically, they will be 'off the table' in the future, unless the police can in some way link it to the Reillys. I strongly suggest that Anne clarify everything, so there can be no comeback. One other point is that the agreement does exclude Anne from having to inform on her father. We know there is a great deal of information she has that falls into this category, so this information is protected.

With all that said, I feel we have a preliminary understanding that sets the foundation for a more formal agreement. The nuts and bolts are that Anne will be interviewed by the police regarding the journals, the Reillys, the bodies of the two girls discovered several months back, the alleged disappearances of at least one boy and maybe another girl and any other information she has, both as a victim and a witness. She must be completely forthright and candid about everything she knows. Her father will be off the table, although she remains free to volunteer any information regarding him that she might choose to disclose. She will also be agreeing to testify in court for any trial that might transpire from her deposition/interview, regardless of the duration. In return, she will not be required to provide information or testimony in the future regarding other findings or legal proceedings regarding the CM. She will also continue to receive any benefits that are subsumed under her original witness protection agreement and will remain eligible for monetary compensation for her suffering, both from any civil litigation filed and any government funds allocated for this purpose.

Finally, I have noticed that when Anne feels stressed, her sense of humor and "practical joking" kicks in hard. Please, could you help her control this. I have told her many times that if she needs to play jokes on someone, play a joke on me, not the police and not "annoy Republicans." I would so appreciate your help harnessing this (albeit delightful) side of her personality. We really cannot afford any more jokes that might backfire, and I am quite nervous about this. Many thanks for your help.

Nathan

I responded to Nathan's letter as follows.

Hello, Nathan.

This agreement appears fair and within reason, based upon my conversations with Anne recently. I will see her again in a couple of days and discuss her concerns and readiness to accept this agreement.

Separately, she has committed to taking things seriously and will not engage in humor or practical jokes, except with you. I will do my best to help her feel prepared emotionally for her meeting with the police next week.

I know that she is staying with you and Cliff, and she doesn't seem afraid this time since she is meeting with the police only and no one from The Christian Movement will know of her presence. Please feel free to contact me anytime while she is there if you need my help or support.

Bob

— CHAPTER THIRTY-SIX —

Once again, Anne found herself traveling back to Portland, but this time with less anxiety. She looked forward to spending time with Nathan and Cliff and to the beginning of the end of years of providing evidence and testifying. In contrast to the woman who had curled into a ball in her window seat and never moved an inch a year earlier, Anne sat on the aisle, ate the pet food the airline offered, and watched a movie that made her laugh out loud several times.

Some of Anne's improved mental state was attributable to knowing she was going to Portland only to provide information and not to face the onerous tasks of testifying or facing members of the church and opposing attorneys. She had learned, to her great relief a few days earlier, that the Reillys would not have any legal counsel present, since they hadn't been formally charged with anything yet and had no knowledge the journals had been turned over to the authorities. The plan, therefore, was to develop a strong case before taking any action.

Perhaps the best part of Anne's upbeat mood came from Nicole's presence in her life. They were still in the early stages of seeing each other, but it had progressed beyond casual dating and gone well beyond any previous life experience for Anne. For the first time, her belief that she would never have a partner, or the kind of deep love that offered, was being challenged, but this was, finally, a really welcome challenge.

As with her previous two visits to Portland, police provided Anne with security, but with less manpower since most of the church ringleaders were in prison. Two policemen met her at the airport. One waited outside in an unmarked car, while, at the end of the Jetway as she entered the terminal, her old pal Mike, from the safe house, waited to greet her.

Seeing her old buddy, Anne smiled. She felt almost excited, a little because she trusted Mike enormously, but mostly because she knew the ride to Nathan and Cliff's would be a hoot.

"Hello, Miss Anne," Mike grinned when he saw her. "Wow, you look so different. I don't know what it is," Mike said with a big grin, looking at her purple hair. "Maybe your life is just calmer, but you look happier."

"I'm just purpler," Anne kidded as their playful relationship easily resurfaced.

Wanting to avoid any awkwardness for Anne, Mike offered his hand rather than a hug, but Anne held his hand with a sincerity that told him she would have been comfortable with the embrace.

"Hey, Mike, how are you?" Anne asked, looking into his eyes, a behavior that confirmed how far she had come along over the past year. "It's really cool to see you here."

"I'm really good, Miss Anne. It's really cool to see you, too," Mike grinned. Then, seeing only a small backpack on Anne's back, he added, "I assume you have luggage checked?"

"Yeah, one small suitcase."

"Then let's head down and get it. My partner's waiting in a car out front, and we're to take you directly to Nathan Cohen's house. Pretty nice digs for a state's witness."

Anne smiled and knew they both remembered the safe house and what that had been like in comparison. She didn't know if Mike knew how close she was with Nathan and Cliff, but she was sure he knew they were a couple since they were very open about it. She also remembered how much Mike accepted people for who they are.

She knew she wanted to tell him about her new friend Nicole, but she wasn't' sure if Mike's partner would be comfortable with gay people. Over the past two years, as Anne found beauty and support in the gay community, she also found prejudice and another closet that was somewhat reminiscent of the way The Christian Movement hid from a larger world that wouldn't have accepted its way of being.

So, they rode out to the house and had lots of laughs. Anne talked about her work and school, and that she had been thinking of applying to law school when she finished university.

"Oh, I always knew you were going somewhere from all this, Miss Anne. What kind of law are you thinking of?" Mike asked enthusiastically.

"I want to work with kids who've been abused or abandoned and be a lawyer like Nathan is, maybe work with the courts and social services," Anne told him.

"Cool, cool, cool," Mike said. His own history of growing up surrounded by gang violence had, once upon a time, similarly motivated him toward the other side of the battleground and law enforcement.

Arriving at the house, Anne was surprised to see just Cliff come out to greet her, but she assumed Nathan must be working late, knowing his dedication. Cliff's reception was very warm, but Anne thought he looked tired. It was so incongruous with the Cliff she knew.

Cliff gave Anne a big warm hug that reflected their closeness. The depth of Anne's response communicated how much she felt without the awkwardness of words.

"Nathan's taking a nap before dinner," Cliff said, after he finally let Anne go. He then picked up her suitcase and carried it up the stairs and in the front door.

Anne couldn't remember Nathan ever having taken naps, but since Cliff quickly started describing the special dinner he was making for her arrival, she put it out of her mind. It was ironic, she thought, that Cliff would think he needed to tell her the meal would be special, since every meal he'd made and served surpassed any restaurant she'd ever eaten at.

"Of course, you're joining the family for dinner," Cliff said, turning to Mike and his partner. He obviously wasn't going to hide his world from anyone, and this was inspiring to Anne. Then, not waiting for a response, since it hadn't been a question, he asked Anne if she would mind picking out her bedroom while he finished preparing dinner.

Anne climbed the now familiar staircase to the magnificent landing. She put her backpack and suitcase in a room she hadn't stayed in previously and headed back downstairs and outside onto the porch to chat with Mike, knowing that Cliff was most comfortable being left alone to perform his culinary artistry as a solo act.

"Dinner's ready," Cliff called about half an hour later.

Anne rose from her seat on the porch, and she and Mike walked into the dining room, where Nathan was already seated in his usual chair at one end of the table.

But Nathan did not stand and come toward her as he usually would have, leaving Anne perplexed and uncertain whether to seat herself or wait for Nathan to greet her. After a moment, she chose to walk over, leaning down to give him a hug when she reached his chair.

Nathan warmly returned her embrace, but she was beginning to have a feeling deep inside that something was far from right. She felt a sudden fear that began to dissipate her awareness, shifting her toward the safety of dissociation, but another voice in her head told her that she wasn't in danger and could stay in the present.

This internal battle to challenge the dissociation that had so protected her life had been waging within her for a while, and she had been learning to use my voice to ask herself a key question—"Do I have evidence that I am in any real danger right now?" So, she held herself in the room.

Dinner lasted almost two hours by the time they finished the last course, consisting of a plate of kiwi, mango, strawberries, grapes, camembert, brie, and a very sharp cheddar cheese, along with three types of what she thought of as "fragile crackers," since half the time they broke as people tried to spread anything on them.

After dinner, Mike headed out, and the other policeman remained on the porch, chatting with Cliff while Anne and Nathan retired to the library to review the anticipated interview for the following morning. However, before they started, Nathan cleared his throat. "There's something I have to tell you that you're not going to like," he said.

In spite of having noticed over the previous few hours that something about Nathan seemed different, Anne's immediate thoughts and fears reverted to her legal situation, and she assumed the agreement was going to be more extensive and stressful than what she'd been led to believe. So, she sat there, in mild protest, with a look of annoyance on her face and didn't say anything.

It wasn't until a few moments later, when Nathan still hadn't said anything, that she knew it was far worse than what she had been contemplating.

"I found out last week that I'm ill, and I have to take a break from work. So I can't accompany you to the interview tomorrow," Nathan said apologetically. "Another attorney is going to be there to represent you. She's a colleague whom I respect a great deal."

The remnants of Anne's annoyance drained instantly as fear sliced through her, both fear for Nathan and fear that he wouldn't be with her at the interview.

"What's wrong with you?" she blurted.

"Well, it looks like I have some kind of growth on one of my lungs, and it appears to be related to another growth they found in my abdomen. I feel pretty okay, but it's obviously serious enough that I have to undergo some kind of treatment."

Knowing this was devastating information, they each managed to not look overly concerned, as if they had been discussing a benign finding.

"Do you know what kind of treatment you'll do?" Anne asked as casually as she could.

"No, but they don't seem to be looking at surgery at this point, so either radiation or chemotherapy. They're still running tests. I'm not in any pain, but I've been a lot more tired the last few weeks, and I've already stopped working. I didn't want to tell you until you were here, so you'd see I'm actually okay—maybe a bit more tired, but okay."

To Anne, Nathan's condition was far from being okay, but she played along as best she could, smiling slightly in response but at a loss for words.

"So, how about if we discuss tomorrow?" Nathan said, wanting to rescue them from the awkward silence.

"Okay," Anne said, torn between confusion and relief.

"I've read the journals, or at least what I could understand, and I agreed to not discuss them with you until after the authorities have interviewed you. In essence, they're hoping you can either corroborate information found in the journals or, at least, help them to understand some of the words and meanings of what's being talked about.

"They appear to be documentation by some of the elders regarding things they did, including things they did to you. After the interview tomorrow and maybe into the next day, since there's a lot of material, you and I can discuss in more detail which parts are about you, if you want to talk more about it."

"Do any of these things have to do with my father?" Anne asked.

"Yes, at least a couple of the writings appear to be by him, but I can't talk with you further about this until after your interviews. I hope you understand that if I tell you any of the details, then the whole idea of you independently corroborating things is, in essence, thrown out the window."

"Yeah, I understand," replied Anne.

"The other thing is that you're going to have another attorney representing you tomorrow, and, in all likelihood, someone else will be appointed while I'm on leave to represent you for anything else coming up."

Anne hooked her feet securely behind the rung of her chair. "Will you still be my attorney?" she asked, the rungs pressing hard into her toes.

"Officially no. I'm on medical leave, and that means I can't retain any formal responsibilities. Unofficially, I'll still be available for your attorney to consult with and for you any time. I'm not leaving your life, just my official role. You're part of our family, and Cliff and I both expect you to be in our lives and that we'll be there for you as best we can."

Wanting to just absorb this wonderful expression of Nathan's love, but knowing it also meant facing a great loss, Anne abruptly asked, "Yeah, but what if you're really sick? Can I still call and talk with you if something is going on that worries me?"

"If I can hear and talk, or write, you can ask me about anything, and I'll do my best to answer. That will depend on my physical health at the time, I guess."

Anne felt numb with disbelief. But she didn't want to burden Nathan further with her own grief, so she merely nodded. "I understand," she managed, knowing his availability would fade soon.

"So, what have you been up to, Anne?" Nathan said brightly.

It was difficult for Anne to talk about her own life in the face of Nathan's illness. Everything paled in comparison to his welfare, and she felt bad talking about living when he was dying, but she summoned her strength for his sake. "I have a new friend," she said cautiously.

"Oh?" Nathan said, realizing right away that Anne was speaking of romance. "Do tell."

Anne almost forgot Nathan's news as she told him all about Nicole and their dating, about falling in love, and her thoughts about law school, a prospect Nathan seemed very pleased to hear about. They also talked about her sessions with Dr. Hirsch and, of course, "the distinguished Dr. Madison." Occasionally, their shared sweet smiles reflected the awkward moments when they touched upon anything in the future, a future that Nathan wouldn't see.

Later, as Anne headed up to bed knowing that her life with Nathan would never be the same again, a great sadness settled over her, along with increasing anxiety at the prospect of sitting with complete strangers the following day to answer questions that would elicit all the memories and, maybe even worse, images she hadn't even remembered or known about.

— CHAPTER THIRTY-SEVEN —

The following morning, when Anne came downstairs, Cliff was preparing breakfast for her and Mike. The sadness that enveloped her not seeing Nathan there momentarily eclipsed the anxiety she was feeling regarding having to go through another deposition and all the memories and images that would be evoked.

"Nathan's been sleeping in lately," Cliff explained, with a sadness in his eyes that he couldn't conceal.

Anne offered a perfunctory, "Well, that's probably good for him," trying to avoid anything else emotional at that moment.

After breakfast, another officer arrived to join Mike in escorting Anne downtown. A half-hour later, they were seated in a waiting room when the door opened and a stylish, yet casually dressed, woman opened the door and introduced herself. "Hello, Anne, I'm Jacqueline Stein, but please call me Jackie," she said with a genuinely warm tone while offering her hand to Anne.

"You know, we share something in common, Anne. Nathan was my mentor and like a wonderful father to me in my early days as part of Protective Services. He's shared with me how difficult this might be for you, having to go into deposition with a stranger, and hoped his trust in me might help you feel a little safer," she added very caringly.

Then, seeing that Anne had remained silent, she changed the subject, reviewing the purpose of the morning's conference and how she saw their respective roles.

"Don't worry," Jackie said, "it'll be pretty relaxed and informal. Such detailed documentation of the perpetrators' behaviors is unheard of, and the journals provide significant evidence, so this will be a more informal process, without any sense of opposition or objections and, hopefully, you shouldn't feel pressured."

"Speak for yourself," Anne thought to herself, and then realized that Jackie seemed really caring and was trying to make her more comfortable.

Jackie then added, "When anything regarding the Reillys is addressed, Anne, you should be aware that your statements might eventually constitute evidence to be used against them," reinforcing the inevitable stiffness and formality that this was really going to be like.

After about fifteen minutes, they joined two investigating police officers and another attorney from the district attorney's office in a small conference room. They proceeded to ask Anne about the meanings of various words and statements, many of which involved speaking in tongues and weren't discernable to her. Her greatest asset to the investigators was to be able to provide translation of unfamiliar terminology that enabled them to better understand the actions being cited. Some of their questions centered around identifying particular people referred to in the journals, either the possible author who was implicating himself or another individual being discussed. There were references to heretofore unknown criminal activities, including the apparent theft of jewelry from homes for the elderly where members of the church served as volunteers. Anne recollected having seen Mr. Reilly come into the house occasionally with strange pieces of jewelry, but this was her only knowledge of such practices.

While the process was not intimidating, it was grueling. It was three hours of intensive questioning until they broke for lunch. However, Anne, while tired, felt relieved that the officers had not focused upon her personal history or any particular acts of abuse toward other girls and, therefore, didn't elicit those memories or images. On occasion, she found herself trying to comprehend why they would have implicated themselves by documenting their actions. She wondered if they may have viewed them as rituals to be preserved, not unlike those recorded in the Bible. Years of separation from the church afforded her the ability to step back and view a larger picture, a picture of men who truly may have seen themselves as doing God's work and above the laws of the larger society as well as men who may have been extremely sadistic and somewhat crazy.

When they reconvened, however, one of the investigating officers said, "We want to at least let you know that five of the journals contain significant numbers of references to the abuse of a very young girl, as young as twelve months, and we are quite certain you are that little girl. Since these events would precede any viable memories you might have, we don't need to ask you about them. We just felt you had a right to know this."

Anne sat there not really knowing what she should feel, if anything, wondering if it mattered that things were being done to her before she could remember, and feeling she didn't want to ever know about any of this. She also wondered if they were awaiting a response, as everyone just sat there looking at her.

Finally, the attorney from the district attorney's office asked, "Do you feel up to discussing the Reillys at this point, Anne?"

"Yeah, I think that would be okay," Anne said, relieved to take her mind off of what she'd just learned and simultaneously wondering if she could ever actually feel up to discussing any of this. It was more about fulfilling her part of the agreement.

The district attorney then turned and directed her focus toward Jackie. "I would like to advise your client at this time, Ms. Stein, that questions regarding the Reillys and her responses are likely to be admitted into court or into their plea-bargaining process, and, therefore, this meeting now will constitute more of a formal deposition, although obviously there is no defense attorney present, nor have the Reillys been formally charged with anything of these findings yet."

"My client is aware of that," Jackie said. "And obviously I will guide her and represent any concerns regarding her own situation and best interests. I also want to clarify that my client, who is without question considered a very reliable and honest witness, is not under oath. Therefore, she is fully free to not answer anything and to stop addressing anything too difficult for her to face at this time."

"That is absolutely correct," the district attorney said, glancing toward Anne and offering a smile. "And we only hope that we can address all the questions we have today, and tomorrow if need be, so that we don't have to arrange further meetings," he added.

Anne took the rather broad hint. Obviously, avoiding answering something today wasn't going to get her out of addressing it and would only serve to prolong her involvement. She was somewhat accustomed to opposing attorneys talking to each other about her. It still seemed kind of strange, but it fit with all the other courtroom games.

"So, Anne, could you please describe the years you spent at the Reillys' home, including any abuse you experienced or witnessed in regard to the children?" the district attorney began.

Anne reiterated the history and responded to numerous questions, after which the district attorney responded, "Your information has been extremely helpful and very much corroborates what we've been able to discern from the journals. You know, it's our hope to use the powerful leverage that you provide as a potential witness to reach an agreement that keeps the Reillys incarcerated for at least several years and gives us time to build an even greater case to keep them in prison for what would, in essence, constitute the balance of their lives. So, on behalf of the state and our office, we thank you for your help today."

Anne was relieved the questioning was over and had found her relative emotional calm during the process satisfying. She had come to feel she was working with these people as part of a team, and it had felt better than any previous experiences testifying. Having to reiterate some of the really painful memories of her years of torture with the Reillys had been difficult, but she had found herself telling a story as if it were about someone else, rather than feeling like she was reliving it. Unlike her dissociative experiences, however, she had remained in the room the whole time. "Dr. Hirsch and Nathan would have been very proud of me today," she thought.

Later that night, however, after another wonderful dinner and a couple of hours of socializing with Nathan and Cliff, Anne retired to her room and found her mind reverting to the things she had talked about that afternoon. So, after several restless hours tossing and turning, she decided to write me an e-mail. She wrote:

It's 3:30 a.m., and I totally can't sleep. See, the thing is, I just don't get how I could possibly have thought it was okay that the Reillys treated people like they did me. It seemed like it was normal and okay at the time, even good, like God wanted them to do it. But I listened to myself yesterday talking to the attorneys about it, and I got more and more upset that I didn't do anything to stop it. According to the police, I moved in with them when I was 20 until I was 23. That's three years. How come I didn't do anything? They all said I was brainwashed, but that sounds like an excuse. I'm having bad dreams. Nathan seems to think we're in this for a long haul. Anyways, I thought I'd off-load my thoughts. See you next week, Anne

After writing the e-mail, Anne fell asleep for several hours and awoke in the morning to find my response.

Dear Anne. I got your e-mail and thought about trying to respond to you, but I would like to wait until you come home, where we can talk in person about what you're feeling, if you feel you can wait. I hope you very much know that I could never view you as having done anything wrong in how you've dealt with all the fear and all the threat. You needed to stay alive, and that was always a way of 'doing anything.' In the end, you survived to become a good and healthy human being, and that is a testament to having done a lot. We'll talk more when you come home, Dr. Hirsch

— CHAPTER THIRTY-EIGHT —

Having heard from Anne during her trip, I knew the deposition had elicited some painful self-reflection. So, when I opened the door to my waiting room, I wasn't surprised to see her looking sad and somewhat shaken. She quietly stood and entered my office and was subdued even when she hugged Madison, something I had never seen before.

"What's happening?" I asked after we'd sat a little while in silence, wondering if something else had gone wrong.

Looking toward the floor, Anne almost inaudibly said, "Nathan's ill, and he has to stop working."

In spite of the enormity of this development for her, my first feeling was less focused on Anne and more of a sinking feeling. Her words were calm, the tone almost benign, but her immense inner sadness had spoken. I managed to move from my own shock back into the room and asked, "What do you know about his situation?"

"He has cancer, and it's spread to his lungs. They're trying to decide what kind of treatment would work the best," she responded listlessly.

As Anne said this, my worst fears were confirmed, that Nathan's prognosis was pretty bad, but I needed to hang in with Anne's seeming need to hope for the best, at least for now. So I calmly asked, "How are you doing with this?"

"I don't want to have another lawyer," Anne said, sounding defeated. "Couldn't he just stay my lawyer and retire from everything else?"

I considered my answer carefully, searching for the right words.

"I don't know what to say, except it sounds like he has a real fight in front of him. And often that fight is harder than the illness. Do you know what kind of treatment they're talking about?"

"I don't think he's having surgery. It has spread too much. He said they were looking at chemotherapy. Do you think that can work?"

She looked somewhat hopeful at that moment, and I was torn between saying what I truly believed and trying to understand her ability to handle that truth. I had never lied or been deceptive with Anne, and I just couldn't destroy that trust, as hard as my answer might be for her to hear.

"Well, I'm certainly not an oncologist, but when I hear about a metastasized cancer that's spread to the lungs of a sixty-seven-year-old man, I think this is possibly the end of his working and the beginning of a fight for his life."

The absence of any reaction from Anne told me that she wasn't surprised. She'd doubtless known this and would have doubted me if I'd said otherwise. So, seeing that she actually seemed more calmed than unsettled by hearing the truth from me, I continued. "For me, I just focus on hoping for some more time for him, and that he finds peace in this process. I also know this is a tremendous loss for you. Nathan and Cliff took you under their wings and into their lives, and they not only protected you but have really cared about you and loved you. Nathan has been sort of your mentor and guide, someone very unique and protective of your life."

"Yeah, it's kind of like losing a dad or maybe a grandfather. I never had one, but he's gentle, like they're supposed to be, and older."

"How can I be most helpful as you face this?"

"I want to know what's really happening, but I know Nathan will want to protect me, so maybe you can talk with him or e-mail him and he'll tell you and you can tell me," she said, characteristically trying to avoid something she found uncomfortable by asking me to do it for her.

"I think a better idea would be for you to tell him you want to honestly know what's happening, and that you want him to see you as having the ability to deal with it now," I said, believing her ability to address him directly would confirm her strength to handle the truth.

"Okay, but will you also tell him?" she persisted.

"How about if I assure him I'll be there to help you go through whatever you need to and that I see you as being able to cope with the truth," I responded, wanting to actively support her in taking this step.

"Okay, I guess that's all right," she sighed and just remained still.

"Would you like to talk more about Nathan?" I eventually asked.

"I don't know. It seems like everyone—Nathan, the district attorney, the police, and you—all think I should implicate my father, and that it would be a way to file a civil suit against his assets. Do *you* think I should implicate him?"

I found myself pausing for quite a while as I tried to compose my response. Most notably, I wrestled with what I felt about her father compared with what she needed. Personally, I despised him, and I had come to feel, quite strongly, that for her to accept herself as a truly good soul, she maybe had to accept him as someone who represented something evil. Ultimately, she would have to live with her choice, both in the near term and for the rest of her life.

At the same time, I knew Anne had the capacity for an honest dialogue regarding such a powerful decision in her life, and I didn't really need to protect her from seeing a different perspective. She was far from being the childlike Anne who had cowered in my waiting room three years earlier, and, more and more, she needed and deserved to be approached as an adult.

So, after pondering my response, I said, "Well, I have a bias here, and it's important that I recognize that and inform you of it. I can't always avoid my biases or feelings, and so I guess it's important to at least clarify them as I answer you."

Anne nodded, watching me intently.

"I deeply believe your father was and still is terribly destructive in his treatment of you. He's broken numerous laws on many occasions, including having committed very severe child abuse, murdering his daughter and very possibly others, creating child pornography that destroys the lives of innocent children, and inflicting immense cruelty upon you. I will never buy that this is about God telling him to act. You know I have always considered that to be bullshit and a cloak to hide behind to justify his deviance."

I could feel my physical intensity revealing my emotions, but I successfully kept my voice even as I continued. "I'd love to see him live out his last moments in a six-by-nine-foot cell reflecting upon what he has done, with the loss of his rights and comforts, just as he imposed upon you for so much of your life."

Realizing that I was actually shaking with the relief of having let out some of the anger that had built in me over the years, I decided to balance what I'd said.

"With that said, none of it means what I feel is what's right or should happen. It's how I feel about what he's done to you, and it's hard knowing he may not face any punishment for what are the true sins here. In no way does that mean you should implicate him or that I need you to do that. You have to deal with the consequences and meaning of that choice, not me. I will certainly be there for you for whatever decision you make." As I stopped, I knew I had just made a speech, and part of me felt very awkward, knowing that really wasn't what therapy was supposed to be about. Then again, this was, at times, different from most of the therapy I had done before.

We both sat there for several minutes, looking at each other intermittently, diverting our attention to the paintings on the wall, the carpet, or anywhere that would relieve the intensity.

"I hope that wasn't too much to have said and that you know my emotions come from caring about you and what has happened to you," I added, realizing that Anne was probably too intimidated to respond.

Anne's tone was immensely gentle, but her expression was pained. "I know that, but I just don't think I can do that to my mother," she said.

"If that's the choice you make, I'll support you, and so will Nathan and Cliff," I said. "In the end, we're all in this for you, and that isn't going to change."

Anne smiled and looked down at Madison, prompting me to add, "And so will he."

"Cool," Anne said, sounding more upbeat. "Can we talk about something else now?"

"Sure," I agreed, sharing in her relief.

"I've been dating Nicole for two months now, and we're sort of calling each other girlfriends. I guess that's the next step beyond dating. I still haven't told her much about my past, and I don't know that she'd be comfortable to hear about it. I'm afraid it would change how she views me."

"What's the view you fear she might have?" I asked.

"That I'm weird or damaged or something, and that I'll never be normal."

"Do *you* still view yourself as weird or damaged and believe that you'll never be normal?"

"Sometimes. I know I'm better than I was, and I'm not really weird. But I don't know if I'll ever not be somewhat damaged or if I'll ever be normal," she responded, looking downward.

"I guess I wonder two things," I replied. "I wonder if you're really projecting your own self-image onto Nicole and thinking she'll be thinking those thoughts, rather than finding out how she might actually feel, and I wonder which worries you more—whether your history would be too difficult for her to handle or whether she would have a negative view of you."

"I'm sure it's both, but I'm more worried about how it might change how she sees me," Anne fretted.

"I understand your worry, but when someone cares about you and starts to love you, which is where she may be by now, then your history doesn't reshape the image of you. It just becomes a piece of the puzzle that is Anne Martin.

"I guess the bottom line is that you can't know until you see what happens. Keep in mind, though, this isn't like something you did that was wrong or something you should feel any guilt about. It happened to you, not by you, and that's a difference. Nicole may feel sorry for you, but she won't feel disappointed in you."

"Yeah, but I don't want to be pitied or have her see me as someone to feel sorry for," Anne protested.

"Fair enough. So, what might I tell you to do right now?"

"That I should tell her I don't want that," Anne said, her eyes rolling upward and her tone parroting my voice.

I grimaced at her. "Oh, great minds think alike," I said. "How about also telling her what you *would* like," I added. "This is really about having an honest dialogue and, ultimately, an honest and real relationship."

Anne sighed and glanced at the clock, looking a little restless, but then she seemed to remember something. "Can I be assertive and not be a bitch?" she asked.

"Where's *that* question coming from?" I asked, surprised.

"Sometimes when Mickie says just what she thinks or feels, she's kind of abrupt and loud, and a couple of guys we know will say 'she can be such a bitch.' It seems like men can do or say what they want, and they don't get called 'bitch.'"

"Well, I hear you asking about two different things. One is about what defines being assertive versus aggressive, and the other is about whether women are viewed and valued differently for the same behaviors. What do you think it means to be assertive?"

"I don't know, just to say what you really want or need."

"That's a big part of it. It's also about being clear and getting your message across. It isn't really about being loud or being angry or abrupt, especially since people end up being aware of your anger or rudeness rather than what you were trying to communicate. So, what is aggression?"

"Being pushy or physical."

"I would give it a more general definition that includes those things. I guess I view aggression as getting in someone else's space, either mentally or physically, like telling them they're hurtful—that's being in their space, rather than saying 'I feel hurt,' which is staying in your own space."

"That makes sense, and Mickie is sometimes telling people what to do or what she thinks of them and can even get too close physically for some people," Anne said, after pondering this for a moment.

"So, what are your thoughts about there being different rules for men and women?" I asked.

"It seems unfair."

"That's more about how it feels to you. Do you think it's right or wrong?"

"I still think it's unfair, so I guess that makes it wrong to me."

"Cool," I said, appreciating her ability to analyze her response. "It probably is unfair. I do believe—and this is just my opinion but it probably would be supported by research—that it is a much greater challenge for women to be equally assertive without being viewed or valued negatively. When men are assertive or even aggressive, they're seen as being manly or masculine, and women are seen as being bitches for the same behavior."

"So, if I'm assertive, then I'll be seen as a bitch," Anne said resentfully.

"You might, but are you wrong just because someone, especially a man, sees it that way?"

"I guess not," she responded, her tone a little hesitant.

"I think your question also originates from a life of surviving by being careful and not looking or acting overtly assertive, but your very survival has depended upon you being assertive in some ways. I guess that sometimes being assertive is less about what you say than what you do to get your needs met."

"So, do you think it's okay even if sometimes people would think I'm a bitch?"

"It's kind of like asking was it okay for black people to assert their right not to be slaves anymore. They had to fear for their lives, not just how they were viewed. So, if you don't want to be enslaved, then you need to be able to be assertive and live with people, once in a while, seeing you as a bitch. Of course, this assumes you believe you, as a woman and, more importantly, as a human, should have the same rights as everyone else. Lecture finished," I added with a smile.

At that point, we both must have reached our limit for the day, because we simultaneously looked at the clock. Anne stood up and said, "See you next week."

After she departed, I sat for a few minutes, pondering what I could say to Nathan. I found myself somewhat anxious, knowing that our conversation would be one of those really delicate and awkward exchanges in life. From too much experience with close friends and clients who were dying, I knew that it was usually far more awkward and difficult for the person who was facing living than it was for the person dying to talk about the truth.

Finally, after ruminating about it, I gave myself permission to just be me and not have to say the exact right thing, and I dialed Nathan in Portland. Somewhat to my surprise, although I don't know why, since my sense was he wasn't seriously symptomatic yet, Nathan answered the phone.

"Hello, Nathan, this is Bob in Boston," I said.

His reply caught me off guard. "Hello, Bob, I figured this would be you," Nathan said with a chuckle.

"Well, I often wondered if you might have psychic powers, since you've been so amazing understanding and anticipating Anne's needs," I complimented him.

Nathan chuckled again. "I wish. But I knew Anne was seeing you this morning, and I figured I'd hear from you soon after. So, how did your session go with her?"

"She's very shaken. But you know Anne. Her outward emotions appear more neutral. However, I'm not so strong. I'm pretty upset hearing what you're facing, and I just wanted to call and say I'm sorry and wish this weren't happening. Is there anything I can do?" I managed to say this without my voice breaking, but I was on that edge. I didn't want Nathan having to take care of *me* right now.

"Thank you very much for your thoughts, Bob," he said. "You know, many people have asked what they can do, and my answer is 'thank you, but nothing really.' However, there is something very important you can do, something I know you will do for me—just be there for Anne for both of us. That will give me an important kind of peace. She's become like the child I guess we once dreamt of having in our lives, and like any parent whose child still isn't quite ready to be on her own, it's so painful to know you're maybe walking out when they still need you."

"I know that has to be a very hard place for you, but I promise I'll do that for you, and for Cliff," I said, choking up.

Nathan somewhat abruptly shifted gears. "You know, someone needs to write the story of her life," he said. "I don't know that Anne could ever face doing it, but it's such an amazing story and one of not just terrible sadness, but also one of such strength."

"I agree," I said solemnly.

"Actually, I think you should write it," he continued, catching me off guard.

For a moment I was speechless. Then I said, "You do, do you?" in my sweetest sarcastic tone. "The only writing I've ever done is in the academic world, and I can't really write a book and treat her as my client."

"I know," Nathan said evenly. "But maybe when Anne graduates from her work with you someday, you'll be able to. It's just a thought I've had, maybe a little bit of a wish," he hinted.

I sat there for a moment, knowing I had asked what I could do for him, and he had just shared a true last wish of sorts. "Well, I'll certainly give it thought, and maybe someday I'll talk with her about it," I said, feeling my response was inadequate but not wanting to promise something I didn't know if I could fulfill.

"So, what are you contemplating in terms of treatment?" I asked, feeling there was little else I could say about his wish.

"Well, in truth, we're close to a decision to not put me through all of that. The cancer has metastasized to my liver and lungs, and the odds of anything doing more than prolonging my death are pretty low. I've had a gilded life, and I'm not going to spoil it with a drawn-out, tragic death. I'm doing okay, but Cliff is devastated and just looks so lost right now. It's really hard, because we're facing such incredible but different fears. Mine is the process of dying, and his is the process of living—without me. We can't really be in each other's space or help each other that much, but we're so loving and caring. We always have been, though, and they say you face dying like you've faced living, but with more intensity. So, we're doing it with even more love and caring."

I absorbed the depth and importance of his words and then remembered Anne's request.

"Well, I promised I would say something on Anne's behalf. She says she wants to know the truth and not have it downplayed, and I'll be there to help her deal with it. Beyond that, she and you need to, in your own way, talk about all of this."

"Thank you. That's important for me to hear from you, because I think that, in part, it says you're feeling she can find her way to handle it."

"I do, and she has incredible strength, as you know." Then, knowing Nathan might easily be tiring by now, I said, "Well, I have a client in my waiting room, but I needed to hear your voice. I'll be in touch over the coming weeks. If there's anything else I can do, I'm truly trusting you'll let me know."

"Okay, Bob. We'll be in touch, and please don't worry about me. I'm actually fairly at peace most of the time, and I have loving support around me."

"I know," I said. "But just know I'm here, and maybe removed enough from your physical world to be a different kind of support. I'll be in touch again soon, Nathan. Bye for now."

I hung up the phone and had one of those basic truth-of-life moments–that no matter what tragedy is occurring for someone, life goes on as always all around them. Nathan was dying, and my next client was waiting.

— CHAPTER THIRTY-NINE —

All of Anne's journeys back to Portland had been very difficult emotionally, fear being the dominant emotion, but this time, as she prepared to visit Nathan and Cliff, she did so with great sadness and apprehension. What would it be like and what would she say, she wondered.

Nathan and Cliff had been totally there for her, yet she had never had an opportunity to reciprocate. As she sat on the plane, she tried to summon the emotional strength and objectivity she had acquired working at the hospice to give back something on this trip.

When Nathan had revealed the seriousness of his illness, she understood he was sharing that he was dying. Everyone had been protective of her since then, concerned with what she could handle. What they all seemed to have forgotten was that in her work at the hospice, she dealt with terminal cancer on a daily basis.

It was difficult to think about how she could ease Nathan's final days while also grieving his imminent departure. Anne also felt very confused about whether she could still ask him legal questions, knowing Nathan would have little energy soon. Having to meet her new attorney increased her apprehension, but Nathan had strongly encouraged that she would be well represented.

Since her days of providing information or testimony were, in essence, over and all of the perpetrators who posed any threat to her were imprisoned, she and Nathan had felt comfortable not requesting police security for this visit. So, for the first time, upon arrival at the Portland airport, she retrieved her small duffel bag from baggage claim, unaccompanied, and proceeded to the limousine Cliff had sent for her. Sitting in the plush interior, she reflected upon the luxuries of Nathan and Cliff's world in comparison to her own life in Boston.

As the limousine pulled into the stately portico, not surprisingly, only Cliff came out to greet her. While she'd expected Nathan to have deteriorated, she was surprised to see how tired and almost lifeless Cliff appeared. His condition, she realized, resulted from the dual impact of taking care of the person he had spent almost his entire adult life with and knowing that the outcome of his caretaking would be to lose him forever.

As she got out of the limo and their eyes met, they smiled sadly and lovingly at each other before holding out their arms for a long hug. It was an embrace that, both knew, marked a shift in their relationship, Cliff now being the one in deep pain and Anne having emerged to greater strength.

Cliff led Anne into the library, where he had set out some tea and cookies, still the consummate host but a far cry from the gay Martha Stewart she had known.

"I wanted us to talk for a few minutes," Cliff began after they'd settled comfortably next to each other on the sofa, "about how he's doing, so you know what to expect. He's deteriorated a lot over the past few months since you last saw him, and he sleeps much of the time. So you'll probably find he's too weak to talk much. He's lucid when he's awake and has been so looking forward to your visit, but ...," Cliff's voice trailed off, and tears streamed down his face. "He says he's going to have to 'say good-bye to our Anne.'"

"I'm sorry. I almost feel like I don't have the right to ... I mean, I've only known him, but you've been together ..." As she heard herself and saw the tears streaming down Cliff's face, Anne felt her own tears for the first time since learning Nathan was dying. Knowing her own sense of loss and abandonment, she couldn't imagine what this must be like for Cliff. "I knew I was coming to say good-bye," she said gently.

"So does he," Cliff said, taking her hand. "Now, I want to give you two time to be alone." Pulling a packet of tissues out of his pocket, he extracted one and offered the rest to Anne. "He wanted to be awakened when you got here," he said, wiping his eyes, "and that will give you a couple of hours until dinner. He's still able to come down for meals some of the time and wants to do that tonight. If he can't, then we'll do a picnic up in our room."

He'd tried to make his voice upbeat, Anne noted, but he'd only sounded hollow. Still, she tried, for his sake, to match his attempt. "That sounds kind of fun," she said. She wanted Cliff to know she was fine to go with the flow and make things easier.

"Okay, so let's go up and wake him, and then I'll leave you two be."

That said, he let Anne, for the first time, help him clear the tea things and carry them to the kitchen. Then they ascended the long staircase to the master bedroom.

Nathan was sitting up and smiling as they entered the bedroom. Anne had little doubt this was to put her at ease, but she was relieved to see him looking better than she had anticipated.

"I can still smile, so I can't be all that bad," he quipped, trying to preclude any awkwardness. Reflecting on the depression and withdrawal that typified most of the patients in the hospice, Anne felt comforted.

"You look much better than I'd expected," she said, matching his smile.

"Well, I'll leave you two alone," Cliff said. "Do you feel up to dinner downstairs tonight, honey?" he asked, lovingly looking at Nathan.

"Of course! It's like a reenactment of the last supper," Nathan responded with a sly grin.

Anne and Cliff indulged his cheer reluctantly but with less resistance than they once would have. Now past the point of feigning unfounded optimism, neither of them challenged this truth.

"So, I was accepted to law school," Anne told Nathan after Cliff had departed for his sanctuary to prepare dinner. Despite his fatigue, Nathan's eyes brightened.

And when Anne shared her intent to study family law and work with child protective services, in part as a tribute to him for having contributed so much to her own welfare, tears streamed down his cheeks. Although he was honored by her choice and proud of her accomplishments, his joy was tempered with the knowledge that he would never be able to see Anne reach her dreams.

Seeing the distress in his joy and his heightened emotions, Anne decided not to ask if she could still talk with him about legal issues. Nathan would not be with her much longer, and she wanted to spend their time together being there for him and for Cliff, however she might do that.

As they headed downstairs to dinner later on, Nathan needed her assistance, providing her a symbolic moment of doing something to nurture him. She realized that giving back didn't have to have a particular shape. It would come in just sitting and talking, helping him walk more steadily, and letting him know her life was going to be okay.

Dinner was diminished to a mere four courses, but was still quite elegant and a perfect last supper. Nathan ate almost nothing and retired right after the meal. Afterward, Anne and Cliff sat out on the deck talking about her life and her future, and only briefly, apprehensively, his future—without Nathan.

— CHAPTER FORTY —

Anne was filled with apprehension of a different kind on the drive downtown the following morning to meet her new attorney. She had come so far, but legal proceedings still evoked a lot of her historical anxiety, a conditioned response to memories and authority.

Nathan had forewarned her that his replacement was very efficient and respected, but that what he possessed in skills and professionalism, he lacked in bedside manner. Anne appreciated the warning but was anything but comforted by the information.

Arriving at the office building adjacent to the courthouse heightened Anne's disquiet, since it had been the scene of so many stressful and frightening experiences. But, this time, it was also strange. Entering Nathan's waiting room, his absence echoed loudly in her mind.

Her heartache amplified the antipathy she already felt for the well-groomed man who stepped briskly into the waiting room a few minutes later. About half Nathan's age, he wore thick, metal-framed glasses and a fashionable pin-striped suit with a stylish tie.

Having grown up in a world where everyone wore uniforms, the attorney's three-piece suit reminded Anne of the rigid clothing worn in the church. This man was all business, which did little to assuage her discomfort.

"You must be Anne Martin?" he asked as he approached her. "I'm Neil Hightower, Nathan's colleague," he said, offering his hand, which she lightly grasped. He invited Anne into his office and attempted to offer some warmth as they were seated. "I know this is very hard for you, no longer having Nathan represent you. I will not be Nathan, but I will do my very best to be there for your legal needs and to answer any questions you have," he said with a tone that was more of a speech than an expression of concern. Nathan's description of him, albeit accurate, had done little to prepare her for the antipathy she felt.

"Thank you, Mr. Hightower," she said politely.

With the awkward pleasantries completed, Mr. Hightower quickly launched into legal issues. "I know that, in all likelihood, you aren't going to have to testify anymore, so we should talk about what legal things might still go on. I'm not sure you're aware, but the Reillys are now in custody and, at the least, facing five years in prison as part of a plea bargain, in large part thanks to your help."

"Nathan told me," Anne offered, her tone sounding disengaged.

"You obviously remain part of the witness protection program, but since anyone who might be a threat to you is in prison, this is likely to remain a formality.

"The last area of importance involves future civil litigation and possible financial compensation, and there are several issues here. I know you and Nathan have discussed all of this, but I want to make sure you and I are starting out on the same page. There are really three tracks we may eventually be able to pursue. You are entitled to compensation from the victims program, possibly both as an adult and as a minor, but seeking both is very unusual and may not be worth it ultimately, since it involves a special request to the courts to allow a simultaneous claim. It's something you and I can decide as we proceed."

Anne cringed at the thought of being part of a "you and I" with Mr. Hightower.

"The other area involves your perpetrators' assets. There are no known or traceable assets from The Christian Movement."

"When did they become *my* perpetrators?" she wondered. "Does this guy even hear himself?"

"The church used all of its known assets to provide its legal defenses or secretly liquidated them. Since the records were kept secret, we may never know what they did with all their assets, and, obviously, Jonas Smith's suicide in prison makes it even less likely we'll find any. The one potential remaining source is your father, but you would have to decide to identify him formally and be willing to testify in a civil trial, not a criminal trial."

"I'm not going to identify my father as anything. I can't do that to my mother, but I want to be put in his will to get an equal share with my brother," Anne blurted out vigorously.

"Nathan told me you were going to say that. So, he and I have talked about how I might approach that issue, but it may involve some help from you. Theoretically, his fear that you might identify him as a perpetrator gives us leverage to convince him to put you into the will. However, legally, we can't attempt to persuade him by threatening him, since this would constitute blackmail. Nathan and I have discussed some ways we might approach that, and we can talk about it if you choose to do so."

"Do I have to decide that right now?" Anne asked.

"No, not at all. But he's eighty-six, so you may not have the luxury of too much time to act on this. This is about money that really is rightly yours, but is also rightly yours to forgo. How about if you think about this, and then we can talk by phone?"

"Okay," Anne said, relieved that she didn't have to make any decisions right away.

"Well, do you have any questions?" he asked, happy to leave this inherited case short and simple.

"Not really. If something comes up, should I call you now?"

"Yes, I'm now your attorney, Anne. So, let's be in touch in a couple of weeks. How about if I call you?"

"Okay," she responded quietly.

"Good-bye, Anne."

Anne rose and again barely grasped Mr. Hightower's offered hand. As she left, she felt intimidated by her new attorney, but she knew he would be efficient, even if he wasn't warm and fuzzy like Nathan.

— CHAPTER FORTY-ONE —

It was one of those spectacular Boston mornings in the early fall, promising the cold of winter but filled with sunshine. I loved the walk to the office on mornings like this and didn't even mind Madison having to leave his mark on almost every tree and bush along the way, as the beauty of the morning took away any sense of urgency to be at work.

After arriving at my office, I sat down to briefly review my e-mail. The first to catch my attention was from Nathan. We hadn't communicated in two weeks, in part because we no longer had to discuss legal issues regarding Anne, and also because his declining health had diminished his ability to communicate.

As I began to read his letter, I knew this was good-bye and that a truly good soul was winding up his performance on earth.

Dear Bob,

As I contemplate the end of my life, I have spent much time reflecting over what I have achieved and the things that have given me cause to be proud of my life's work. As I look back, the one thing I consistently return to is my time spent with Anne and the progress I have seen her make over the past few years.

Bob, I do not know if you are aware, but soon after I was appointed to represent her, we presented a motion requesting she be made a ward of the court.

Whilst it was decided that this was not the best course of action at the time, the decision was made not because it was felt she was competent, but, rather, because it was agreed she would not make a credible witness as a ward of the court.

I tell you this simply because I want to impress upon you the incredible change that has occurred. When I first met Anne, she did not talk (now there's a change), and whenever possible she retreated to a corner of the room and sat huddled in a ball, rocking back and forth. She was scared of everything and everyone, and I thought there was no chance she could turn it around.

One of the most worrying aspects of her situation was her total refusal to engage in any kind of medical treatment or therapeutic care. I remember two policewomen having to hold her down while a doctor examined her and drew blood. On more than one occasion, we had to crush up antibiotics and hide them in her food. I now receive regular reports from Anne, and am constantly amazed that she is comfortable seeing doctors—what progress!

When she left for Boston, I was certain she would fall flat on her face, so you can imagine how pleased I have been with her progress. I am convinced that this progress, although driven by her determination, has been made possible thanks to the outstanding care she has received from you and people you have referred her to. It is most important to me that I thank each one of you for taking care of Anne. Cliff and I both feel very protective of Anne and are thrilled that she has not only received such good care, but also that it is from people who seem genuinely concerned for her and aware of her individual challenges.

I would like to, in my own small way, thank these people for their care and compassion, and I am asking for your help in this matter. I am shipping Anne some wine from our Napa cellar and am asking her to give you a few bottles, in the hope that you will kindly pass on my thanks and best wishes to the people who have cared for her. Of course, I am including a bottle for you. Please express my heartfelt gratitude to each one of them.

I am, of course, most grateful to you. On a personal level, you made it possible for me to negotiate the agreement that brings an end to this chapter of Anne's life, and I am particularly grateful for your help in curbing her sense of humor at inappropriate moments.

I do hope to be in touch with you occasionally during the next few months. Cliff and I are both extremely fond of Anne, and it makes my current situation easier knowing she is in such a good place.

Many thanks.

Nathan

As I read this letter, I had so many emotions. I felt incredibly sad for the end of Nathan's life and so moved by his devotion to Anne. Tears streamed down my cheeks, but this time I let them fall. I felt so saddened by the images of two policewomen having to hold down a terrified Anne—to protect her against her will. I felt proud of my work with her and so much hope for her life going forward, along with wonderment about how her history would affect her. I also realized that there was still so much to her history and her experience that was sealed inside her, some of it too painful and too difficult to be allowed to surface and share with anyone. Without ever having met in person, Nathan and I had become both colleagues and friends, sharing in our respect for each other and our care and respect for Anne. After reading Nathan's letter and experiencing a powerful sadness, I had to put my emotions in writing.

Dear Nathan,

I just read your letter this morning, and it moved me to tears. I realize there is little time, and I so want to meet you. Life works so mysteriously, as does death. Each end of the spectrum creates the power of the other (if that makes sense), and for some reason I am meeting you at one end of that spectrum.

E-mail can't replicate personal contact, but it does have the power to connect us. I would like you to let me know your honest thoughts if I were to (spontaneously) venture your way for a few days. I have given it a lot of consideration and would like to fulfill your request to write a book about Anne's life—and our work together. Of course, this is something that Anne and I need to talk about, and she would need to feel it is right for her.

I have little doubt that this book will be dedicated in part to you, and I would love you to be some part of it, and meeting you would enable that. However, I also would fully understand that a visit from a relative stranger might not be fitting right now.

In the interim, I send my thoughts to both you and Cliff.

Bob

A few days later came the last communication in our young and wonderful friendship.

Dear Bob,

What a beautiful e-mail from you. Thank you. My health is currently deteriorating, and I feel weak and sleepy much of the time. Sadly, I do not believe I could manage a visit, but I am so touched that you thought to spend your precious time and money to visit an old man.

I must admit, I feel very old these days, but it is not such a bad thing. I firmly believe there is some form of existence after we leave this life and am convinced that we will, in some way, be connected then—I certainly hope so. My voice is beginning to deteriorate, and speaking is becoming more difficult. I am consistently out of breath and, as I said before, am generally lackluster, but I have started to write down my thoughts about my experience with Anne, from the first time I met her, and the challenges and pressures I felt, etc.

I hope these notes (which I will send to you once finished) will be of some value, at least providing some insights you would not otherwise have had. Thank you again for all your kindnesses.

I can see why Anne has blossomed under your care, and my hope and prayer is that you will both stay connected after the book is finished and I am not around to keep an eye on her. I feel dreadfully paternal toward her. Does it show?

Cliff and I send our very best wishes to you. All good wishes.

Nathan and Cliff

Nathan died a few days after sending this letter. He died as he had lived, quietly and with dignity, with his life partner by his side. He died having been highly honored and decorated for his life service, and, I believe, he died carrying a smile for Anne.

Over the next couple of weeks, I arranged to bestow the bottles of wine to the people he had intended them for. I am not a wine connoisseur, but I could see that these were highly rated vintages from a very prominent collection, and I mused that they were an apt reflection of Nathan, a reserved but truly memorable and fine human being.

— CHAPTER FORTY-TWO —

Anne and I met more sporadically after dealing with Nathan's death. She had weathered the loss and the transition, only occasionally taking potshots at her younger and less personable new attorney. Much of this was a testament to her tremendous gains in self-confidence and self-respect. She clearly no longer looked at me as the authority and was expressing herself in many areas of her life, rarely with any real fear. It felt like we both knew that she was ready to graduate.

I felt like she was ready to fly, and I had great confidence that she would do so with the strength of an eagle. Our sessions together had become more about sharing her experiences and were less emotionally oriented. She had been emotionally quite stable for most of the past year, the only exceptions having been significant environmental stressors, including having been assaulted and having to consult with her new attorney.

I felt it was important that she learn to trust herself without me being there in the ways I had been, including turning to Nicole as her primary support. A therapist is almost always something we psychologists call a "transitional object"—someone who is an anchor of some kind while a person goes from one path or place in life to another. Madison had provided a comfort and an anchor, allowing Anne to feel safe with me over time, and I had provided those vital needs while she became more comfortable with the real world.

I had been pondering for the past two weeks how I might bring forward the idea of us bringing therapy to a close, knowing I had made a clear commitment to never abandon her. During the past month, I had envisioned how to present a marriage of ideas. I had decided to propose that we continue in life together, but in a different form, a collaboration to write the story of her life. I truly had no idea how she would perceive my proposal or react to it, but I was prepared to accept her decision, since that was the commitment I had made to her.

I was also clear that if she chose to go forward with the book, I would lobby strongly for her to continue to work with someone to process the emotions, memories, and psychological experiences that our undertaking would trigger. In addition, I felt she would need someone to help her deal with feelings regarding me being in this very different role in her life.

I had never taken a step remotely like this one in my eighteen years as a therapist and found this decision anxiety provoking. I certainly had former clients who had entered my social circle in one fashion or another, but this represented a powerful new connection with someone who had been my client for more than three years. Over the previous couple of months, I had consulted with several colleagues regarding this step, and I knew I was venturing along the edges of acceptable and comfortable practice in my field.

The ethical issues were less of a concern, since I wasn't violating any prescribed standard per se, but the clinical effect on Anne of continuing or altering the nature and structure of the relationship was salient and very important to me. Maybe of equal importance, I had absolutely no idea if I could ever finish or even enjoy such a large project. I just knew that Anne's story was important to tell.

So, when Anne entered my office on this particular morning, I had done a great deal of thinking about where our session might go. Anne appeared to be in very good spirits, and I didn't know how to feel about it. Part of me said that she was truly in a good place to consider this proposal, and part of me feared I might bring her down. As we sat down, Anne took charge of our initial direction, bringing up two simultaneous occurrences of importance to her.

"I have to tell you what happened this week," she said excitedly. "I was accepted to law school, and they're offering me a full scholarship and will even pay for books and everything. Isn't that cool? And Nicole's throwing me a party for graduation. I've never had a party before, and that's so cool."

I looked at her shining eyes and the way her whole body leaned into her words as if she couldn't wait to get started and compared her in my mind's eye to the terrified woman who'd once sat before me.

"Wow, I don't know where to start in congratulating you," I said. "Look where your life is, and how much you described in the last thirty seconds."

Anne looked pleased and uncomfortable, pleased to hear the great pride I held for her and uncomfortable with that level of praise. "Yeah, I know," she said quietly.

"You just described a life that includes a woman who is really there for you now, and you have loving friends to share the joy and the inevitable challenges. You also described an amazing feat. You began school for the first time in your life four years ago, and you've been offered a scholarship to law school. That alone is incredible. And maybe, most importantly, you have real pride in what you're describing, and that's so great to see."

As I spoke, I knew that, while emotions were pouring out of me, Anne remained, at least visibly, stoic. It was still a stretch for her to absorb so much praise, because for thirty years she'd heard the opposite. But I no longer had to protect that past image.

"So, will you come to my party?" she grinned.

"Absolutely, I wouldn't miss it," I said, my voice reflecting my excitement.

"Cool, because I wouldn't be having it if it weren't for everything you've done for my life," she said matter-of-factly, as was her way. But for me it was high praise, and it made me feel very proud, both of Anne and of myself.

As we paused for a few moments, I decided I would bring up my topic for the day.

"So, I have something I want to put on the table, so to speak. But it's just an idea. You retain the veto power, okay?"

"Yeah?" Anne said, a skeptical, almost fearful look on her face.

"Well, I have a proposal that we continue to work together, but in a different way. It would still mean we'd be very much a part of each other's lives, but rather than be your therapist, I would write a book about your life and our work together, something that Nathan asked me to consider doing."

I had thought that by now I could predict Anne's responses, and, in the very least, I had anticipated some awkwardness and concern on her part. So, when she merely said, "That sounds very cool. When are you going to start it?" I was fairly surprised.

"Well, we're not there yet. We're still talking about a decision that we both would need to make to do this. But you almost sound fine with it," I said carefully.

"I think it's really pretty cool. Would we get to meet regularly to do this?"

"We could meet as often as we wanted to or as the work needed. There wouldn't need to be a schedule, but we could do that, too. Do you have any concerns about us stopping therapy together or about having a book written about your life and being involved in the process?"

"I worry it will bring up a lot of things for me, and I'd have to think about them again," she said truthfully.

"That's almost certain," I agreed. "And it's one of the things that needs to factor into whatever decision you ultimately make. However, I've already been concerned with this and would want, maybe even insist, that you work with another therapist while I'm writing the book, so that you have a place to deal with anything that comes up, including your relationship with me."

"Who would I see?" Anne asked curiously, showing none of the resistance she once would have.

"Actually, I've given it a lot of thought, and there's a colleague of mine who I think is wonderful. He's a very good therapist and someone you'd feel safe with—and he has a really cool dog, almost as cool as Madison," I added, smiling.

"Is he like you?" she asked, hopefully I thought.

"No, he's much taller," I smiled playfully.

Anne gave me one of her sarcastic smiles. "Very funny," she said.

"I think you'll find him very different from me, in his style and his expression. But I think you'll find that he's very similar in really caring and being there."

"Is he a gay man?" she asked quickly.

I smiled again. "Yes. You don't think I would have ignored that criterion, do you?"

Anne just smiled back.

"So, tell me your thoughts and feelings about this," I prompted.

"I'm fine with it, but how soon would we do this?" she asked, her tone a little less certain.

"That's up in the air. But if we decide to take this path, then I'd like you to meet my colleague first. His name is Harry. If you both feel comfortable and we know that resource is in place, then you and I can decide on a time frame. My thinking, off the top of my head, is not for a couple of months, though. We need time to make this transition emotionally as well as logistically."

"So, how do I meet him?"

"Well, first, let me ask you, do you feel this is a good direction for you and for us?"

"Yeah, if you do."

"I guess I wouldn't have brought it up if I didn't, so that says I'm supportive of it, but the impact will be much more on you and your life," I said, wondering how much that was true. We had grown used to our time together over the years. Also, a little voice inside of me almost instinctively knew it wasn't necessarily an accurate statement for another reason. I anticipated that over the coming years, I would find the process of revisiting my work with Anne and crafting it into a book as profound an experience as having worked with her in therapy.

"Then I'm cool with it," Anne said.

"Well, let's start by having you get in touch with Harry, and I'll give him a heads-up beforehand. After you two meet, we can see how you're feeling with all of this. One of the things I'll share with him is that you need to talk about how this change in our relationship feels for you. I'll give you his number before we finish today."

Then, because I wanted to hear all about law school before our session ended, I changed the subject. "So, tell me your thoughts about law school, now that you know you're going," I said.

"I'm really scared. I don't know if I can do it, but I'm thinking of doing a joint Master of Social Work and Juris Doctorate program, since that would be perfect for working to help protect kids who've been abused or are in foster care. I could help them both psychologically and legally," she said.

"Well, in truth, I'd like a dollar for every time you've been scared about something you had to do and were stellar. I could retire a lot sooner," I smiled.

Anne just smiled, too, and I think we both knew she could do it. On this day we had planted the seeds of the future—hers, mine, and ours.

— CHAPTER FORTY-THREE —

Looking like a terrified and wounded animal trying to protect itself from a predator, Anne had entered my office three years earlier. Having once lived a life defined by fear, she was now a woman who carried herself with confidence and a sense of self-directed purpose.

I often found last sessions, when I had worked with someone for a long time, to be very emotional. Today was different, more of a graduation than a good-bye, since we would continue to see each other as my work began on the book.

I knew it would take me a few months to extricate myself from other obligations to enable me to undertake such a large endeavor, so I had agreed to meet together periodically in the interim until she felt more comfortable working with Harry, provided she no longer see me as a paying client. The plan was for her to begin working with Harry in a couple of weeks and, hopefully, shift her psychotherapy needs to him in a month or two, so that she would have that support in place before we approached issues in my writing that might be difficult for her.

What was most difficult for me to discern were Anne's deeper feelings regarding the decision to stop our psychotherapy together. In spite of her sharing in the decision-making process, there was a great inequity between us in terms of future consequences and personal impact. Whereas I had become as equally connected to her in many ways as she was to me, and although I had very positive and caring feelings for her, she had uniquely relied upon me for a long time and had come to depend upon our sessions as both a sanctuary and a place to resolve difficult emotional experiences and choices. Consequently, as we processed our decision, I knew that she felt some sense of loss and abandonment of what had been my primary role. I also knew that her loss was, at least partially, mitigated by the knowledge that we would continue seeing each other and having another type of relationship that would likely endure for a long time.

I struggled with whether or not the latter was appropriate. I knew that Anne would have to bear the psychological challenge of continuing our relationship, while I would have to bear the clinical and ethical responsibility. And as was often true with powerful and important choices in my life, I knew there would be unforeseen consequences that could be positive and negative. Such decisions were never black and white. Deep down inside, I could only hope that having consulted both of our minds and hearts, to chart our course, that we would someday look back and feel our choice had at least been okay, if not truly right.

But Anne and I were not the only part of the equation. There was also another sort of closure happening—the one between Anne and Madison. My "four-legged co-therapist" had clearly become an integral part of the process, and I wondered if he knew something different was happening today. But as Anne's and my eyes rested upon each other, absorbing the significance of being in our respective roles for the last time, Madison seemed oblivious to anything but the tummy rub he had positioned himself on the couch to receive.

"Well, I'll begin," I said. "I've given a lot of thought to this day over the past few weeks, and I think I feel like a parent who's done all he knows to give his child all the tools he can, who's inspired in her all the hope that he can imagine, and who now needs to step back and let her fly. I know your wings are strong, so I have no real worry. But I don't know what the form of our lives will be like later on, and I think that's one thing a parent doesn't get to know at this stage." I momentarily paused, a little overcome.

"You know I'm not one for all the emotional words or to show what I feel, but inside I feel you've given me so much and the chance to have a real life, one of my own," Anne said, her eyes welling with tears for one of the few times I could ever recall.

It was clear she wanted to hold them back. I, on the other hand, felt my own tears streaming down my cheeks. This moment was truly about both of us, and really these were tears of immense pride and joy for Anne, and for myself.

Then, as spontaneously as her tears had appeared, she said, "I made a quilt about therapy."

I had so loved all the quilts she had created, both for their artistic beauty and for their meaning, but they had always been about her experience or other important figures in her life. I guess I had always wondered if she would make one about us, and maybe I'd secretly hoped so.

Anne retrieved the quilt from a paper bag and unfolded it on the floor between us.

"I made it from scraps of fabric that I would normally have thrown away. It's like having had to put the scraps of my life together to make something out of it. It was kind of ironic, because it didn't look like I'd have enough scraps to really make a whole quilt, and that's kind of what I felt when I started therapy. The colors are mostly this blue and the yellow. The blue is calming, and the yellow is sensible."

Wow, I was struck by the two attributes of me that stood out the most for her, calm and sensibility. Those were good things to be as a psychologist, but I guess I wanted to be more about caring than anything else, and for a moment I wondered if that had been somewhat overshadowed. I had cared so deeply for Anne for so long, but I wondered if maybe that was too much for her to truly absorb.

I had always been intrigued by the metaphors of Anne's quilts. Made out of scraps—I'd wondered if they represented disparate pieces of her psyche and that she now possessed sufficient resources to become whole again. She had made not only quilts, but also a whole person.

My thoughts reminded me of a ritual I often practice when my sessions with long-term clients end. I took out my notes from our first couple of sessions, so we could see how far Anne had traveled.

"So, what do you remember of the person who came into my office more than three years ago?" I asked.

"I remember being terrified and sitting in the corner and going between fear and shutting down and wanting to disappear, and I remember my friends telling me you wouldn't hit me, but I didn't really believe that," she said. "And I remember you looking like you were being really careful and having to do most of the talking."

"You remember it well," I agreed. "What does that image feel like to think about now?"

"It feels like someone I knew a long time ago, and it feels like it was yesterday. Because that person is still there and will always be there, I think."

"Is that okay?" I asked gently.

"Yeah, mostly. Because she isn't controlling my life anymore."

"Well, the one thing I see very much in common with that person and the one in front of me now is that you've always been very brave and very strong, but you were much more fragile and lost then. I don't think you're lost anymore. You have your own identity, which is connected to the important things around you, like Nicole and law school and equality with your parents and people in your life. That's pretty whole in my book. You really were more about fragments and scraps, and now you're a quilt sewn of the fragments and scraps that hold you together as a whole being.

"I think my other image is that I had a little child in front of me, a child whose emotional world was arrested maybe when she was about five. That child saw the world as so terrifying, and she had lost her bigger sister. But today I see a woman who has a healthy respect for the world's dangers, but who doesn't let the fear of them control her. Maybe she's even become her own bigger sister to that little child."

As she had done through all our time together, Anne just smiled as a way of saying she understood and appreciated my image of her.

"So, I know we've talked about this over the past couple of sessions, but I wanted to ask once more what this feels like today—our stopping this phase of our relationship and moving to a different one."

"It feels mostly okay, but I guess I'll have to see what it's like. You said we could still talk, but it wouldn't be a real therapy session, so when can we do that?"

"I don't know that I have any more of an image than you do, so when would you like to meet up next?"

"Maybe next week, since I don't meet with Harry for a couple of weeks," she said.

"That sounds fine. So, where would you like to meet other than here?"

"Will Madison be with us?"

I had the pleasant feeling that the three of us were a little family when she said that, and I suspected she shared this feeling. "Would you like him to?"

"Yeah, for sure if that's okay."

"I never imagined it any other way, but I guess you two are saying good-bye to this phase of your relationship today, too, so we need to always include him in the plan," I grinned.

"That would be cool. Maybe we could meet at one of the coffeehouses you and Madison hang out at."

"I was thinking exactly that. So, before we wind up today, we'll figure a time and place and begin our new life together, the three of us."

Spontaneously, with a smile, Anne reverted to my earlier question about what she remembered. "I also remember that I knew you weren't a real doctor, but I still wondered if you maybe had body parts in your freezer," she chuckled.

"And how do you view that image now?"

"Well, I've never seen your freezer, so I'm not absolutely sure. But I'm not worried about it anymore."

She said this with a straight face to ensure I'd never absolutely know for sure if she still wondered about how safe I was. It seemed that her response had reflected a strength in having learned to cope with uncertainty—even about me. I also felt it was fine to leave this alone, but I wanted to underscore the sentiment.

"Well, I think the greatest challenge in front of us is for you to someday see us as equal people, not as doctor and patient, and to feel free to ask or say anything. I know that takes time and just being together differently," I said.

"Yeah, I think that will be hard to do, especially since I've always known you'd be there if something came up or if I was really upset," she agreed.

"I still will be, but as your friend, and hopefully I'll find a way to let you be there for me when I need that, since it's part of equality."

"That would be really cool," Anne exclaimed.

I sat for a moment and thought of those words. They were almost her motto and a hallmark of Anne. I thought it was the perfect sentence on which to end. "So, how about if we wind up this chapter of our relationship and meet at Java Time next week?"

Hearing those words, Madison jumped up to offer his good-bye. Anne stood and leaned down and gave him a long and loving hug, to which Madison responded with several licks of her cheek, the last one catching a tear that had dropped.

Anne then turned and, for the first time ever, we gave each other a hug. Neither of us said anything, but so much was communicated in that moment, as much as had been communicated when I had first opened the door to my waiting room more than three years earlier and no words were said.

As Anne shut the door behind her, I felt so many things, but the most prominent feeling was one of real pride—pride for Anne and pride for myself.

But that's not where Anne's story ended, although it is perhaps where the next chapter in our story together began.

— CHAPTER FORTY-FOUR —

On one spectacular October morning shortly after Anne had given me the wondrous quilt representing our three years of therapy, I was driving with Madison to Provincetown, hoping to spend the weekend reviewing my notes and sketching my ideas for this book.

As we reached the lower part of the cape, I found its serenity, sheer beauty, and quietude striking, even after decades of making this same trek. It was one of those days referred to as Indian summer in the Northeast, and Madison felt it, too. I could tell by the way he, having claimed the rear of my SUV as his domain, lifted his wet, black nose toward the open land and marshes of Truro, knowing we were getting close to the beaches and woods he had always so loved romping around.

At twelve, Madison had less energy than he'd had before, and for the past eighteen months, his occasional seizures had become more frequent. But today he was excited enough that, when he could tear himself away from the window, he'd stick his muzzle in my ear as if to say, "Hurry up!"

As we rounded the familiar bend toward my house, I reached back to give his head a rub. "We're almost there, guy," I said, enjoying his excitement as much as the prospect of a walk on the beach, followed by a hot tub under the stars, but no hot breath, no warm tongue met my outstretched palm.

"Madison?" I said, knowing, in that moment, that he must be having one of his seizures, reflected by the leg spasms, slumped head, and glazed eyes that afflicted him. I glanced in the rearview mirror. I could see him, but he was down like a water buffalo. There wasn't even any visible chest movement to indicate his breathing. "He'll be fine," I told myself.

The seizures were always frightening, but they passed. This time, however, somewhere inside, I knew this was different and I was losing my little guy. Dazed, I turned and headed for the animal clinic. Luckily it wasn't too far. Madison and I had been there once before, when he had his first seizure.

It was only a few minutes before I pulled into the parking lot, threw open my door, and rushed into the clinic. "My dog's in the car. He's …," I stopped. I'd intended to say he was having a seizure, but in that moment, I'd realized I couldn't feel his energy anymore.

The medical assistant waited patiently while I stood there dumbly. "What seems to be the problem?" she asked after a moment.

My response startled both of us. "He's dead," I said with an eerie calm.

Grabbing one of the other medical assistants, she rushed out to the car and opened the rear hatch. There was no movement, no furry face, no pounding tail.

Madison was gone. He lay there, so still, so peaceful, and tears poured down my face. Somewhere beyond my shock, I remember thinking that Madison had chosen to leave this world after his work with Anne was done. Perhaps he had held on until then, knowing that now that Anne felt completely safe with me and within herself, he could pass on as he needed to.

My walk on the beach that evening bore no resemblance to the joyous caper I'd imagined. The waves broke endlessly on the shore, and the starry night seemed so distant—a cold, remote beauty indifferent to the suffering of mere mortals.

Later, sitting stunned and alone in my house, I contemplated whom I needed to contact. Who had been a part of Madison's life? The list wasn't small, but before I tackled it, there were a couple of calls I knew I had to make. The most difficult of these was, of course, to Anne.

In many ways, Anne's last few years had centered around three beings—me, Nathan, and Madison. Nathan had died, and I had moved on from my role as her therapist. Now I was about to tell her the last member of the triad had passed on. I knew she would be strong and weather the news, but it would still be a tremendous loss for her. I also knew there was no way I had the capacity to console her, as every time I realized anew that I would never again have Madison to hug, I broke down.

But I picked up the phone and dialed. "It's Madison," I managed when Anne answered. There was no reason to say more, and I could not have if I'd tried.

Instead, it was Anne who spoke. "He's free now," she said. "Just like me."

For the first time that day, I cried to someone. Anne just listened. She was there for me.

Although I didn't realize it at the time, in retrospect I see that Madison's passing had facilitated a new passage in our relationship. Anne became my friend that night, and it would be as friends that we subsequently began our journey to write this book.

As I headed out to Race Point Beach the next morning, a place Madison and I had long cherished both for its beauty and for the time to run along the sand and water as best friends, I felt the sun shining down and the world seemed more benevolent. And as I opened my notebook to begin this book, a very simple thought moved through my being. No matter what we endure—the painful, the beautiful, the beginnings, the ends, the fears, and the hopes—life goes on for each of us in our own way.

EPILOGUE

In the early stages of writing this book, I considered making the title *Why?* This was the first question Anne began to ask as she began to accept that all the abuse and cruelty weren't directed by God or the teachings of the Bible and weren't deserved. As the therapy evolved, a second "Why?" came into focus: Why does a particular individual not only survive, but successfully move forward compared with so many others who are irreparably damaged by serious childhood trauma? The first "Why?" is likely more rooted in philosophical, sociological, theological, and historical understandings, whereas the latter "Why?" seems more understood within the realm of psychology, which includes genetic, developmental, and environmental determinants, and human behavior, most notably when one looks at the concept of "resilience."

A basic definition of resilience is: the ability to recover or quickly return to a healthy or functional state after experiencing a setback. Its root word implies springing back to a similar shape or position. My own particular focus and research in this area, however, has been more specific to the characteristics of women who are resilient after experiencing significant abuse and/or trauma.

The key strengths that are most often found in these women include:
- strong intellectual capacity (not necessarily correlating with formal education);
- physiological strength;
- strong and, at least temporarily, healthy defense mechanisms (e.g. dissociation and a sense of humor);
- the ability (not necessarily measured by anything tangible) to not only survive, but to move beyond survival and thrive;
- the ability to develop and retain strong supports, both in childhood, especially if the perpetrator is a primary support, and in adulthood;
- sustaining "enough" prominent emotional damage to be motivated to seek psychological treatment;
- the almost "innate" desire to help and support others stemming from one's own painful experiences;
- some kind of authority over memory—that is at times protective and might represent some level of denial;

- the ability to make sense of and understand the traumatic childhood
   experiences that lead to awareness;
- the ability to experience emotion, even when it can't be expressed;
- the conversion of adversity into the capacity to cope with future
   adversity.

Other important characteristics involve:
- the avoidance of future abusive relationships and/or knowing the need
   to quickly exit these circumstances;
- a healthy oversensitivity to threat;
- the ability to assess how to behave in threatening situations to
   mitigate further injury or harm;
- learning to be assertive and view oneself as equal.

Anne clearly possessed these strengths and characteristics, having very
strong innate intelligence, physical strength, the ability to dissociate and
employ humor as a means of managing negative emotions, a strong will
to move beyond survival, and the use of her experience to inspire her life
goals and a greater capacity for developing healthy and loving interpersonal
relationships. She also possessed another characteristic that is a more typical
rather than essential component of resilience—a very strong connection to
animals, maybe as a safer substitute for affection and connection compared
with humans.

Probably the one way in which she differed significantly from most of
the resilient women depicted in the research was having difficulty making any
real sense of her experience that could lead to a greater/beneficial awareness.
This is likely to be more difficult for her because it brings her into conflict
with her spiritual beliefs and the values that defined her whole childhood.
It is probably easier when someone can focus on a single perpetrator versus
an entire culture. I think this aspect of her resilience remains a work in
progress.

In addition, the task of trying to understand *why* one has been abused
is complicated by numerous factors. There is an inherent desire to arrive at
a singular and logical conclusion, but the answers are often multifaceted
and illogical. Human nature is to try to make sense of things, even of what
ultimately doesn't have a rational basis. Accepting a painful or significantly
adverse experience as simply unfair or having been in the wrong place at the
wrong time often proves unsatisfactory, in part because it denies any real
sense of control over one's safety or life. Most of us live with the illusions of
control and predictability in spite of having very little control over the large
and powerful aspects of our lives. These illusions offer a (perhaps false) sense
of security. In truth, we have very little control over the larger issues—our

births, our deaths, our genetic composition, huge concepts called luck and fairness, and a myriad of other influences.

Sometimes, for resilient women, the ultimate conclusion is to let go of being able to know why—as a way of moving on. This is not necessarily the same as the desire to know why, which might endure. Being able to accept that horrible and wonderful events often occur randomly and aren't controlled by spiritual, natural, or human causes, often involves rewriting the world one has known (i.e., accepting that life may simply be unfair and that bad things happen to good people).

Anne's self-blame is very much in accord with what is believed by many women who have been abused. In my recollection, she never used the word "victim" to describe herself. It remains a highly controversial word, one that can imply helplessness and an enduring negative self-image. In many respects, it is the opposite of self-blame. Whereas "victim" typically implies the absence of any real control, self-blame lends itself to a notion of perceived self-control. Another role of self-blame is that it can serve to protect the child/individual from further anger and punishment by the abuser while simultaneously providing an enduring negative self-image.

When a psychotherapist works with a child who is in danger of being abused, the therapist needs to find a crucial balance between helping the child to not engage in self-blame and to simultaneously find ways to feel some sense of power or ability to diminish the impact. Just the act of shifting blame to the perpetrator requires effort and conscious motivation, and typically doesn't occur until adulthood, often through the encouragement of psychotherapy and support groups.

Some resilient women describe having found value in the trauma or tragedy, such as: an enhanced appreciation for life later on; having been strengthened by developing the capacity to survive; learning who are their true supports; and being motivated toward a more caring sense of others through greater empathy and understanding of pain and difficulty.

As I neared completion of this book, I sat down with Anne and asked her two questions that would remain crucial to her life and her comfort. My first question was simply, "As you look back now, why do you think this happened to you?" Without any hesitancy, Anne responded, "Because I was in the wrong place at the wrong time." When I asked if there were any other answers as to why this happened to her, she responded, "No, that's all." Irrespective of all the complex and controversial understandings that were possible, she had placed her why into a very real and basic place that she could live with.

My second question related to how she now viewed or experienced spirituality and religion. Her response was, "Religion and spirituality have a place in my life now, but it doesn't change people like it says it does. Organized religion makes a lot of claims and provides a good veneer for people. In some ways, the church feels like the most unsafe place when we take our kids, because it remains in a position of great trust, yet still children can be and are harmed there. I still feel like I should believe in God, and I think I do."

As I contemplate my own responses to these two questions, they would be quite different, and considerably more complex, but in the end, the answers and the ability to find solace and meaning are more important to Anne than to myself. Maybe that is the essence of this thing I do called psychotherapy. By the time I finished writing the book, I realized how much impact Anne's life and our work together had created for me. In many respects, writing about the abuse was more difficult since my focus wasn't on someone else, as is the nature of my role as a psychotherapist, and I was more in touch with the details and my own images.

My work continues, as does my learning, and I will always remain the observer, albeit one who has been changed by the years I spent with Anne.